Loneliness and the Crisis of Work

ERRATA SHEET

- The author of Cooperatives, Mental Health and the Critique of Wage Labor is Cristopher Morales Bonilla

- The author of The Phenomenology of Parasocial Relations and Loneliness – Buber and Stein is Thomas J. Spiegel

Loneliness and the Crisis of Work

Edited by Pritika Nehra

Cambridge Scholars Publishing

Loneliness and the Crisis of Work

Edited by Pritika Nehra

This book first published 2021

Cambridge Scholars Publishing

Lady Stephenson Library, Newcastle upon Tyne, NE6 2PA, UK

British Library Cataloguing in Publication Data
A catalogue record for this book is available from the British Library

ISBN (10): 1-5275-6912-8
ISBN (13): 978-1-5275-6912-6

Contents

Part III. Concerns from the Pandemic

Introduction

Pritika Nehra

Freud was once asked what he thought a normal person should be able to do well. He responded: "Lieben und arbeiten," which translates neatly into English as, "To love and to work."[1] This is the normalcy that is lost in the contemporary world. Following this loss/absence of the stability of work and that of love for the other, as the most intimate form of belonging among human beings, it is difficult to distinguish between social pathology (Loneliness) on the one hand and normalcy/social order on the other.

The volume is a collection of twelve articles that philosophically reflect on the new forms of structural domination, vulnerabilities, and alienation in the contemporary social relations of work. The essays are categorized under three sections: the first section presents theoretical perspectives on the theme, the second section includes essays on loneliness and the crisis of work with particular reference to a critique of capitalism, and the last section offers emerging concerns of loneliness and work under the global Covid pandemic.

Reflecting on what role the activities of work perform in human lives, it was Hannah Arendt, who linked work with the enterprise of world-building. Contrary to what Marx had hoped, one can also ask: is it possible to get rid of work in an ideal society? How does one understand the legitimacy of work? In the background of these concerns, the volume seeks to address the crisis of work/social labor and loneliness within contemporary capitalist work settings (Academia, corporations, etc.) to understand new modes of domination, vulnerabilities, exclusion, and meaninglessness in the present times. The essays present a socio-political and collective dimension of precarious work, unemployment, and loneliness which are often characterized as a matter of individual failure.

---

[1] Qtd. in Elms, A.C (2001). 'Apocryphal Freud', *Annual of Psychoanalysis*, Vol. xxix, 2001: 9-10.

In the context of work, the term 'crisis' subsumes a broad range of issues spanning from economics to ethics. Therefore, 'Crisis' is used in a plural sense here, which is not seen as an economic dysfunction of the society *per se* but also as a 'lived crisis' within social, political, and cultural domains. Some of these lived experiences include the industry of precarious contractual positions, the speed-up culture of performance-oriented academia under the market forces, the digitalization of intellectual work through videos/power-point accumulations as a cookbook of the teaching pedagogy, the failed possibilities of any effective political resistance, the regulatory environment of constant surveillance through regular appraisals, intellectual bullying within the academic circles, lack of care, and the existential anxiety and dread. There is an inadequacy in addressing these lived experiences of the crisis within the existing discourse on the matter. Further, we find that popular descriptors of the problem like 'crisis' and 'social pathology' are redundant as they fail to motivate any actual social and political critique, once they acquire a social standing. Consequently, we refer to the terms 'crisis' and 'social pathology' with caution, since once we interpret our experiences as a crisis/pathology, we end up attributing a normative meaning to it.

In this volume, we deliberately deviate from the narrow understanding of loneliness as a mere social pathology. The main reason for this divergence is that the idea of pathology in a general sense implies a converse state of 'normalcy' or a state, where there is no need for a treatment for a specified problem. We approach Loneliness as a problem that is not discovered by the critic based on a utopian vision of future social health but in a degenerating social/political system that is already showing objective signs of dysfunction in the present. Through such an approach, we also intend to consider how to interpret loneliness as suffering coming out of a dehumanizing experience at workspaces and the causes thereof. Loneliness is thus characterized by the fact that it cannot be properly diagnosed or treated at the level of the individual. It is associated with what Adorno calls, cases of domination (*Beherrschung*), which he later extends to his analysis of politics and society. The key thrust of the volume is to examine how the contemporary work crisis and loneliness can be seen as inseparable from domination and vulnerabilities in the first place so that some transformation can be brought about in the discourse concerning these issues, which sideline any focus on these issues behind the veneer of stress management, psychiatric treatment, and counseling as the only form of available care.

The first section includes five chapters that present theoretical perspectives on the theme of loneliness and work. Pritika Nehra's paper sets the tone to the volume in her explication of political concerns of loneliness by connecting loneliness and precarious work of the academic with intersubjectivity, freedom, and structural domination. Charles Djordjevic and Georgias Karakasis offer new perspectives on the conceptual understanding of work. Djordjevic suggests a task-oriented approach to work that connects the subjectivity of the worker with new ways of interacting with the world (tradition). He proposes an ethics of soul-craft in a deliberate creation and re-forming of the self to connect with others. Such a soul-craft is not easy but comes at the price of difficulty/hardship in the becoming and being of a person. Karakasis insists on integrating joy in work to avoid alienation of the worker from the activity of work and the product of work. He compares two different kinds of alienation in the works of Marx and Heidegger to further his point. The last two chapters in this section by Anton Rennesland and Navjot Kaur discuss the loneliness of the academic. Rennesland views the loneliness of the anonymous academic in an encouraging, positive light as paving a way to thinking in solitude, a divergence from capital's normalcy, a slowness contrary to capital's speed, and cultivation of emotions of rage. In contrast, Kaur views the loneliness of the academic as a negative response to capital-driven academic structures without having the necessary preparedness or self-enrichment to deal with it. She suggests an overall change in attitude and expectations concerning academic work to combat this situation.

Instead of a commonplace negative characterization of loneliness, Pritika Nehra's *The Political Concerns of Loneliness* posits loneliness as a response to intersubjectivity that underlines political considerations of belonging. She views that Solitude and loneliness emerge as affinities to the self through our encounter with an 'other.' Social or civil freedom from loneliness requires the presence of others who are trustworthy and non-dominating. This is further linked with political concerns of plurality and sameness. Drawing from Hannah Arendt, she elaborates that loneliness is a peculiarly dehumanizing experience in the paralyzing impact on the capacities of thinking, speech, and action. Her critique raises concerns about democracy at the workplace: 'to consider how unjust socio-political structures are bound to create social pathologies; how we respond to vulnerable others in the work settings and maintain exceptions about their silence and invisibility with impunity.' In the present times, when we are experiencing increasing concern about mental health issues and stress management at workplaces, we also find that the socio-political conditions that form the background for these pathologies take a back seat. We are continuously captivated by a picture of politics that on the one hand celebrates the voices of the vulnerable but on the other hand also consistently undermines them and obscures their agency, which creates them in the first place. The negative experiences of suffering in an already degenerating socio-political system that contributes to our pathological social reality are kept at bay by making its victims invisible, lonely, and superfluous. Political equality allows everyone to express their differences in the public domain whereas the sameness of our biological make-up homogenizes us as humans having the same fundamental needs for survival. Loneliness also brings into question the dualism of the external world and the internal reality of human beings (subjectivity and the world) more sharply. It makes us think about our bodily embeddedness in the world. Nehra views that the importance of uncovering the political concerns of this suffering and making it visible lies in its potential to change our approach to loneliness at workplaces to resolve it.

In *Making things difficult: Work on/and soul-craft*, Charles Djordjevic explores a radically different conception of work and the human condition that purposefully imposes hardship on people. He views work as one of the 'precondition[s] for becoming and being a person within a specific community'. He discusses two different approaches to work: the activity view and the Task-oriented view of work. The activity view of work regards work as nothing more (or less) than the 'filling up' of Newtonian time with labor power for mere survival. This view of work becomes strangely 'a- or anti-social, something one does out of sheer necessity and, ergo, something that occludes intersubjectivity, freedom, and subject formation'. To avoid this, he suggests changing to the Task-Oriented approach to work. He argues that this view of work is a constitutive condition for forming a particular sort of community. Extrapolating from Kierkegaard and later Wittgenstein, he criticizes the idea that hard work is some sort of anathema to the human condition. He draws from Kierkegaard's conception of 'being a self and belonging to a community must involve a particular sort of temporalization–narration.' Narratives have a unique structure based not on homogenous chunks of time, but end-states, repetitions, and suffering. Narration work requires that the end-state that structures task-oriented work not be 'naturalized' but be adopted explicitly by the worker as her goal. It requires a willed repetition that guides work and 'presupposes both that the workers have a reflective understanding of the content of their work as well as a sense that they transcend the mere activities that constitute it'. He draws affinities from Foucault's thoughts on ethics as soul-craft, i.e., the deliberate creation and maintenance of a particular sort of self. And it is precisely this form of ethics that connects task-oriented work with subjectivity, tradition, and one's belonging to a unique kind of community. By tradition, Djordjevic implies not a grasp of dead propositions/dogmas but 'enacting ways of interacting with the world'. Tradition secures a narrative understanding of time and 'is realized by repetition wherein an end-state is (re-)affirmed by a person as she constantly (re-)orders her activities in its terms.' He links his critique further with anthropological research into the 'Islamist' movement in Egypt, drawing from the work of Saba Mahmood and Talal Asad. He argues that lowering the price of admission or hardships may lead to loneliness. Task-oriented work relies not on the workers' ability to express themselves but on their constitutive ties to their tradition. One way to deal with the endemic sense of loneliness, and the pathologies it engenders, is precisely by willingly joining a task-oriented work community. A natural outcome of membership in task-oriented work communities is that these will inflict suffering as they re-form the self. But it is precisely this re-formulation that constitutively connects a person to others via tradition.

Georgios Karakasis' *Rediscovering Joy in Work*, insists on the necessity of reintegrating joy in labor. Drawing from Marx and Martin Heidegger, the chapter examines how workers in the modern capitalist society are alienated both from their product and from their productive activity. The worker is alienated from the product of his work because his work is now totally automatized and mechanized. The worker is also alienated from himself/herself as a worker, having lost the joy of work as the creation and the relationship with the creation. Karakasis suggests that the joy in labor and recovery of the connection to labor as creative activity can be found only through freedom and the will to treat nature and the product of labor as the reflection of the completion of self-consciousness. He concludes that the goal of the modern capitalist human being is to tame the world, make it bend to his rules, and make the whole world creation of the human beings image. Drawing a comparison between the two kinds of alienation (as discussed by Marx and Heidegger), He writes: 'While for Marx, the worker separates himself from the world due to the alienation taking place during and after the productive activity, according to Heidegger the modern capitalist human being, due to the limitless capacities offered to him by technology, separates himself from the world through his desire for utter domination and control. The beings no longer stand against us as the unsurmountable objects, as the enemy that has to be overcome, but now become mere resources and the entire world an enormous warehouse always ready-at-hand to satisfy our incessant needs and desires. Even the distinction between subject and object disappears in this vortex where everything, human being included, becomes resources and raw material; everything becomes "standing-reserve".'

Anton Rennesland's *Cynical Reason in the Academe* uncovers the academician's vulnerable condition through Peter Sloterdijk's critique of the Enlightenment project concerning the discontent with capital. He finds that in this peculiar (pseudo-)enlightenment, reason emerges as cynical, falling short of actual enlightenment and embracing false consciousness. The dictates of the capital and the neoliberal stronghold have commodified the university as "University of Excellence" concerning itself not with spaces of the enclosure but with specializations, services, and control. The academician has become *Anybody* (*Das Man*), tantamount to citations, published articles, and students' evaluations. Rennesland discusses this peculiar loneliness of the academician under this veil of anonymity. He views that becoming-*Anyone* disburdens us of the more serious questions of life. Existentially, it eradicates identity and uniqueness, and in theory, leaves each alone to fend for herself. He reflects on our cynically blind religious dedication to Capital's language. The system reinforces itself by providing the same images and expressions that numb consciousness: 'It prompts a paranoia in each to outdo the other, to be cunning in playing the rigged game because without enough performance one is easily replaced.' What matters in the University of Excellence is not how hard the academician plays Capital's game but her behavior in playing. In face of Capital's dominating language, the academician vexes between the fear of non-compliance and dedication to one's discipline. A consequence of this obedience is that we experience alienating assimilation by growing nearly identical to each other with the same dreams, goals, and even causes of suffering.

Rennesland nudges us to reconsider the academician's loneliness from a mere existential offshoot to her magnifying lens when engaging with society: 'This magnifying lens affords her a seriousness not at what Capital provides, but ironically a seriousness of not taking things too seriously, a humor that releases us from our emotional comfort zones and affords us a shift to another plane, a cultivation not of diffused emotions but rage within this novel economy of garrulous discontent and resentment'. Loneliness as a divergence ought to be reckoned as a reminder of nature lost. It provides silence amidst Capital's commotion and a release from *Anyone*'s tyrannical overabundance. Paving a way for the positive potential of loneliness, Rennesland writes that from this lonely state, one realizes how thinking is at work in solitude. Isolation stands as a stimulus of thought, a slowness in contrary to Capital's speed. The authenticity of the cynic thus is the divergence from Capital's normalcy, and the academician's loneliness is not just a divergence but is in itself the difference, the opportunity to traverse to other planes for a reassertion of critical thought.

In *On the peculiar nature of work crisis in Academia*, Navjot Kaur attributes capitalism as the reason for the precipitation of a crisis in Academy. She finds that there is a shift in the perception of the nature of intellectual work from Aristotelian *praxis* to *poiesis*, which is contrary to the very essence of academic engagement and fosters loneliness. She views that the recognition of loneliness as a task of inwardness. She finds that in most cases the individual is responding in some or the other manner to the felt deficiency without actually having the necessary personal preparedness to deal with it. The preparedness to deal with it comes from 'the constant endeavor by an individual to enrich oneself, of developing one's creative faculties which allow his smooth transition into a thinking being'. Unable to find solace in one's response to the onslaught of affections the nature of which is not clear to oneself, one becomes a victim of the structures of manipulation working to keep one ignorant and passive.

Loneliness is a genuine response of an individual to the manipulative structures. It signifies one's discontentment with the affairs around. She draws from Berdyaev on the sad state of affairs of an academic environment where a genuine attitude of contemplation finds no appreciation. She proposes a change in attitude and expectations from the overall work, nature, and environment of the University to a change in the understanding and execution of academic work from what is in Aristotle *praxis* to *poiesis* form of activity. In the pressures of performance appraisals, the time and peace required for the roots of knowledge to grow are lost. The ad-hoc nature of teaching appointments has made the University an avenue for the exchange of benefits and mutual adjustments. Besides, she views that the protestant work ethic which feeds capitalism creates a fundamental discrepancy between the genuine expression of the self and the work culture. Work as a refinement of one's self, as one's constant endeavor at self-beautification is lost in the urgencies of the capital-driven academic structures.

The second section includes three essays that discuss loneliness and the crisis of work under capitalism in different contexts. Jedan Christoph's study on responsible capitalism demonstrates how large-scale and unrecognized loneliness is collectively produced by an invisible frame that structures work under capitalism. Cristopher Bonila focuses on the crisis of minimum wage labor under capitalism. He suggests transforming hierarchical jobs under capitalism to deal with this crisis. Irene Ortiz finds that considering precarious employment under capitalism as a matter of individual choice or personal failure is a fallacy. Highlighting the collective dimension of socio-political processes of discrimination, technological changes under capitalism, and globalization in creating unemployment, she offers hope in collective action and solidarity of the vulnerable groups.

Jedan Christoph's *The Invisible Frame* analyses 'the nexus of loneliness and work in the context of today's 'responsible capitalism' in an empirical-philosophical way. The study combines conceptual insights and interview data conducted with 'Ellen,' HR manager in a multinational energy company. Acknowledging that loneliness is not an inexorable ingredient of the human condition, through the study he argues the point, how loneliness is collectively produced 'by the ways in which we allow work to be organised'. The study shows the numerous instances of the darker side of work. Christoph finds that the employee-facing side of 'responsible capitalism' is the combination of two potent ideologies, neoliberalism and the human potential movement in management studies. Combined, they provide a 'frame' that structures policies, programs and perceptions, yet—and this is crucial—without the individual even noticing this. This frame is 'invisible to all intents and purposes yet it informs the thinking of participants to an astonishing degree.

The uncertainty of employment turns every worker into a hunter for possibilities and chances. Those who cannot keep up, become the prey. However, life as a hunter does not produce meaning and no occasion for reflection and sense. Drawing from Zygmunt Bauman's analysis of work and loneliness, he finds an odd mixture of acute observations and a disturbing undertone of quiet resignation in the present. Such large-scale and largely unrecognized loneliness forms the backdrop to a vast variety of practices around us today. Towards a more specific analysis, Christoph asks: 'Which ideological constructs inform the structure of modern work to produce this omnipresent loneliness?'

In *Cooperatives, Mental Health and The Critique of Wage Labor*, Cristopher Morales Bonila discusses the crisis of wage labor as a social phenomenon that manifests itself in many ways. Its main characteristic is the destruction of the equivalence between work and survival, that is, the possibility that a worker can have a job but cannot guarantee the minimum necessary to have a decent life. However, this is not the only feature of the crisis of wage labor. It is also shown in the emergence of numerous mental illnesses associated with wage-earning activity itself. Depression, anxiety, sleep disorders, etc., have become some of the most notable consequences of the new ways in which work is managed. Bonila raises concerns over the key issue: How can we solve such a crisis? He finds that the transformation of many hierarchically organized jobs into cooperatives is proving, in many experiments throughout the world, to be a way of reducing the occurrence of such mental illnesses.

The bare life of the unemployed by Irene Ortiz analyses the mechanisms through which people are forced into unemployment and loneliness in societies that tend to prioritize social recognition through wages and the type of work. She discusses the example of social movements that try to revoke the situation of loneliness and ostracism through collective mobilization and the resignification of precariousness. The case insight is the transformation brought about by the platform, People Affected by Mortgages, *PAH* in Spain in changing people from victims to activists and offering them roots and belonging. She also insists on not forgetting the important role that the capitalist system plays in the tacit condemnation of precarious people. Ortiz recommends that any claim that views the most precarious people, with worse working conditions and lower wages as a matter of individual choice is a fallacy that we must denounce.

There is no freedom of choice when the option is to choose between working under the conditions set by the employer and not being able to pay the rent for your accommodation. In this sense, Ortiz finds that it is important to recognize the abyss that separates her reading of the unemployed from that which only underlines the meritocratic system, where wealth is the result of effort. She finds that free choice is a chimera in an already degrading system, where what is presented is the imposition of working to survive. The absence of work, especially if an unemployment benefit is being collected, is understood as an individual failure. The responsibility, therefore, falls on the unemployed person, who not only has economic problems but also lacks social recognition. Thus, we avoid thinking about the labor market, the work system, and, ultimately, the economic system. Ortiz finds that it is not only a situation of economic precariousness but also an emotional one. Therefore, 'not only is the debate on unemployment monopolized by different types of expert and excludes the unemployed themselves, but in addition, the media broadcast strongly stigmatizing material about the jobless, concentrating on the responsibilities of the individuals themselves and not on the profound changes suffered by the country in a very short space of time.' She views that any attempts to analyze the unemployment situation without considering technological changes within the capitalist system, as well as the impact of globalization, as an error. In this way, the process of depersonalization of those excluded from the world of work has consequences on their psyche and on the way, they connect with their environment. Precisely due to the processes of discrimination, stigmatization, and depersonalization suffered by unemployed people, Ortiz invests in their potential for collective action and solidarity in restoring their dignity as a group that has been unjustly mistreated.

The last section includes four chapters on various concerns on the theme of work and loneliness in the context of the pandemic. Somyabrata Chowdhury discusses the concern of the subjectivity of migrants workers, both in their bodily life and in their reflective consciousness. With particular reference to Work from Home during the pandemic, Joseph Arel examines the relationship between alienated labor and home. Loneliness experienced during such a scenario invokes revolt and resistance against being separated from a genuine connection with the others and to the self. Tyler L. Jaynes discusses the legal concerns of labor performed by AIS (Artificial Intelligence Systems) concerning labor market expectations of patients with AIS-dependent bionics in the context of the pandemic. Thomas Spiegel takes up the concern of the digitally enabled parasocial relations that claim to curb loneliness. He finds it as an unfulfillable promise and rather cautions us against them in that parasocial relations may be conducive to the rise of totalitarianism.

Somyabrata Chowdhury's *Migration and Subjectivity* analyses the historical conditions of migration concerning its changing function in economic and social theory from the end of the 19th century to the present. He suggests a new political understanding of migratory subjectivity in terms of collective desire and emancipation instead of the purely historical determination of the migrant. He begins by analyzing the historical circumstances under which the physical movement of the migration takes place and then, presents the structural amplitude or range that supports the physical movement of migrants with the circumstances in which they take place. He finds that the most obvious example of such structural amplitude is the development of the global circuits of capitalism in at least the last hundred years that have led to both emergent patterns of the migration of labor and accelerated intensity of the very idea of migration. Chowdhury's analysis raises concerns over the modes of being of the migrant's existence both in its bodily life and in its reflective consciousness. He raises key questions about the migrant's subjectivity: 'Does the migrant consent to the larger logic of history that produces her migratory experience? Or even more directly and obscurely, what does the migrant want?Suppose one were to imagine that having gone through the historical and physical experience of migration the so called migratory subject that is the migrant refuses this experience…what form of subjectivity would correspond to this refusal?' He foresees that we might quickly put forward the hypothesis that this refusal marks the threshold of a political possibility. He views that this possibility can only arise from a passionate and difficult traversal of the historical and structural conditions of migrant's existence but it arises also as a certain intellectual refusal of the very conceptual terms of migration commonly used to describe the experience of migration.

He does not prescribe a political "solution" to the problem of migration but hopes to get a little closer to the 'real of history' that makes it possible to both de-familiarise ourselves to the so-called natural conditions of migration and also allows us to think of the minimal existential counter-conditions for a politics released from the dogma or fetish of migration imposed by capitalism today.

Joseph Arel's paper assesses the relationship between alienated labor and the home with particular reference to a world in which working from home is the norm. Unlike workspaces, home secures for us privacy of space and time. In the vicinity of one's own home, one can live as one desires, creatively or even as strangely as one wishes. He views that through the home, we retain the possibility and at times the reality of a measure of freedom made possible by having our own space, a place where we can shut the door and separate ourselves from work. This may change, however, in a world where working from home is increasingly the norm. Drawing from Marx, Arel writes that although our time away from work is where feeling at home is possible, the nature of alienated labor has made it difficult to feel at home. Work from home presents the possibility of a more totalizing form of alienation. When the ability to distinguish between the time at work and time away from work becomes vague, the integration of work into time off work is made more complete. Arel infers that 'If our time at work is alienated, and if we begin to feel as though we are always at work, then all of our time is alienated'. This implies an omnipresence of the office. All spaces are public spaces with the demands that this puts on us. The freedom of home becomes less and less a possibility. The private space of home becomes public through the surveillance of the camera or microphone, or even simply the requirement that all space available becomes workspace.

Besides, Arel cites a further form of dissociation found in our ability to relate to or understand the meaning of what we are doing. It refers to the inability to achieve some degree of mutual recognition since intimacy requires the active participation of the self and others. Arel elaborates: 'If I am alienated in my home, and this alienation seems to run around the clock, there will be no time where I am my self. This means that I will lose touch with myself, finding only an alienated self or, as Marx says, I will 'feel free only in my animal functions.' Following an intersubjective understanding of selfhood, Arel argues that, far from showing a particular weakness of ourselves as individuals, loneliness testifies to our nature as fundamentally a being-with-others. From out of the alienation of our labor, exaggerated by much of the WFH labor, comes a revolting signal from our nature. On a positive note, he views that the loneliness experienced urges resistance against being torn apart from a genuine connection to others and, as a result, to ourselves.

From Specialized to Hyper-Specialized Labour by Tyler L. Jaynes focuses on the legality of labor performed by artificial intelligence systems (AIS), and concerns for the labor market expectations of patients with AIS-dependent bionics. He argues for a legal distinction between augmented human groups and AIS to protect the computer, human, and laborer' interests in this realm. With the transition of the pandemic-gripped labour market *en masse* to remote capabilities to avert from national or international economic meltdowns, a concern arises that many job seekers simply cannot fit into the new roles being developed and implemented. Beyond the loss of on-site work, the market is unable to reverse the loss of many roles that are, and have been, taken over by artificial (computer) intelligence systems (CIS). The "business-as-usual" mentality that many have come to associate with pre-pandemic life supposedly took these losses into account, much to various societies' detriment during this international crisis. And unlike at the turn of the millennium, the market has come to realize that it cannot function without advanced CIS. Arguments can be made that humanity's currently most sophisticated CIS come nowhere near replicating the nuances that would prompt one to classify the system as being "human-like," and that they will remain this way for the foreseeable future. Jaynes argues what is conveniently ignored in this assessment is how not even three generations have passed since computer systems became an integral aspect of daily life. While the loss of work for humans as a result of this advancement of technology may not immediately reach concerning levels, it still raises concerns for how society should react to a lack of non-specialized work and the value of "humanness" in the labor market whether nationally or internationally. Jaynes's work intends to explore these concepts and provide anticipatory guidance on how humanity should adapt to post-pandemic life.

Underlying these transformations is the endless struggle to balance between repetitive functions that can be entrusted to a human and the ceaseless progression of artificial (or computer) intelligence systems to take these tasks either partially or entirely out of human hands.

Thomas J. Spiegel's chapter *Parasocial Relations, Loneliness, and Alienation in Digital Technologies,* takes up the question of parasocial relations, namely, What truly are parasocial relationships? How do they differ from regular interactions on a deeper level? What is the social ontology of parasocial relationships? Spiegel views loneliness as a secondary, yet fundamental existential condition of being human that consists in the absence of the second person. Trivially, loneliness is problematic in many different ways. Parasocial relations promise to curb loneliness through connecting people digitally to (re-)introduce the second person. Modern parasocial relationships are those which are qualitatively different in important aspects that are closely connected to the kind of lopsided interactivity and reciprocity enabled by internet-powered mass media, specifically influencer culture of Instagram or TikTok and interactive video and streaming services like YouTube and Twitch.

Drawing on the work of Martin Buber and Edith Stein, Speigel argues that parasocial relationships of the kind enabled by contemporary social media technologies do not qualify as relationships of the kind which would be able to dissipate loneliness. This is because they do not feature the second person at all. He writes: 'The specific mode of interactive engagement, while pretending to traverse the 'gulf' between the first and the second person, serves to mask this fundamental disconnect – a disconnect which is not present in genuine I-Thou relationships.' They offer merely an unfulfillable promise of companionship in an increasingly atomized social world. The article closes by pointing towards the connection between loneliness and totalitarianism famously posited by Hannah Arendt to the effect that parasocial relationships, rather than combatting loneliness, might be conducive to the rise of totalitarianism.

PART I.

THEORETICAL PERSPECTIVES

THE POLITICAL CONCERNS OF LONELINESS

PRITIKA NEHRA

> 'No man is an island,
> Entire of itself,
> Every man is a piece of Continent,
> A part of the main.'
> —John Donne[1]

> 'You'd be surprised how quickly the mind goes soggy in the absence of other people. One person alone is not a full person. We exist in relation to others. I was one person: I risked becoming no person.'
> —Margaret Atwood[2]

> 'It isn't running away they're afraid of. We wouldn't get far. It's those other escapes, the ones that you can open in yourself, given a cutting edge.'
> —Margaret Atwood[3]

Loneliness brings into question the dualism of the external world and the internal reality of human beings (subjectivity and the world) more sharply. It makes us think about our bodily embeddedness in the world. Loneliness is not merely a subjective response but more importantly, it is a response to the intersubjectivity of the world. Through the lens of Hannah Arendt's views, first I develop a phenomenology of various lonely states viz., isolation, solitude, loneliness, superfluousness, and virtuality to demarcate them from each other. Then, I proceed to establish how each of them connect with intersubjectivity within a common, shared world and the political conse-

---

[1] Donne, John (1624). 'Devotions Upon Emergent Occasions, Meditations XVII' in *Donne's Devotions*. Cambridge University Press: 98.

[2] Atwood, Margaret (2020). *The Testaments*. Vintage: 132.

[3] Atwood, Margaret (1996). *The Handmaid's Tale*. Vintage: 18.

quences of experiencing these states of loneliness. Instead of a negative characterization of loneliness as a subjective emotion of lack/absence/loss[4], I propose to view loneliness as a response to the intersubjectivity of the human world which calls for political considerations. Instead of approaching the subjectivity and the world as separate, I consider both the internal human experience and the external socio-political world as connected. The experience of the other plays an important role in not just loneliness but all experiences of the ego. It is important to know what triggers the rupture or gap that dislocates the ego from itself ('the two-in-one') in case of loneliness. What makes loneliness a dehumanizing experience is its impact on the capacities of thinking, speech, and action. The critique also raises concerns about democracy at the workplace: to consider how unjust socio-political structures are bound to create social pathologies; how we respond to vulnerable others in the work settings and maintain exceptions about their silence and invisibility with impunity. In the present times, when we are experiencing increasing concern about mental health issues and stress management at workplaces, we also find that the socio-political conditions that form the background for these pathologies take a back seat. We are continuously captivated by a picture of politics that on the one hand celebrates the voices of the vulnerable but on the other hand also consistently undermines them and obscures their agency, which creates them in the first place. The negative experiences of suffering in an already degenerating socio-political system that contribute to our pathological social reality are kept at bay by making its victims invisible, lonely, and superfluous. The importance of uncovering the political concerns of this suffering and making it visible lies in its potential to change our approach to social pathology.

1. Solitude, Loneliness, Superfluousness, Isolation, and Virtuality

Solitude *(Einsamkeit)* and loneliness *(Vereinsamung)* are concerned with the experience of intersubjectivity, i.e., how to *inter-act* with other human beings. Loneliness as a phenomenon emerges whenever there is a lack/absence of a tangible common world and connectedness. It is the nearness to others that is lost in loneliness. However, it is not enough to say that loneliness is merely the absence of a common social world and inter-connected-

---

[4] This approach is common among psychologists. Recently, loneliness as an emotional condition of absence has been proposed by Roberts, T. and Krueger, J. (2021), Loneliness and the Emotional Experience of Absence. *South J Philos*. https://doi.org/10.1111/sjp.12387

ness and that it can be understood in negative terms only. Instead of a negative characterization of loneliness as a lack/absence/loss, I posit an understanding of loneliness as a response to the intersubjectivity of the human world. Such an understanding has important implications in our understanding of political freedom and democracy concerning situations of exclusion from the socio-political spaces and domination as freedom's other. The tangible common world and interconnectedness are not merely some desired material 'social goods'[5] or subjective psychological needs that can be externally refilled as a cure to loneliness but they express a relationship to the human socio-political world. The condition of absence of a common social world and intersubjectivity is a political question in the sense that it relates to the concerns of freedom, belonging and equality, i.e., an absence of considering another person as an equal fellow human or even a complete human being (as in case of slaves in the ancient times and stateless people); of abandoning her/him from the space of listening and caring. How does everyone in society become unavailable or absent for the lonely? How does the lonely become invisible to others? Although, the other people are still around, and yet they cease to mean in any relationship to the lonely person or one ceases to belong to the world? One is lonely when the important others are not present for any real meaningful conversations leading to a lack of belongingness required to participate in a common world[6].

Loneliness always refers to a sphere of social intercourse, wherein one is deserted by all human companionship ('abandoned by everything and everybody') whereas isolation refers to reaching an impasse, when the political sphere of a person's life is destroyed. One can be isolated and lonely without being alone. Isolation renders one impotent for collective action, that constitutes one's political agency. It happens during tyrannies when 'human capacities for action and power are frustrated' (Arendt 1994, 474). One can also be isolated and alone but not lonely, i.e., despite the inability to act collectively, one can still act on one's own and create new objects for consumption by the human world. Isolation marks the impotency to act collectively but one can still act individually. Isolated people are powerless by definition. Although the political contacts are broken, yet all contacts are not severed. The sphere of private life and the capacities for experience,

---

[5] For example, Roberts, T. and Krueger, J. (2021) in their paper 'Loneliness and the Emotional Experience of Absence.' *South J Philos* write that one of their aims in the paper is 'to highlighting the range and depth of the social goods that may be experienced as absent in this complex emotion'.

[6] How do conversations cease to be meaningful? I shall take up this concern further in the section 4 on conversations with the lonely.

fabrication (work), and thought are left intact. However, isolation in the form of labor[7] disables the presence of others as it disallows even a common material world of objects. This kind of isolation in the form of labor paves the way for loneliness.

In the state of loneliness, one can neither act collectively nor alone. It is the state of uprootedness that is a harbinger of superfluousness, a state of having no place/belongingness in the world[8]. There is no common shared world with anyone, marked by a loss of sense of time and place or any society or hope of being visible/heard by others. Superfluity is the limit condition under which no form of politics is possible as the agency of the superfluous is obscured in the political sphere. It marks a relation of abandonment and how domination is fluidly connected with the social spaces by rendering the superfluous and lonely to invisibility and nakedness of bare life. Loneliness, a social pathology is associated with domination in that it underlines that there is something wrong in the socio-political domain of intersubjectivity. Loneliness alters our reality into a spacelessness and atemporal existence in the experience of the present moment ('now'). It is a breaking up of the lifeworld as a means to illuminate our concrete existence in going beyond the 'idle talk'.

Solitude requires being alone, in the sense of absolute independence. However, loneliness 'shows itself most sharply in company with others' (Arendt, 1994, 476). Solitude opens up doors to thinking dialogue with oneself while still being connected with the human world of others through an imagined community. But it is not the same as isolation, which is the fertile ground for killing solitude. Isolation kills the social connection with other humans when one is not able to see one's reflection in the eyes of others[9]. Solitude is something to be sought but it shouldn't always be found because solitude

---

[7] Arendt defines labor as an activity done for preserving biological necessities for self-preservation. Labor is also ascribed to slaves in ancient times. (Arendt, *The Human Condition*, 7, 83-84)

[8] In *The Origins of Totalitarianism*, Arendt writes: "To be uprooted means to have no place in the world, recognized and guaranteed by others; to be superfluous means not to belong to the world at all. Uprootedness can be the preliminary condition for superfluousness, just as isolation can (but must not) be the preliminary condition for loneliness. Taken in itself, with our consideration of its recent historical causes and its new role in politics, loneliness is at the same time contrary to the basic requirements of the human condition *and* one of the fundamental experiences of every human life." (475)

[9] However, one can also be physically isolated and socially connected as in the case of the present covid-19 pandemic globally.

can also become loneliness. This happens when all by oneself one is abandoned by one's self. In loneliness, the self disappears and one ceases to be. While the self is intact in solitude and engages in thinking dialogue with oneself; in loneliness, the self disappears due to the lack of affirmation by others, who are equal and trustworthy and one ceases to trust one's thoughts. It brings anxiety and fear. In response to the question of how to *inter-act* with others, solitude seeks a way inwards by engaging with the world through thinking, loneliness seeks a way outwards through collective action/agency which is denied to it. Both are a response to the plurality of the shared human world. Organized loneliness is more lethal than the unorganized impotence of those who are ruled by tyrannical forces.

Virtuality is the disembodied, technological space of mere appearance. A virtual presence/absence creates fragments/manifolds of assembled identities without any wholistic view. Virtuality also creates a specific kind of identity which is non-haptic and disembodied.

These experiences of fragmented temporalities and intersubjective distancing impact the political existence of human beings in a shared common world. Solitude and isolation screen out any external collective action. Loneliness limits the possibility of any individual or collective action. The horizon of possibilities of virtually distanced, disembodied collective and individual actions is also curtailed in being open to manipulations within the digital space of technology and thereby, lacking any space in the real world. These experiences of loneliness/isolation/superfluity/solitude/virtuality result in framing a new form of limited or no political existence in the human world concerning a curtailed intersubjectivity.

2. Loneliness and Intersubjectivity

In an ontological sense, human beings exist in a relationship with the world. In this sense, Solitude and loneliness are varied forms of existence in the world. Although, we no longer live in Arendt's description of 20th-century totalitarian crisis, the historical ground for fragmentation and atomization of the society, yet we find that the world is increasingly inhabited by large populations of lonely, isolated, solitary humans that remain invisible to one another in their full humanity. Solitude and loneliness emerge as our affinities to the self through our encounter with an other (either a radically different 'other' that invokes solitude or an 'other' who is same enough to abandon the ego to loneliness). It would be a mistake to infer that since loneliness is a subjective experience, intersubjectivity or the connection with others is inessential to it. The experience of the other plays an important role in not just loneliness but all experiences of the ego. It is important to know what triggers the rupture or gap that dislocates the ego from itself (the two-in-one) in case of loneliness.

Loneliness is not just social alienation but also a self-alienation, namely, that we no longer belong to ourselves too. It is symptomatic of a feeling of no longer belonging to the world and that there is no place for the lonely on the face of the Earth. It leads to a loss of trust in oneself and a loss of confidence in the world. An easy way to avoid the domination of the exclusionary forces acting on the lonely is to find solace within when no place in the world is available to you but freedom from loneliness cannot be achieved either in isolation or solitude. Social or civil freedom from loneliness requires the presence of others who are trustworthy and non-dominating[10]. For a way-out of solitude, the internal two-in-one dialogue needs to stop for which one needs the other for the 'two-in-one' to become one again, i.e., one unchangeable individual whose identity can never be mistaken for that of any other.[11] (Arendt 1994, 476) It happens when the outside world intrudes upon our thinking and curtails the ongoing flow of thought. Loneliness emerges only when one is confronted with an other, who is just like the ego that leaves the ego unchanged. Adrian Costache explains it in very lucid terms:

> "… solitude and loneliness ought to be defined as a rapport to oneself through an other. Such a rapport becomes solitude when the other encountered is a radical alterity displacing the ego from the self and subjecting it to a complete transformation (This also explains why solitude is sought after and always takes the form of a re-collection.) And it takes the form of loneliness when the other encountered by the ego is just an other like the self, an other which leaves the ego completely unchanged even though it introduces a gap within itself. In solitude one becomes two-in-one through a third while in loneliness one encounters a same and is multiplied three times. According to this logic being neither alone, nor lonely means arriving through a third person not to a two-in-one or a multiple of one but straightforwardly to a

---

[10] In *Republicanism: A Theory of Freedom and Government*, Philip Pettit views social or civil freedom as "the status associated with living among other people, none of whom dominates you" (Pettit 1997, 66)

[11] In *The Origins of Totalitarianism* Arendt writes: "For the confirmation of my identity I depend entirely upon other people; and it is the great saving grace of companionship for solitary men that it makes them 'whole' again, saves them from the dialogue of thought in which one remains always equivocal, restores the identity which makes them speak with the single voice of one unexchangeable person." (Arendt 1994, 476)

> two. Being neither alone, nor lonely means arriving to a two through a third." (Costache 2013, 138)

Arendt makes a distinction between equality and sameness. While equality is a political concept that refers to a normative ideal, sameness implies the similarity of the natural givenness of our biology as human beings. Equality is an artificially agreed-upon political notion. Since humans are different from each other in their social, cultural, economic circumstances, we agree politically to allow everyone the treatment of equality in the public sphere and equality before the law. Political equality allows everyone to express their differences in the public domain whereas the sameness of our biological make-up homogenizes us as humans having the same fundamental needs for survival. In this sense, equality is not opposed to difference but it opposes sameness. Reducing the political space of human affairs to the sameness of life of bare necessities (i.e., the life of *animal laborans*) is extremely dangerous as it extinguishes the space for all differences and plurality and thereby, creates the experience of loneliness.

3. Thinking alone

In face of the lack of intersubjectivity, the most affected faculty is that of thinking[12]. We enter alien modes of speech and thought, where there is no common ground for understanding with others and self-understanding. But does loneliness lead to thoughtlessness?[13] The answer to this question lies in the fact that in loneliness we trade our capacity to think for rhetorical and performative speech that barricades any thought. This inability 'to stop and think' (Arendt 1978, 4) while immersed in loneliness further frustrates all communication with others. Since there are no strong forces of habit, tradition, common sense, or religion that can bring people together into a fold of any sort of belonging in the present times, there is an increasing yearning

---

[12] Arendt writes, "The only capacity of the human mind which needs neither the self not the other nor the world in order to function safely and which is as independent of experience aa it is of thinking is the ability of logical reasoning whose premise of the self-evident. The elementary rules of cogent evidence, the truism that two and two equals four cannot be perverted even under the conditions of absolute loneliness. It is the only reliable "truth" human beings can fall back upon once they have lost the mutual guarantee, the common sense, men need in order to experience and live and know their way in a common world." (*The Origins of Totalitarianism*, 1994, 477)

[13] Martin Shuster takes up this question in his article 'Language and Loneliness: Arendt, Cavell, and Modernity' *International Journal of Philosophical Studies* Vol. 20(4), 2012: 473–497.

for a home and belonging among the rootless and lonely people. Any opportunity of membership into any form of a community (even if that involves obeying a certain norm and a logical set of operations) is irresistible for the lonely because it gives a temporary meaning to her/his life. In the absence of intersubjectivity and plurality of our socio-political world, the internal dialogue that one has within the self is the last trace of company. This internal two-in-one dialogue is also the space of solitude in which thinking takes place[14]. It is a secure, private space where active thinking is possible. Often, we seek such solitude in crucial moments in life as this inward journey offers opportunities for discoveries of resources and avenues within us[15] But this internal dialogue after the withdrawal from the socio-political world does not offer any salvation for the lonely. This is because there is an added dimension of suffering along with solitude in the case of loneliness. Thinking under conformism and pressure changes its outcome. One must also note that thinking is not the same as rationalizing. Arendt describes thinking as 'a kind of action' which arouses us to kick out of the clutches of mass conformism[16]. It is the force of thinking that draws us out of dark times to act when everyone else is swept away unthinkingly. However, standing apart from the crowd does not imply standing alone as thinking is brought to fulfillment only when one enters the public space for action. Without a free space for speaking, questioning, and answering others, thinking ceases to flourish. Thinking is reduced to a set of logical operations for the lonely. Although one can deliver oneself out of the thoughtlessness of loneliness by the sheer ability to replace it with the illuminating thoughtfulness of solitude, it is not a solution to loneliness as it calls for the presence of others who are equal. In loneliness, both the ability to recognize the plurality of the self within and the plurality of the others in the world are lost simultaneously.[17]

---

[14] Arendt writes that thinking originates in 'absolute solitude' (Arendt 2005, 20-21). Yet, she is skeptical of any thinking that takes place outside the world (any transcendental space or a view from nowhere as they are unavailable to human beings). Although thinking demands separation from the affairs of the world, yet it is always about the talkative and contested spaces of our human world.

[15] Arendt quotes Cato in *Questions on Moral Philosophy* to emphasize this active solitude: "Never am I more active than when I do nothing, never am I less alone than when I am by myself" (Arendt 2003, 99)

[16] "When everybody is swept away unthinkingly by what everybody else does and believes in, those who think are drawn out of hiding because their refusal to join in is conspicuous and thereby becomes a kind of action." (Arendt 1978, 192)

[17] In the words of Arendt, 'Self and world, capacity for thought and experience are lost at the same time' (Arendt 1994, 477).

4. Conversations with the Lonely

All our experiences of the world are mediated through linguistic speech and gestures, signs, symbols which too can be interpreted linguistically. Arendt emphasizes the importance of speech in humanizing the world: 'we humanize what is going on in the world and in ourselves only by speaking of it, and in the course of speaking of it we learn to be human.' (Arendt 1995, 25) Speech also concerns the ethical struggles of our life when we try to express ourselves in dark situations where language alienates our experiences off the world. To be impoverished of others also makes us lose our voice and having nothing to say.

Arendt had the stateless person in mind while discussing loneliness. She also mentions the slave in ancient times in this context. Drawing a comparison between the stateless person with the slave, she is of the view that the slave is still exploitable and useful to others for various reasons of labor and work and has some rights (for example, the master cannot kill the slave but nobody will ask questions about the murder of a stateless person), which are completely denied to the stateless person. In the context of precarious work as the contemporary analog to slavery, the position of speech is reserved only for the authority figures while the jobholders need to understand only orders and not speak as any such speech is automatically registered as defiance. They can only make noise or revolt (akin to an *animal laborans*) but the capacity for speech is reserved only for the authority in control. It is a problem of not acknowledging the speech of the other and not considering them as a complete human. The lonely are often speechless for this reason. This idea of leaving the essence of being human (as capable of thinking, speech/*zōon logon ekhon*, and action/*zōon politikon*) untouched, impinges on their human dignity making them superfluous. It is dehumanizing and tyrannical to not allow any political action from individuals.

Speech is not mere talk or content of the conversation but it is the pleasure in the person that makes a conversation meaningful. That is why many people become unavailable for conversations with the lonely because they cease to have respect or trust in them. They no longer stand unto their words. It is hard to take advice from a hypocrite or share your thoughts with someone who makes you feel insignificant or who is snotty enough to think of themselves as all-knowing. The tone of such conversations also implies considering oneself as educating another, of knowing better or being better than the other, which sounds like a play for emphasizing power. Such conversations are akin to advertising boards, where one is always speaking to a passive audience and do not seek any active participants[18]. Such presumptuous people labor under a false belief of knowing better and considering themselves as the center of the universe. These nuances of conversation are often ignored in considering alienation and how they affect the other. An openness to the world and a space for free speech are the prerequisites for healthy public conversations. Yet, we find that there are very few chances of a meaningful conversation not just for the lonely but even for the non-lonely people, who discourage such attitudes. One may also ask here: What is it that makes pleasure possible in another person? About this, Arendt writes, "Pleasure, which is fundamentally the intensified awareness of reality, springs from a passionate openness to the world and love of it." Regarding conversations, she also writes: "Gladness, not sadness, is talkative, and truly human dialogue differs from mere talk or even discussion in that it is entirely permeated by pleasure in the other person and what he says." (Arendt 1995, 15) This feeling of a genuine gladness and pleasure in the fellow humans is amiss in the world of loneliness.

5. Agency and Loneliness in the context of Work

Next, I discuss how unequal work relations, precarious employment, everyday experiences of disrespect and micro-aggressions undermine human agency in uneventful ways[19]. Work corresponds to the 'artificial' world of man-made things distinct from the natural surroundings. Individual human life is housed in the boundaries of the artificial world of workmanship. Work provides an artificial world that lasts through generations of endless human life cycles and transcends the utility of objects of use. It is a world-building activity. The most important task of the activities of work is 'to offer mortals a dwelling place more permanent and more stable than themselves' (Arendt 1998, 152). The activities of human beings can be preserved in lasting things produced by work. Work in this sense also acts as a storehouse for human memory. Work is needed to ease the burden of labor and to preserve the immortality of human actions in things produced by human artifice. The human condition of work is worldliness. Arendt emphasizes the importance

---

[18] Myisha Cherry presents a fine discussion on these concerns of conversations in the context of race, class and gender in her book, *Unmuted: Conversations on Prejudice, Oppression, and Social Justice* (2019). OUP.

[19] Andrew Schaap discusses 'how struggles for appearances are limited and shaped by the social conditions within which they are enacted' in his paper 'Inequality, Loneliness and Political Appearance: Picturing Radical Democracy with Hannah Arendt and Jacques Rancière' *Political Theory*, 2020.

of work in the work of writers, artists, poets, historians, etc without which the story of humanity shall not find a place anywhere else:

> 'If the *animal laborans* need the help of homo faber to ease his labor and remove his pain and if mortals need his help to erect a home on earth, acting and speaking men need the help of homo faber in his highest capacity, that is, the help of the artist, of poets and historiographers, of monument-builders or writers, because without them the only product of their activity, the story they enact and tell, would not survive at all.' (Arendt, 1998, 173)

There is no human life without labor, no human world without work, and no freedom without action. The only ground on which Arendt rejects the artificial world of human fabrication is that it is built on a means-end approach (However, she also acknowledges that there are non-utility based products of work as well, e.g., art). This approach threatens the stability of the world of objects as every product is meant for the sake of further ends.

Although our workspaces have changed enormously in the present times engaging with innovation and creativity yet we find that they have not changed much of their social spaces. The problem with the social space of work is that it is modeled on the household, where everyone has one interest and there is no space for disagreements and differences. It unites people together in 'the form in which the fact of mutual dependence for the sake of life and nothing else assumes public significance' (Arendt 1998, 46). In the household, the head of the family rules, but in the case of society, the opinion of the majority leads. The dominance of the majority in society implies conformism to a given set of codes and conventions of behavior by everyone. But since it is ruled by no one but all, there is nobody to take responsibility. Arendt herself witnesses this cult formation within academia, which she referred to as the rule of cooperation[20] among intellectuals that can also lead to phenomena such as intellectual bullying. She argues that it is tyrannical to not expect any disagreement and action from individuals. There is

[20] 'And cooperation meant that your friends cooperated. The problem, the personal problem, was not what our enemies might be doing, but what our friends were doing. This wave of cooperation...made you feel surrounded by an empty space, isolated. I lived in an intellectual milieu... and I came to the conclusion that cooperation was, so to speak, the rule among intellectuals... I left Germany guided by the resolution that 'Never again!' I will never have anything to do with 'the history of ideas' again. I didn't, indeed, want to have anything to do with this sort of society again.' (Arendt qtd. in Elisabeth Young-Bruehl 2004,108.)

a gap between belonging and responsibility in the social realm. While everyone belonged to the social realm, there is nobody to take responsibility for.

Privacy or secrecy in the issues concerning work implies a deprivation from an objective relation with others in the public sphere, where one is free to belong or separate from others. One of the outcomes of this deprivation from speaking in the public about workspaces in the present society is the experience of extreme loneliness. It not only deprives people of the external public world but also from the protection of the private, where one could remain prosperous and wealthy. The precarious conditions of academic work whereby individuals are prevented from identifying with their work render them substitutable/replaceable. They are unable to see their work as making any meaningful difference. The social conditions of inequality and loneliness increase vulnerability and compulsive patterns of behavior (the alienating pathologies of work). Impersonal solidarity and self-responsibility fostered by the membership of a profession is an antidote to such alienation. How else do we account for the moral meaning of work? This points to the role of public institutions which should ideally facilitate struggles for equality across social differences yet we find that such institutions fail to nourish any solidarity. Academia is organized to serve only a few while the many remain on the margins.

Arendt writes that the world has entered 'the last stage of laboring society, the society of jobholders' [which] demands of its members a sheer automatic functioning, as though individual life had been submerged in the overall life-process of the species and the only active decision still required of the individual were to let go, so to speak, to abandon his individuality, the still individually sensed pain and trouble of living, and acquiesce in a dazed, 'tranquilized', functional type of behavior' (Arendt 1998, 322). We have witnessed the hubris of the technological/scientific mind, which has taken over all means of the world of production. Work has become more demanding and less fulfilling due to the lack of security by professional institutions against arbitrary interference[21]. However, this does not mean that there is a particular dominator, who commands such arbitrariness rather any would-be authority takes the garb of the dominating figure in this situation. The

[21] This does not mean that security is the only parameter of freedom. In *Statelessness, Domination, and Unfreedom: Arendt and Pettit in Dialogue*, Christian Rostbøll's writes: 'The subject that is to be free can appear only in a human world in which others are responsive to one's actions and opinions. In this way there is a further positive dimension to freedom than mere security and protection, a dimension of intersubjective relationships and human responsiveness.' (Rostbøll, 26)

dominated has nobody or nowhere she can press the claims, not because she does not have access to any constitutional or human rights but because nobody would listen and care as it has become the normative condition. The academic precariat has no status apart from being a replaceable worker or standing at the brink of the membership in the professional community lacking 'a right to the statuses and powers that make our freedom secure and allow us to be free to avoid the ills and evils that result from the loss of such a status.' (Bohman 2008, 203). This view is also encapsulated in Arendt's conception of natality or the ability to begin anew that acknowledges the possibility of being recognized as someone in an accepting and responsive community[22]. The lack of social status and unfreedom of the precarious worker is not because of an absence of security from domination *per se* but because the social structure is designed in such a way to provide positive privileges to some as opposed the others. It is not that some people can dominate the precarious worker in capitalist societies but what is more important to note is that they also have the accepted right to do so with impunity. It is also a concern for questioning their legitimacy: on what grounds do some have the right to dominate others? The social pathology in the form of loneliness results from such domination which is 'the product of social structures and institutions, of the capitalist division of labor' (Rostbøll, 26). Precarious, meaningless employment is not something that people have but it is something that happens to them as an onslaught of a structurally unjust socio-political world. Nobody signs up to be lonely.

This is associated with the larger crisis of capitalism in our present times in addition to racism, casteism, misogynistic and patriarchal tendencies. The widespread loneliness in a mass society where people are deprived of any possibility of a meaningful action exposes them to arbitrary violence as a consequence of being substitutable/replaceable in such a system. The capitalist processes uproot people paving a way for unemployment, loneliness, and homelessness. There is a structural inequality between those who control the game and those who do the bidding.

6. Avoiding Loneliness

The point of this critique is to emphasize that human existence has a public dimension that involves others with differences who too share freedom to speak, think and act irrespective of their precarious situations. The way to

[22] In *The Human Condition,* Arendt explains that beginning 'is not the beginning of something but of somebody, who is a beginner himself' (177)

avoid loneliness is paved through a political change in the structural inequalities and injustice that create the vulnerable, precarious conditions of work and also the stateless people. It is important to see the otherwise invisible and vulnerable others as actual people with perspectives and as having knowledge, which can be mutually beneficial for everyone in a healthy society. The solution to the problem of how to overcome loneliness (or how to protect people from internalizing the sense of their superfluity) lies in creating pluralistic spaces for trust and belonging with an attitude of care for the world rather than domination from above. However, as a caution, one should reject a togetherness that is based on the sameness of lonely individuals as it is a breeding ground for totalitarian practices. To combat loneliness, one must also secure the sanctuaries of solitude (a friendship with the self) that cradle thinking in dark and lonely times. Friendship with others is a way of building solidarity to overcome loneliness. Two characteristic features of such friendship are openness to others and plurality. It creates feelings of mutual pleasure and joy rather than pain and suffering. One can also view it as a willingness or fellow feeling to share the joy of being in the company of equals, which is far superior from the pain and suffering of the lonely when lacking this company. The pleasure in the company of others depends on the foreignness of the plurality of our public spaces and not sameness of our biological form.

Arendt criticizes the modern Behavioral sciences which 'aim to reduce man as a whole, in all its activities, to the level of a conditioned and behaving animal' (Arendt 1998, 45). The solutions offered by the behavioral sciences to problems of modernity like loneliness and lack of space for excellence in deeds 'concerns only a possible change in the psychology of human beings—their so called behavior patterns—not a change of the world they move in.' (Arendt 1998, 49). The social realm removes all differences and insists on equality in terms of behavior and conduct[23]. There is no space for

---

[23] Further referring to the inadequacy of psychological approaches to social pathologies, Verovšek quotes Azmanova to point out, 'once crisis and social pathology become the status quo, the inability of these descriptors to motivate social and political theorizing can lead to a "crisis of critique" (Azmanova 2014: 357)' (Verovšek 2019, 2).

Loneliness is a social problem that is not discovered by the critic based on a utopian vision of future health but in a system that is already showing objective signs of dysfunction in the present. The crisis of work relations is a moment of action and key decision making that will decide whether we will be able to resolve the problem of loneliness or not. It also decides how we will diagnose this as suffering coming out of a dehumanizing experience at the workspaces and the causes thereof.

individuality and differences in it. One of the characteristic features of the public realm is its individuality. In Arendt's words:

> "...the public realm itself, the *polis*, was permeated by a fiercely agonal spirit, where everybody had constantly to distinguish himself from others, to show through unique deeds or achievements that he was the best of all (*aien aristeuein*). The public realm, in other words, was reserved for individuality." (Arendt 1998, 41)

This *agonal* character of the public realm is destroyed with the rise of the social realm in the modern age. The Public sphere itself becomes a political problem of exclusion and meaninglessness in the present case.

The question of freedom and political power can be phrased in terms of intersubjective involvement and membership and the conditions of non-domination. What does it mean to belong to a plural human community? Is it mere instrumental participation or does it include any intrinsic value to it in appreciating the human capacities to think, speak and act? Although work is not the only way of forming belonging as one can also associate with others outside of work in the political sphere and also instrumentally through the democratic procedure that secures their freedom against any arbitrary domination and decisions. But one can also ask: 'Can one combat the irresponsibility of the professional intellectual whose inmost tendency is to "[fabricate] ideas about everything" by a contrivance of thought that defers intersubjective engagement?' (Cuthoys 2017, 2)

Conclusion

The lonely person implies an enclosed wordless mind and raises questions about meaning and the dependency on other minds for a conception of an intersubjective and shared social reality. Human existence is structurally oriented toward others. Loneliness also brings into question the dualism of the external world and the internal reality of human beings (subjectivity and the world) more sharply. It makes us think about our bodily embeddedness in the world.

The lonely states illuminate our concrete existence. It is the private sphere that illuminates the uniqueness of an individual that is intimately connected with experiences of inequality in the political sphere and discrimination in the social sphere of mass conformism. I have proposed a view of loneliness that is not a negative characterization of the phenomena *per se* marked by an absence but I view this lack as a response to the intersubjectivity of the human world that is a marker of dehumanization and unfreedom. Loneliness brings forth the question of how to be alone and how to be with others i.e. friendship with the self and with the others. Thinking in solitude unfolds our internal dialogue with the self and leads to the invention of new avenues within which can help us in critical situations in life. Loneliness raises concerns about something going wrong in the political domain. The role of philosophy here is to guide us on how to befriend ourselves in the dialogue with ourselves and to be friends with others to create and repair belonging in an otherwise broken world.

References

Alberti, Fay Bound (2018). One Is the Loneliest Number: The History of a Western Problem. Aeon. https://aeon.co/ideas/one-is-the-loneliest-number-the-history-of-a-western-problem

Arendt, Hannah (1994), *The Origins of Totalitarianism*. Harcourt: 474-476

Arendt, Hannah (1998). The Human Condition. Chicago:7, 41, 45-46, 49, 83-84, 152, 173, 177, 322.

—. (2003). 'Some Questions of Moral Philosophy'in Jerome Kohn (ed.) *Responsibility and Judgment*, New York, NY: Schocken, pp. 49–146.

—. (1995).'On Humanity in Dark Times: Thoughts on Lessing' in Arendt, Hannah. *Men in Dark Times*, Harcourt: 15, 25.

—. (2005). *The Promise of Politics*. Schocken:20-21.

—. (1978). *Life of the Mind.* Harcourt:4.

Atwood, Margaret (2020). *The Testaments*. Vintage.

—. (1996). *The Handmaid's Tale*. Vintage: p.18.

Berkowitz, Roger (2009). 'Solitude and the Activity of Thinking.' SSRN Scholarly Paper ID 1336242. Rochester, NY: Social Science Research Network. https://papers.ssrn.com/abstract=1336242.

—. (2020). 'Loneliness and the Loss of the Common World.' *The Hannah Arendt Center*. Accessed May 11, 2020. https://hac.bard.edu/amor-mundi/loneliness-and-the-loss-of-the-common-world-2020-05-07.

Bohman, James (2008). Nondomination and Transnational Democracy. In C. Laborde & J. Maynor (Eds.), *Republicanism and Political Theory* (pp. 190- 216). Oxford: Blackwell Publishing.

Borren, Marieke (2013). "'A Sense of the World': Hannah Arendt's Hermeneutic Phenomenology of Common Sense." *International Journal of Philosophical Studies* 21 (2): 225–55.
https://doi.org/10.1080/09672559.2012.743156.

Cherry, Myisha (2019). *Unmuted: Conversations on Prejudice, Oppression, and Social Justice*. OUP.

Christian F Rostbøll, 2014. 'Statelessness, Domination, and Unfreedom: Arendt and Petit in Dialogue' in C Dahl and T Andersen Nexö (eds) *To Be Unfree: Republicanism and Unfreedom in History, Literature, and Philosophy*. Bielefelt: Transcript Verlag, 19-36.

Costache, Adrian. 2013.'On Solitude and Loneliness in Hermeneutical Philosophy.' *Meta: Research in Hermeneutics, Phenomenology, and Practical Philosophy,* Vol.5, No.1:130-149.

Curthoys, Ned (2017).On Active Solitude: Caring for the Self in Hannah Arendt's Moral Philosophy. *Graduate Faculty Philosophy Journal*, Vol.38, Issue 2: 1-23.

Donne, John (1923). *Donne's Devotions*. Cambridge University Press: 98.

Delistraty, Cody (2016). How Loneliness Generates Empathy and Shapes Identity. *Aeon.*

Ekbia, Hamid (2020). 'Solace in Solitude.' *Los Angeles Review of Books*. Accessed May 11, 2020.
https://lareviewofbooks.org/short-takes/solace-in-solitude/.

Elisabeth Young-Bruehl (2004). *Hannah Arendt: For Love of the World*. Yale:108.

Gadamer, Hans-Georg (1988). 'Isolation as a Symptom of Self- Alienation,' in *In Praise of Theory. Speeches and Essays.*Yale: 101-113.

Jaffer, Nabeelah (2018). Loneliness Is the Common Ground of Terror and Extremism. *Aeon.* https://aeon.co/essays/loneliness-is-the-common-ground-of-terror-and-extremism

Lucas, Sarah Drews. 2019. "Loneliness and Appearance: Toward a Concept of Ontological Agency." *European Journal of Philosophy* 27 (3): 709–22. https://doi.org/10.1111 /ejop.12432.

Pettit, Philip. (1997). *Republicanism: A Theory of Freedom and Government.* Oxford, NY: Oxford University Press.

Roberts, T. and Krueger, J. (2021), Loneliness and the Emotional Experience of Absence. South J Philos.
https://doi.org/10.1111/sjp.12387

Schaap Andrew (2020). 'Inequality, Loneliness, and Political Appearance: Picturing Radical Democracy with Hannah Arendt and Jacques Rancière.' *Political Theory*, 49(1), 28–53.
https://doi.org/10.1177/0090591720920215

Shuster, Martin. 2012. 'Language and Loneliness: Arendt, Cavell, and Modernity.' *International Journal of Philosophical Studies* 20 (4): 473–97. https://doi.org/10.1080/09672559.2012.713379.

Verovšek, Peter J. forthcoming. "Social Criticism as Medical Diagnosis? On the Role of Social Pathology and Crisis Within Critical Theory." *Thesis Eleven*, 072551361988866. https://doi.org/10.1177/0725513619888663.

Worsley, Amelia S (2019). "A History of Loneliness." *The Conversation*. https://theconversation.com/a-history-of-loneliness-91542

MAKING THINGS DIFFICULT: WORK ON/AND SOUL-CRAFT

CHARLES C. DJORDJEVIC

> "You must do something, but since with your own limited capabilities it will be impossible to make anything easier than it has become, you must, with the same humanitarian enthusiasm as the others have, take it upon yourself to make something more difficult"
> —Kierkegaard, *Concluding Unscientific Postscript*, 186

> "I don't know why we are here, but I'm pretty sure that it is not in order to enjoy ourselves"
> —Wittgenstein, cited in Peter Hershey *The Beginning of the End*, 109

Often, work in the contemporary world is cast as inherently exploitative and antithetical to community formation. Though it is undeniable that many forms of work are rightly criticized on these grounds, I explore a radically different conception of work. Specifically, I discuss a type of work that purposefully imposes hardship on people. I argue that this form of work is a constitutive condition for forming a particular sort of community. Based on this, I then criticize the idea that hard work is some sort of anathema to the human condition. Indeed, as we shall see, one way to avoid anomie may well be this sort of work.

Section one sets the stage. I examine why many have come to view work as inherently problematic. Section two turns to a radically different conception of work and the human condition, extrapolated from Kierkegaard and later Wittgenstein. In section three, I link this account to ongoing anthropological research into the so-called 'Islamist' movement in Egypt, drawing mainly from Saba Mahmood and Talal Asad. Finally, in section four, I discuss what I call, for lack of a better term, the price of admission, and argue that lowering it may lead to loneliness.

I. The Activity View of Work

It seems clear that our current conception of work is a late development. Indeed, philosophical reflection[1] and anthropological[2] and historical[3] data suggest that work in different historical periods or across different cultural configurations, is understood in very different terms. Given this, it is necessary to work through the current conception of work. By doing so, I hope to articulate how we intuitively make sense of work and why work and community are cast as diametrically opposed.

To begin, one of the oddest features of the current conception of work is that it lacks an internal end-state. In effect, work is understood as a brute activity one engages in to secure goods that are external to it. This can be seen in certain truisms. One works to make a living; one is paid by the hour (not for completed tasks); and so on. Let us call this "the activity view of work."

Commenting on this, Graeber notes that the activity view of work requires "two conceptual leaps.... first, to think of the [worker's] capacity to work, his 'labor-power,' as a thing that was distinct from the [worker] himself and, second, to devise some way to pure this capacity out, as it were, into uniform temporal containers– hours, days, work shifts."[4] In other words, the activity view requires that we reconceptualize both the nature of time and, relatedly, the introduction of labor power. Let us take each in turn.

For time, research suggests that time is often understood as dependent on activities. Anthropologically, Evans-Pritchard notes that for the Nuer "[t]he daily timepiece is the cattle clock, the round of pastoral tasks, and the time of day and the passage of time through a day are to a Nuer *primarily* the *succession of these tasks and their relation to one another.*"[5] Broadening this point, Thompson further contends that "[i]t [this task-oriented view of

---

[1] E.g., Hannah Arendt *The Human Condition* (Chicago: University of Chicago Press, 1998), 79-174. Note that, though I think Arendt's distinction between work and labor is critically important, I ignore it here as, by her own admission, we have conflated these in ordinary life and philosophical reflection

[2] E.g., David Graeber *Bullshit Jobs: A Theory* (New York: Simon & Schuster, 2018), passim

[3] E.g., E.P. Thompson "Time, Work-Discipline, and Industrial Capitalism" *Past & Present* No. 38 (Dec. 1967), 56-97

[4] Graeber *Bullshit Jobs*, 88

[5] E.E. Evans-Pritchard *The Neur: A description of the Modes of Livelihood and Political Institutes of a Nilotic People* (Oxford: Clarendon Press, 1940), 101- Emphasis mine.

time] is perhaps the most effective orientation in peasant societies… [Indeed], there is a sense in which it is more humanly comprehensible than timed labour. The peasants or labourers appear to attend to what is an observed necessity."[6] And, interestingly, this conception of time may have underlaid Aristotle's argument that "[t]ime is a measure of motion and of being moved, and it measures the motion by determining a motion which will measure the whole motion."[7] Notice that this view of time renders the activity view of work unworkable. Time is not indifferent to activities but derived from them. Ergo, the idea of chopping time into uniform chunks that are independent of various activities and then paying someone in terms of these chunks is absurd.

In marked contrast, our current intuitive conception of time is different. It is epitomized by Newton, who bluntly declares that "[a]bsolute, true, and mathematical time, in and of itself and of its own nature, without reference to anything external, flows uniformly."[8] In other words, time is a feature of reality in its own right that does not depend on activities or changes. Moreover, it is equally clear that Newton views this feature is homogenous, quantitively accessible, etc. In turn, this means that parsing out time into bundles that do not depend on activities makes good sense. In effect, the "hourly" in "hourly wage" is pegged precisely to Newtonian time.

However, this is not yet far enough. In effect, the "wage" in "hourly wage" turns on the idea that the activities by which one fills up Newtonian time are commensurable. Without this assumption, inter-work comparisons so that standard wages become possible is not viable. For instance, if tin can making and child caring are incommensurable because the works are different in kind, then the idea of paying a care giver and a tin can maker by the hour becomes increasingly hard to make sense of.

To rectify this, an abstraction is introduced– labor power. Labor power is the "capacity for labour is to be understood the aggregate of those mental and physical capabilities existing in a human being, which he exercises

---

[6] Thompson "Time, Work-Discipline, and Industrial Capitalism", 60.

[7] Aristotle "Physics" *The Complete Works of Aristotle Vol. 1: The Revised Oxford Translation*, ed. Johnathan Barnes (Princeton: Princeton University Press), 220b33-221a8

[8] Isaac Newton *The Principia: Mathematical Principles of Natural hilosophy* trans. By I. Bernard Cohen and Anne Whitman (Oakland: University of California Press, 1999), Scholium 1

whenever he produces a use-value of any description."[9] In other words, labor power is a stipulated metaphysical power that human beings have, in virtue of their metabolic relationship with the world, and which, though differing in quantity, cannot vary in quality. Precisely because both a tin can maker and a child carer expend effort to work, this expenditure can be understood in terms of labor power. Critically, this view casts workers (be they tin can makers or child carers) as, at base, metaphysical resources that support the working process, understood as the filling up of Newtonian time with activities.

In turn, Graeber notes that this metaphysical posit requires an "abstraction of man's labor from both his person and his work."[10] For the content of a person's work, it is clear that the only salient feature is the expenditure of effort, not the end-state of the work, its internal structure, and so on. Indeed, were this not the case, the same inter-work comparative breakdown would emerge because the work's content might structure work into different kinds. For the person the only salient feature of work is the quantity of labor-power someone can bring to bear on a job. This holds in abeyance the idea of skills, working on oneself, and so on. We return to this in section II and III.

Given this, the activity view of work and community formation may well (often do) conflict. This is because the activity view of work cannot provide a reason for working that is internal to it. One fills up Newtonian time with effort, not because of the end-state, but because one is forced to by, e.g., coercive externalities. Indeed, "[p]eople have to be compelled to work; if the poor are to be given relief so that they don't actually starve, it has to be delivered in the most humiliating and onerous ways possible, because otherwise they would become dependent and have no incentive to find proper jobs."[11] In turn, this compulsion, 'privatizes' work in a crucial sense. As Arendt points out, the only real analog we have for an activity with no other point than its being done out of necessity are brute biological processes where the sole 'aim' is to sustain and reproduce the organism. Thus, activity work is best understood as "the human body… [being] thrown back upon itself, concentrates upon nothing but being alive, and remains imprisoned in its metabolism with nature without ever transcending or freeing itself from the recurring cycle… This privacy… is essentially the privacy of

---

[9] Karl Marx *Capital: Vol. 1,* ed. Frederick Engels, trans. Samuel Moore and Edward Aveling (Moscow: Progress Press, 1887), 119.
[10] Graeber *Bullshit Jobs*, 302 fn 17
[11] ibid, 81

appropriation."[12] In other words, since work is nothing more (or less) than the 'filling up' of Newtonian time with labor power, and since the only 'point' of this is mere survival, work becomes strangely a- or anti-social, something one does out of sheer necessity and, ergo, something that occludes intersubjectivity, freedom, and subject formation.

II. The Task-Oriented View of Work

In the last section, I briefly adumbrated the activity view of work. Given this viewpoint, it is unsurprising that so many contemporary debates cast work as profoundly antithetical to the community formation. Indeed, people are cast as mere metaphysical resources who work because they would starve to death if they did not. There is simply no room here for the idea of work as forming communities via work.

However, both Arendt ent and Graeber stress that criticisms of the activity view of work often cede far too much to its conceptual architecture. In effect, both pro-activity work advocates and their critics usually take for granted that Newtonian time must be held in place. Indeed, the debate between 'work time' and 'free time' assumes Newtonian time and then fights about how to apportion it properly. This holds in abeyance a radically different conception of work as well as how this work might well be a precondition for becoming and being a person within a specific community. Let us call this different account, "the task-oriented view of work." Let us develop it.

To begin, Thompson notes that a task-oriented view of work "appears to show the least demarcation between 'work' and 'life.' Social intercourse and labor are intermingled– the working-day lengthens or contracts according to the task– and there is no great sense of conflict between labour and 'passing the time of day."[13] Relatedly, Arendt reminds us that, even in the activity view of work, there is

> "[t]he fact is that the human capacity for life [and the activity work processes that underwrite it] in the world always implies an ability to transcend and to be alienated from the processes of life itself, while the vitality and liveliness can be conserved only to the extent that men are willing to take the burden, the toil and trouble of life, upon themselves."[14]

---

[12] Arendt *The Human Condition*, 115

[13] Thompson "Time, Work-Discipline and Industrial Capital", 60

[14] Arendt *The Human Condition*, 121

She adds, "Man cannot be free if he does not know that he is subject to necessity, because freedom is always won in his never wholly successful attempts to liberate himself from necessity."[15]

Given this, there may be a way to change from activity work to task-oriented work, a different kind of work. In turn, this task-oriented work might function as a precondition for communities, not a coercive acid that destroys them. And to address these issues, let us turn to Wittgenstein and Kierkegaard.

To begin, the opening sections of *Philosophical Investigations* develop a language-game, the builder-game, that can be understood in terms of the activity view of work. The game consists of Builder-A barking orders, holding signs, and so on, and Assistant-B fetching them.[16] The reason Builder-A does what she does, the point of the exercise, and so on, are left strangely opaque. Wittgenstein famously calls this game primitive[17], and, following Cavell, the primitiveness of this game might be meant in several ways, two interdependent ones being of interest for us.[18] First, the game may be primitive because A and B display strikingly non-human behavior. Indeed, Cavell casts them as proto-humans who merely respond to some perceived brute necessity. Second, Cavell notes that "[t]he child [who plays with her words and elders] has a future in language; the builders have next to none."[19] And this lack of a future stems precisely from the fact that intersubjectivity is non-existent here. B's only interaction with A is silent obedience, one that a robot may equally well perform. And A's relation to B is perhaps best understood as sheer domination.

However, Wittgenstein goes on to elaborate a qualitative shift in this game, one that, for our purposes, helps us begin to make sense of a task-oriented view of work. Wittgenstein asks what happens if a new sign is introduced into this game without any training, specified reference, role in the endless self-same activity, etc.

---

[15] ibid

[16] Ludwig Wittgenstein *The Philosophical Investigations* trans. GEM Anscombe, PMS Hacker and Joachim Schulte (Oxford: Wiley-Blackwell, 2009), e.g., §§ 2, 6, 7.

[17] ibid, § 2

[18] Stanley Cavell "Declining Decline" *This New Yet Unapproachable America: Lectures After Emerson and Wittgenstein* (Chicago, University of Chicago Press, 1989)

[19] Ibid, 99

> Let's assume that "X" is such a sign, and that A gives this sign to B– well, even such a sign could be admitted into the language game, and B might have to answer them with a shake of the head (One could imagine this as a kind of amusement for them)[20]

Notice that the constitutive rules Wittgenstein has relied on to specify the game up to this point have been shattered by him. In effect, A and B now face a new situation. Relatedly, notice that "X" is also strangely outside of the activity view of work, specifically the process it betokens, as these rules have defined it. The endless recycling of activities that fill up Newtonian time seems confronted by something that is strangely different from the activities. "X" has no role in these activities. Finally, third, notice that "X" is admitted into the game, into work, indeed, does work, precisely through a mode of intersubjectivity. For the first time, B responds to A. Moreover, B's response is not at all akin to a malfunctioning machine presented with an unworkable bit of data. Instead, B's reaction is playful, a form of amusement for them both.

In turn, this qualitative shift opens up several new vistas. First, it seems that Arendt is precisely correct. "X," A, and B, all transcend the activity view of work exactly because something independent of the brute need to stay alive, and the non-rational processes that secure this, opens up. Second, part of what enables this new form of intersubjectivity is recognition. In effect, what allows A and B to cope with "X" is exactly that A and B recognize themselves (and each other) as independent of the work process. Third, in turn, this recognition is best understood as constitutively normative in that it changes the status of A and B via a shift in recognitional practices. In effect, A and B cease to be mere appendages of the work process whose behavior is determined solely by the need to survive. Instead, A and B now count as intentional agents who are capable of intelligible actions. A holds up "X" not out of brute necessity but to, e.g., get a rise out of B. And B reacts to "X" partly by assuming and reconstructing A's intention to be funny. Fourth, critically, and, again, echoing Arendt, this normative recognition is only possible against the background of the work activities themselves. "X" can only perform this feat when A and B are reflective and share an awareness of the rules that determine the work process, that "X" has no set place, etc.

Given this, a task-oriented view of work has some striking features. As Thompson noted above, the distinction between 'work' and 'life' becomes

---

[20] Wittgenstein *Philosophical Investigations*, § 42

unclear. A's use of "X" and B's response enable each to display features of their personality. Second, the twin abstractions required for labor power to work begin to misfire. Again, it is not a metaphysical capacity that A is trying to get from B, but distinctive features of B's personality, and vice versa. And, equally clearly, the content of the work also becomes salient. And this is because the use of "X" presupposes that both A and B understand explicitly what they are doing, the rules that constitute the work process, etc.

However, later Wittgenstein's account is non-temporal in that he does not make clear how A and B might conceptualize time. Ergo, to understand how time might change in a task-oriented work, we need a supplement–Kierkegaard.

To begin, recent literature in Kierkegaard studies has emphasized that his conception of being a self and belonging to a community must involve a particular sort of temporalization– narration.[21] And this narrative time is rather different from Newtonian time. Intuitively, a story about my life is not an indifferent list of all events, interactions, etc., that occur in Newtonian time. Instead, narratives have a unique structure based not on homogenous chunks of time, but end-states, repetitions, and suffering. Let me take each in turn.

To begin, one striking feature of narratives is that they require end-states to function. This is because the unity of a narrative turns precisely on the fact that some events are salient, and others are best discounted. And the only way to systematically decide which is which by reference to an overall end-state that determines if certain activities further, fall away from, or are indifferent to the end-state. Marrying someone is likely highly salient, whereas tying my shoes probably is not. And what makes this distinction principled is the end-state of the story itself.

However, there is a dis-analogy between works of fiction and the work of life that Kierkegaard insisted on.[22] Specifically, whereas a fictional story likely has a predetermined end-state, life most certainly does not. Moreover, Thompson's thought that task-oriented work requires that "[t]he peasants or

---

[21] E.g., Anthony Rudd *Self, Value and Narration: A Kierkegaardian Approach* (Oxford: Oxford University Press, 2012); John Davenport *Narrative Identity, Autonomy, and Mortality: From Frankfurt and MacIntyre to Kierkegaard* (New York: Routledge Press 2012), 92-130.

[22] Danial Watts "Kierkegaard, Repetition and Ethical Constancy" *Philosophical Investigations* Vol 40(4) (Dec. 2017), 414-439.

labourers appear to attend to what is an observed necessity"[23] is no longer viable as people in the (post-)modern age find naturalized teleology untenable, for a host of reasons.[24]

Given this, making narration work requires that the end-state that structures task-oriented work not be 'naturalized' but be adopted explicitly by the worker as her goal. And, for Kierkegaard, the only way to make this work is repetition. Indeed, "he who wills repetition… and the more empathically he is able to realize it, the more profound a human being he is."[25] Notice that this will to repetition, this constant (re-)affirmation of an end-state that guides work, does both ensure that the activities have a teleological structure and that the agent achieves a form of diachronic consistency in that all her activities are unified precisely by her willed end-state. Notice also that this will to repeat emphasizes the person's choice and repeated (re-)affirmation of it in her activity. Indeed, one critical insight of Kierkegaard's here, it seems to me, is that the nostalgia for a (possibly never-existent) 'natural teleology' or 'organic community' is useless. One repeats, one does not 'discover,' the end-state.

In turn, this will to repeat does, in fact, cause suffering for the person. Though we develop this more fully in section III, for now, I make one note. The suffering endured by the will to repeat the end-state is a mark of one's chosen commitment to this very end-state.[26] In effect, it is precisely because the person has committed herself to an end-state, and willingly repeats it, that she suffers for it as, e.g., changes, tight corners, etc. open up.

Hence, we see that the task-oriented view of work is radically different from the activity view. Task-oriented work presupposes both that the workers have a reflective understanding of the content of their work as well as a sense that they transcend the mere activities that constitute it. Further, it

---

[23] Thompson "Time, Work-Discipline, and Industrial Capitalism", 60.

[24] For aspects of this story, see Albert Hirschman *The Passions and the Interests: Arguments for Capitalism Before Its Triumph* (Princeton: Princeton University Press, 2013), passim; Charles Taylor *Sources of the Self: The Making of Modern Identity* (Cambridge: Harvard University Press, 1989), 211-390; Alasdair MacIntyre (Notre Dame: Notre Dame University Press, 2007), 36-78.

[25] Soren Kierkegaard *Fear and Trembling/Repetition* trans. Howard and Edna Hong (Princeton: Princeton University Press, 1983), 123.

[26] E.g., Soren Kierkegaard *Concluding Unscientific Postscript to the Philosophical Fragments* trans. Howard and Edna Hong (Princeton: Princeton University Press, 1992), 431-525

reconceptualizes time from Newtonian time to narrative time, thereby ordering the work process in a reflective, rational, and teleological manner.

III. Task-Oriented Working on Oneself and Working to Form One's Community

In the last section, we used later Wittgenstein and Kierkegaard to reflect on how one might shift from activity work, and its 'privatization,' to task-oriented work. This section discusses how task-oriented work and being part of a unique kind of community interdepend with one another. To do so, I focus on Saba Mahmood's and Talal Asad's ethnographic discussions on people's participation in so-called 'Islamism,' or the Islamic Revival Movement (hereby IRM), in Egypt.[27]

To begin, Mahmood points out that the normative assumption that "all human beings have an innate desire for [a particular conception of] freedom"[28] is hard to square with her ethnographic data. This stems, in part, from the fact that IRM females willingly adopt practices that impose suffering and valorize submission on themselves. To make sense of this, Mahmood draws on later Foucault's thoughts on ethics as soul-craft, i.e., the deliberate creation and maintenance of a particular sort of self.[29] And it is precisely this form of ethics that connects task-oriented work with subjectivity, tradition, and one's belonging to a unique kind of community. Let us take each linkage in turn.

For subjectivity, Mahmood contends that IRM females sense of their "agency is predicated upon her ability to be taught, a condition classically referred to as 'docility.'... [a] term [that] literally implies the malleability required of someone in order to be instructed in a particular skill or knowledge– a meaning that carries less a sense of passivity that struggle, effort, exertion, and achievement."[30] In other words, their understanding of agency is best construed in terms of difficult-to-acquire skills/virtues. And these skills/virtues are inculcated precisely by a task-oriented work whose internal end state, i.e., being pious, is conceptually related to the work itself.

---

[27] I have several reasons for avoiding the use of 'Islamism' including certain political connotations it has in Euro-US contexts.

[28] Saba Mahmood *Politics of Piety: The Islamic Revival Movement and the Feminist Subject* (Princeton: Princeton University Press, 2005), 5

[29] E.g., Michel Foucault *The Foucault Reader* ed. Paul Rainbow (New York: Pantheon Press, 1984), 333-390

[30] Mahmood *Politics of Piety,* 29

Indeed, "the very processes that secure a subject's subordination are also the means by which she becomes a self-conscious identity and agent."[31] Notice that this aligns with later Wittgenstein in that this sort of task-oriented working on oneself presupposes self-reflective persons who explicitly understand the point of their work.

To make further sense of this, consider an analogy with learning to play the violin. Learning to play the violin has an end-state, mastery of the violin, that the agent both explicitly understands and willingly adopts. In turn, this transforms the repeated practicing on the violin into self-conscious actions that, eventually, enable the person to master it.

In turn, this task-oriented view of working on oneself, or working to acquire the very skills, dispositions, virtues, etc., that the end-state encodes, connects one to a tradition. By "tradition," I follow Asad and emphasize its discursive aspect wherein it is

> "primarily a matter of linguistic acts passed down the generations as part of a form of life, a process in which one learns and relearns how to do things with words… and learns and relearns how to comport one's body and how to feel in particular contexts. Embodied practices help in the acquisition of aptitudes, sensibilities, and propensities through repetition… Through practices one can change oneself"[32]

In other words, a tradition is not a storehouse of dead propositions that an agent can simply grasp. Instead, it encodes specific tacit knowledge that is transmitted precisely by task-oriented work. One becomes part of a tradition not by endorsing dogmas but by enacting ways of interacting with the world. In turn, this connects with Kierkegaard. In effect, a tradition is realized by repetition wherein an end-state is (re-)affirmed by a person as she constantly (re-)orders her activities in its terms. Moreover, it also secures a narrative understanding of time precisely because all of one's activities are coherently ordered diachronically to achieve the end-state.

Again, by analogy, task-oriented work on the violin allows for narration in that certain practices, like playing the scales, over and over, become salient. Moreover, the task-oriented work is structured teleologically in that a conceptual-temporal ordering is internal to the process. One can only learn to play a song after one has mastered the scales. And, finally, this

---

[31] ibid,17

[32] Talal Asad "Thinking About Tradition, Religion, and Politics in Egypt Today" *Critical Inquiry* Vol 42 (Autumn 2015), 166

interdepends with tradition in that it is precisely a musical tradition that determines which sounds count as notes (scales, songs, etc.) and encodes what practices (moving one's fingers thus-and-so) can inculcate the requisite abilities.

In turn, and most critically for us, this tradition enables a unique form of community. Specifically, the social roles that constitute this form of community are not accidental or arbitrary ones that an agent happens to fall under. Instead, they are inherently normative, as they are ethical achievements, i.e., end-states reached via task-oriented work. In turn, this inherent normativity must presuppose that one can go wrong. And "going wrong" is only meaningful provided that there is, in the tradition, a standard and epistemically-objective [33] normative metric that clearly articulates which practices engender what end-states as well as how and why someone might fail to live up to them, in spite of her self-understandings, best effort, etc.

Hence, what binds such a community together is precisely this shared normative metric, embedded in the tradition, that makes one's and other people's practices count as correct viz. the end-state. In turn, this connection between a practice and an end-state is underwritten by constitutive rules that determine which activities are part of the task-oriented work and engender the desired end-state. And these rules are, themselves, supported by recognitional patterns, embedded, embodied, and shared in the tradition, that allow for sanctions, corrections, rectifying deviations, and so on. In effect, what holds the community's normative metric in place is precisely that members of the community enforce it via imposing discipline on each other. Moreover, this discipline is conceptually connected to suffering exactly because a person who is willingly repeating an end-state, and trying to realize it in her practices, has placed herself under such a normative metric and so is open to sanctions and corrections.

By analogy, to be a member of the violinist community requires that one occupy the social role, being a violinist. In turn, this role is the outcome of task-oriented work that achieves precisely this end-state. And this connection between end-state and task-oriented work is underwritten by a shared normative metric that determines if one is counted as a violinist by other musicians. In turn, what grounds this is precisely normative recognitional patterns that enable sanction, correction, refinement, encouragement, and so

[33] John Searle *The Construction of Social Reality* (New York: Free Press, 1995), 10-13

on. Being a violinist is not just making arbitrary sounds but producing correct notes. And the correctness conditions for the notes turn on the disciplinary practices embedded in learning how to play, shared within a musical community.

Given this, it is clear that a task-oriented view of work enables a unique form of community, one with a radically different understanding of suffering corrections and sanctions. This community is established and maintained precisely by a shared normative metric that constitutively connects end-states and practices together. And this constitutive connection manifests itself exactly in the disciplinary practices a community relies on and inflicts suffering on people. And, critically, such an overt and explicitly normative community, structured by and in task-oriented work and disciplinary suffering, is utterly different from community as it is commonly understood, a point we develop in the next section.

IV. The Price of Admission

In the last section, I adumbrated anthropological data that shows that a very different form of community, one predicated on a shared task-oriented view of work, is possible. I close by arguing that the suffering and hardship that joining, remaining, and continuing such communities requires are not antithetical to persons but a precondition for them and may well help cure loneliness.

To begin, it is clear that IRM females (and members of other religious groups) as well as, to a lesser extent, violinists (and other communities that emphasize skill, tradition, and apprenticeship) do, in fact, impose suffering and hardship on people. Indeed, Mahmood (among others[34]) points out that, from a secular liberal perspective, it is challenging to make sense of the idea that an educated Egyptian female would deliberately wear uncomfortable clothing, go out of her way to eschew interactions with most males, fast, etc.. This stems partly from the fact that such behaviors do not readily lend themselves to models of intentionality wherein an agent's actions are understood in instrumentally rational terms. Prima facie, these females are not maximizing pre-established preferences via rational computation of means/end. Instead, they seek to remake their sense of subjectivity precisely

---

[34] E.g., Mahmood *Politics of Piety*, 1-39; Lila Abu-Lughod *Do Muslim Women Need Saving?* (Cambridge: Harvard University Press, 2012) 35-47; Leila Ahmed *A Quiet Revolution: The Veil's Resurgence, from the Middle East To America* (New Haven: Yale University Press, 2011), 68-130.

by submitting to a shared tradition and opening themselves up to the disciplinary practices embedded in their communities. Given this, the 'price of admission' for such a community is high and demanding.

However, critically, it is precisely this price of admission that works against anomie. To see this clearly, let us briefly consider several genealogies that clarify how many Euro-US people think about agency and intention.[35] These genealogies agree that one critical move made by political philosophers and proto-economists at the dawn of modernity was the radical reduction of human agency to, in effect, a desire-fulfillment matrix. In this view, a desire is taken as given and has a definite intentional object that determines which state-of-affairs would sate it. Hence, the utterance "I desire that p" takes "that p" as a proposition that represents a possible and intelligible state-of-affairs. Given this "desire" is then understood as odd sort of attitude that is inherently motivational. In effect, "to desire" is, perhaps, best understood by analogy with itches– one has it, and then one acts to sate it, in virtue of brute features of embodiment. In turn, intentionality is then conceptualized in terms of these inherently motivational pro-attitudes (e.g., itches) that are then paired with beliefs. And the function of beliefs is conceptualizes in terms of instrumental rational calculation wherein they re-present various possible plans (or whatever) so that the pro-attitude (the itch) can be sated. All agency reduces to getting what I want. And, strangely, what I want has very little to do with me but is, e.g., a god-given preference set, a product of brute biology, etc.

The issue with this reduction is, simply, that task-oriented work communities become unworkable. Simply put, the idea of forming and fostering constitutive relationships between people such that their preference sets are radically modified is challenging to articulate. Such relationships would (i) problematize the semantic content of the desiring state (ii) drastically reconfigure the motivational aspect of desire itself and, worst of all (iii) render instrumental calculation impossible. And this is precisely because the self that emerges after being subjected to the disciplinary practices in a tradition is not the same self that goes into it.[36]

Critically, though, it is precisely the sort of constitutive relationships that, it seems to me, help rectify social anomie. Exactly by insisting that one is not

---

[35] See fn 24

[36] For a discussion of related issues in contemporary economics, see Thomas Schelling *Strategies of Commitment and Other Essays* (Cambridge: Harvard University Press, 2007).

a good Rousseau-ian subject who simply putters around the state of nature but, first and foremost, a violinist, an IRM participant, etc., one immediately lionizes exactly the relational aspects of the self that cure loneliness.

Moreover, as Asad points out, task-oriented work communities do this in a controlled and systematic manner. Thus, "[w]hat Shaykh Usama [one of Asad's conversation partners] was trying to describe [in terms of IRM theology]… was the idea of intention itself being constituted in the repeated acts of body-and-mind within a social context."[37] In other words, for IRM, and other task-oriented work communities, intentionality and agency do *not* stem from god-given preference sets people are endowed with. They are forged and re-formed within inherently intersubjective contexts. And part of what task-oriented work communities do is re-formulate the overall social contexts so that specific intentions are constructed in the first place. And it does so precisely by demanding submission to the authority of the tradition and imposing discipline on subjects in its name. One learns to be a violinist by forcing oneself to engage in exercises that one does not yet fully understand, embedded in a musical tradition. And doing so actually creates the skills, dispositions, intentions, and so on, that allow one to reconstitute oneself as a violinist. And this reconstitution removes loneliness precisely because one can now relate to other musicians. Obviously, this is yet more radical for religious work task-oriented communities.

In sum, the sense of the self that task-oriented work creates is not based on the subject's ability to, e.g., express herself (and the underlying assumption that there is a pre-discursive self and that social relations are antithetical to it as they limit its ability to 'be natural') but on precisely their constitutive ties to their tradition. And, precisely because the tradition is shared, an individual's counting as a member of it is a constitutive relationship that forms and fosters a self-interpretation, precisely in relation to others in the tradition. And these constitutive self-making social relationships ameliorate loneliness because they ground self-interpretation on task-oriented work that is inexorably social.

V. Conclusion

In conclusion, there are two critically important points to make. First, if this brief account is persuasive, then it seems that one way to deal with the endemic sense of loneliness, and the pathologies it engenders, is precisely by willingly joining a task-oriented work community. These will inflict

[37] Asad "Thinking About Tradition, Religion, and Politics in Egypt Today", 176

suffering as they re-form the self. But it is precisely this re-formulation that constitutively connects a person to others via tradition.

Second, it is imperative to bear in mind that task-oriented work communities may well inculcate deeply problematic norms, skills, values, etc. Indeed, Kierkegaard was at pains to make this clear.[38] However, for Kierkegaard, achieving individuality presupposes as a background condition such task-oriented communities. In this, I think Kierkegaard would agree with Picasso's famous quip that one must learn the rules like a pro (by submitting to the authority of tradition), so one can break them like an artist.

[38] E.g., Soren Kierkegaard *Two Ages: The Age of Revolution and the Present Age, a Literary Review* trans Howard and Edna Hong (Princeton: Princeton University Press, 1978), 60-112

Rediscovering Joy in Work: Marx and Martin Heidegger on Worker's Alienation

Georgios Karakasis

1) Introduction

The goal of this chapter is to examine from an ontological point of view how workers in the modern capitalist society are alienated both from their product and from their own productive activity getting, thus, trapped in the web of necessity, feeling no joy or homeliness while at work.

I will start by outlining Marx's theory of the alienation expounded in his *Economic and Philosophic Manuscripts of 1844*. Having presented the phenomenon I will show how the alienated modern worker, unsatisfied and frustrated by the lack of meaningfulness of his labor, may eventually conceive the society and the world surrounding him as an enemy, as the enemy that enchains him to necessity's reign, distorting, thus, the meaning of his labor and his relationship to the product he creates.

Then, based on Heidegger's later philosophy, I will set forth how modern capitalist society, through the means of technology and its distorted essence as Positionality, is converting every being, human being included, into mere resources and raw material, binding human labor and productivity to an exclusively utilitarian and results-driven mentality.

Finally, I will stress the utmost importance of seeking and inserting joy in our work as a way of recovering our relationship with the world and with our own alienated and fragmented selves. Feeling joy is not to be perceived as one among many other elements that should characterize labor but as the stable ground upon which the worker may finally come to find himself again and relate to his products in a genuine and fulfilling manner.

2) The loss of the self in labor: Marx on the alienation of the worker

One of the pillars of our western capitalist society is work. People work, produce and through their labor the society is able to develop, advance and offer us the commodities we all need and/or desire in our lives. The worker is the core of every productive activity and, notwithstanding the progress of technology, he will always be the indispensable personal factor of every possible production and advancement. Still, even though the worker is such a crucial figure for the well-being of our societies, we could not pretend that workers, in most cases, enjoy the benefits of their labor. Quite the opposite, work is closely tied to necessity and to the acquisition of all those necessary means for survival and continuity of our physical existence. There is no doubt that there are many people who like their job, feel fulfilled when working and would not change their job for anything in the world. There are also some millionaires, who manage to become even richer thanks to their work and their devotion to it. On the other hand, there are far too many people who do not have a job or those feeling asphyxiated by necessity's shackles in their work. For the latter, work is not a creative, fruitful and enriching experience; quite on the contrary, it is a constant reminder that our survival depends on our labor and on those able to offer us the means of production. We need money to live and nourish our families thus we need work and we depend on those who can offer us jobs. Necessity and dependence are two of the main characteristics of modern labor. No matter the importance of finding an enjoyable and creative job, when necessity calls, as it happened in the 2008 global financial crisis, we would all bend our will to what necessity and our survival demand. The Great Depression during the decade of the 1930s and the actual economic turmoil provoked by the Covid-19 crisis prove that even finding a job nowadays should be considered a success, expelling the prospect of finding the "job of our dreams" into the sphere of a utopia.

Nevertheless, despite the economic issues many workers and their families are met with, our society is a profoundly consumerist one since people ceaselessly demand new products and services for their incessantly emerging needs. We produce, we consume, we temporally cover our needs and after our needs have been satisfied, we start demanding once again setting in motion the afore mentioned chain of demand and production. Thus the worker becomes the necessary cog for this mechanism to work. The fact that he does not like his job or that feels drained and mortified by it does not matter; the only thing that matters is that the production has to go on offering people new and various ways to cover necessities they do (or not) have. Without the worker the whole capitalist structure would fall into pieces but the primordiality of his role is lost in the faceless mechanized and highly bureaucratized modern labor system whose fetters are, as we have seen before, necessity and dependence. In addition, the more the worker produces, the more people and society demand of him while underestimating or hardly ever recognizing the cruciality of his contribution to the whole process of production. Quoting Marx:

> The worker becomes all the poorer the more wealth he produces, the more his production increases in power and range. The worker becomes an ever cheaper commodity the more commodities he creates. With the *increasing value* of the world of things proceeds in direct proportion the *devaluation* of the world of men. (Marx 1988, 71)

The worker, following Marx, becomes through his labor a commodity whose only task is to produce more and more, while, at the same time, the importance of his producing act is undervalued and the only thing that matters is the product of his activity; a product that is no longer his, a product the worker is alienated from both during and after the activity of production. In other words, in modern society the worker is alienated from the product of his work and due to the fact that his work is now totally automatized and mechanized he is also alienated from himself as a worker, having lost the joy of work as creation and the relationship with the creation.

In order to better comprehend what alienation[1] is in Marx's thought we should first understand the relationship between labor and nature as well as the result/product of labor as an objectified reality which reflects-or better said, should reflect-the creativity and the self fulfilment of the worker's productive activity. Quoting Honneth,

> According to Marx, human beings' central feature is their capacity for objectifying and realizing themselves in the product of their labor; it is only by this act of objectification that individual subjects are in a position to achieve certainty of their own powers and thereby attain self-consciousness. Thus the possibility of freely and willingly experiencing their own labor as a process of self-realization forms the deciding precondition for a good life.

---

[1] In this chapter there is no space for a thorough presentation and interpretation of this really important concept in Marx's thought. For more complete analyses on the subject see also: Wallimann 1981, Mészáros 2006, Khan 1995, Mandel and Novack 1973. For a philosophical examination of Hegel's and Marx's understanding of the phenomenon of alienation see: Sayers 2011. For a study on the relation between technology and alienation in Marx's though see: Wendling 2011.

> However, this condition is destroyed by the establishment of the capitalist mode of production, since wage labor robs the active subjects of any control over their activity. Capitalism therefore represents a social form of life that sets human beings in opposition to their own essence, thus robbing them of any prospects of a good life. (Honneth, 2007, 14)

Labor, seen in this light, is not to be conceived as the frenzy of unending production to satisfy the needs of a greedy capitalist society. Labor's product is a mirror of the human productive activity, the energy of the human being as a worker that desires to shape nature and the world in such a way so as to see in it the reflection of his own creativity and freedom. Labor's objectified presence in the product should be the accomplishment of the worker's self-consciousness through the recognition of his own being in the result of his own activity. This way nature as well could participate without mediation in this act of worker's becoming self-conscious of himself through his own productive activity. Quoting Marx, "The worker can create nothing without *nature,* without the *sensuous external world.* It is the material on which his labor is manifested, in which it is active, from which and by means of which it produces (Marx 1988, 72)". Furthermore, according to Marx,

> It is just in the working-up of the objective world, therefore, that man first really proves himself to be a species *being*[2]. This production is his active species life. Through and because of this production, nature appears as *his* work and his reality. The object of labor is, therefore, the *objectification of* man's *species life:* for he duplicates himself not only, as in consciousness, intellectually, but also actively, in reality, and therefore he contemplates himself in a world that he has created. (ibid. 77)

The whole physical world is the place where human being as worker releases his creativity and his labor so as to make of the world an image of his own being and personality. The worker wants to recognize himself in his product and the objective world grants him the possibility of doing so

---

[2] By species being Marx distinguishes the natural man from the man that is distinguished from all the other living beings. Quoting Ollman:
Alongside natural man, the other half of Marx's dichotomy is species man. As a species being man can be distinguished from other living things, for he now possesses qualities which are uniquely his own. In Marx's words, man is a being for himself (fuer sich). Therefore, he is a species being, and has to confirm and manifest himself as such both in his being and knowing.' By describing man as a being 'for himself, Marx is referring to man's selfconsciousness, to his awareness of himself as an individual active in pursuing his own ends. This is how he confirms himself through knowing. (1996, 82)

through the beings that surround us. In this case human being is not exploiting nature, draining from it its energy and life, but he lets nature become a part of his own being and essence, the necessary mediator through which the worker achieves his self-consciousness and self-completion. Furthermore, this productive activity of shaping nature, namely labor, is a conscious and free act, which distinguishes human being from the other beings around him. Marx comments the following regarding this distinguishing feature of the human being:

> The animal is immediately identical with its life-activity. It does not distinguish itself from it. It is *its life-activity.* Man makes his life-activity itself the object of his will and of his consciousness. He has conscious life-activity. It is not a determination with which he directly merges. Conscious life-activity directly distinguishes man from animal life-activity(…) In creating an *objective world* by his practical activity, in *working-up* inorganic nature, man proves himself a conscious species being, i.e., as a being that treats the species as its own essential being, or that treats itself as a species being. Admittedly animals also produce. They build themselves nests, dwellings, like the bees, beavers, ants, etc. But an animal only produces what it immediately needs for itself or its young. It produces one-sidedly, while man produces universally. It produces only under the dominion of immediate physical need, while man produces even when he is free from physical need and only truly produces in freedom therefrom. (ibid. 76)

Thus labor, in its most genuine and primordial form, is a conscious and free world-forming activity that liberates the worker from the shackles of necessity, consequently liberating nature from its ceaseless exploitation. Freedom, self-awareness and the desire for self-completion are the cornerstones labor should be built upon. This kind of labor attunes the worker to nature and to the rest of the co-workers since the world becomes the canvas on which labor, as purely creative and productive activity, appears as the painting of each single worker's vision. Through labor the world gets the form each worker freely and consciously grants it having made good use of nature's offering. Only through freedom and the will to treat nature and the product of labor as the reflection of the completion of their self-consciousness can workers find joy in their labor and recover their connection to labor as creative activity.

In the capitalist society, however, nature and workers are restricted to their twofold role of filling needs and demands, drastically altering their relationship with the environment and with their co-workers. Quoting Max Horkheimer, "The history of man's efforts to subjugate nature is also the history of man's subjugation by man (Horkheimer 2004, 72)". One of the ways through which this subjugation happens is the phenomenon of alienation.

According to Marx, the alienation can be understood in the following way:

> Labor produces not only commodities: it produces itself and the worker as a *commodity*—and does so in the proportion in which it produces commodities generally. This fact expresses merely the object which labor produces— labor's product—confronts it as *something alien,* as a *power independent* of the producer. The product of labor is labor which has been congealed in an object, which has become material: it is the *objectification* of labor. Labor's realization is its objectification. In the conditions dealt with by political economy this realization of labor appears as *loss of reality* for the workers; objectification as *loss of the object* and *object-bondage;* appropriation as *estrangement,* as *alienation.* (Marx 1988, 71)

During the alienation the worker, instead of recognizing his own self and personality in the product of his work, feels alienated and separated from the latter since it is no longer his but now belongs to others. The product that was supposed to mirror the worker's creativity now stands against him, as something alien, as a creation that stands against the creator. This brings forth the gravest ontological consequences of the subject-object distinction. While in labor as attunement to nature the worker can recognize his activity and his own self in the product, through the phenomenon of alienation, the object not only stands opposed to the worker as an object but is also becoming something alien to the worker, a product that has shattered every possibility of getting related anew to the worker. This violent shattering deprives the productive activity of its own essence since it takes away from it what rightfully belongs to it, namely the completion and the objectified product. Likewise, the worker also loses a part of himself due to the tearing apart of his product away from him. This violent separation taking place among the worker, his labor and the product of the activity highlights the distorted relationship between the worker, nature and the world. Marx comments the following concerning this distortion:

> All these consequences are contained in the definition that the worker is related to the product *of his labor* as to an alien object. For on this premise it is clear that the more the worker spends himself, the more powerful the alien objective world becomes which he creates over-against himself, the poorer he himself— his inner world—becomes, the less belongs to him as his own. It is the same in religion. The more man puts into God, the less he retains in himself. The worker puts his life into the object; but now his life no longer belongs to him but to the object. Hence, the greater this activity, the greater is the worker's lack of objects. Whatever the product of his labor

> is, he is not. Therefore the greater this product, the less is he himself. The *alienation* of the worker in his product means not only that his labor becomes an object, an *external* existence, but that it exists *outside him,* independently, as something alien to him, and that it becomes a power on its own confronting him; it means that the life which he has conferred on the object confronts as something hostile and alien. (ibid. 71)

The fact that the product of the worker's productive activity alienates itself from the former has serious ontological consequences that affect the relationship the way the human being as worker perceives his labor and the whole world. Namely, when capitalism obliges the workers to incessantly offer their labor in order to maintain and enhance its own expansion, then the workers are deprived of any possibility of a genuine relationship to their product and witness how their productive activity loses its significance and joy since the only thing that matters is the final product; a product, nonetheless, that no longer belongs to the worker and hardly ever does the latter receive the credit and the thanks for the amount of work he has dedicated to it. The greatest the product, the darkest the shadow that overshadows the worker who becomes aware of the fact that his effort and his struggle to make the production possible are heavily overlooked in a society which only desires products, results and more needs to satisfy. This distorted relationship between the worker and the product caused by capitalism eventually creates a rupture inside the worker himself who now no longer perceives labor as a world-forming activity and the product as an expansion of his own being. The world now becomes the enemy, a battleground full of objects/products that have been alienated from their creator constantly casting into doubt the latter's significance and degrading his role to a mere faceless producer. Seen in metaphysical terms, in capitalism the object dominates the subject blocking every possible path that could lead to the re-appropriation of the product by the worker. The worker witnesses the emergence of his fragmented self in the world through the products and he is not capable of healing the broken bond that was binding them together during the productive activity. This is why, the very beginning of the alienation is not to be found in the product of labor but in the worker's productive activity itself, in labor. Quoting Marx,

> What, then, constitutes the alienation of labor? First, the fact that labor is external to the worker, i.e., it does not belong to his essential being; that in his work, therefore, he does not affirm himself but denies himself, does not feel content but unhappy, does not develop freely his physical and mental energy but mortifies his body and ruins his mind. The worker therefore only feels himself outside his work, and in his work feels outside himself. He is at home when he is not working, and when he is working he is not at home.

> His labor is therefore not voluntary, but coerced; it is *forced labor* (..)External labor, labor in which man alienates himself, is a labor of self-sacrifice, of mortification. Lastly, the external character of labor for the worker appears in the fact that it is not his own, but someone else's, that it does not belong to him, that in it he belongs, not to himself, but to another. (ibid. 74)

The outcome of forced labor is that the two main features that should be at the core of every productive activity, namely a conscious subject and his acting freely acting, are now getting distorted. Of course, the worker is free to deny work and the feeling of uncanniness the latter provokes. If the worker does not feel at home when working, he could reject this way of life and look for new paths. Nevertheless, that is the same as abandoning his family by not having the most basic means to fill their everyday needs. Probably one person that has inherited a lot of money and properties could decide to reject the capitalist kind of labor and live according to the rules set by himself. A lower-class worker, however, who knows that losing his job means losing his only means of making money and survival would probably act in a different way. Thus the worker in the capitalist society has the freedom to reject labor but hardly ever does this freedom materialize since most of the workers are already chained to labor by necessity and dependence. In a few words, freedom exists but as the possibility that ought to be a reality, as the ideal that has yet to be fulfilled. Freedom is what each job should provide but the strict necessity is what characterizes far too many jobs in the modern capitalist society; and, what is worse, workers are conscious of the fact that they are trapped in this vicious circle of necessity and alienation.

A worker that feels alienated from his productive activity, from his labor, may be well aware of the fact that he has no power over what he creates and this is why he feels "mortified" and "ruins his mind" as Marx comments. Of course, there might be jobs whose mechanistic and automatic character may not require a total and constant self-awareness during the productive activity, just like Charlie Chaplin in the movie "Modern Times" endlessly screwing loose bolts onto pieces of metal. There are many workers, however, that are always conscious of the fact that they are spending their time, energy and effort, creating something that will be torn from them later on. There lies the danger of the worker's perceiving the world and his surrounding as a distorted version of his creation, as a broken bond of what should be united and attuned. The worker feeling violently detached from his productive activity is turning against the creation/object that has turned against him; he is turning against the world and the world's manifestation through labor. The reason why Marx's analysis of alienation is so important lies in the fact that the worker, through his labor, is progressively becoming the enemy of both his product and the act of production itself, since he no longer sees his creativity, personality, devotion and being reflected on the product, on his own creation. The demand for production becomes an imposition made upon the worker by capitalism and the frenzy of the consumerist society. The worker instead of seeing in his products the reflection of his creativity and of his *techne*, he sees the distorted version of everything he has given shape and created. The products are no longer created in the worker's own image since they are not the fruits of a free, enjoyable and creative activity; they are the offspring of necessity and dependence. Thus labor, suffocating inside the strict limits of demand, offer and profit, instead of helping the worker shape the world as his abode, constantly alienates him from his own activity and product converting the world into an alien place full of products that no longer have meaning for the worker. Labor, in capitalist society, instead of bringing the worker closer to the world and vice versa, converts the latter into the enemy, shattering every possibility of the worker's self-completion and fulfilment through his work. The worker could feel everywhere at home except at work since at work is where his freedom is strictly restrained by necessity.

3) Positionality and alienation: the worker as an automaton

Marx's analysis of the phenomenon of alienation and the rupture happening inside the worker between his own self and the alienated product, takes us to another German philosopher who highlighted the existential and ontological challenges the human being is facing in the era of modernity and technology, namely Martin Heidegger. Even though Heidegger's philosophical thought could sometimes stand on the opposite side of Marx's philosophy, both thinkers are crucial for our better understanding of the dead ends workers deal with in our capitalist society[3]. Despite the fact that Heidegger did not analyze labor as thoroughly as Marx did, work still emerges as an important aspect of Heidegger's philosophy with a great emphasis placed on its ontological significance. The worker and the labor for Heidegger are ways through which the human being decides to uncover and shape the world. Through work we manage to unconceal the meaning of the world and seek

[3] For an interesting book concerning the philosophical relation of those great thinkers' ideas see: Hemming 2013.

for our place and being in an unhospitable and challenging environment that brings us, quite often, to our limits. It is in this world where the human being struggles to find his abode having no guarantee that this will ever be possible. It is in this world that we strive against nature, release our power against it facing the possibility of our own shattering against it.

This abode-seeking struggle, however, is altered by another kind of alienation that violently tears away the human being, the worker, from his world and product. The alienation makes its presence felt in Heidegger's thought in a variety of ways: through human being's getting lost in the triviality of idle talk of the everydayness of the others, as "they"[4]; through our metaphysical entanglement in the subject-object distinction that does not let human beings finally get attuned to Being; through Being's distorted essence as "Positionality (or Enframing)" where technology becomes the gathering force that converts every being, human being included, into mere ready-at-hand resources, or, finally, through the greatest peril of the oblivion of Being, and the abandonment of beings by their own Being dooming them to a meaningless presence whose sole goal is the perpetuation of the "now" and the lived experience. Where Marx saw fragmentation of the worker due to his alienation both from his product and from his own recognizing himself in his creations, Heidegger also saw the danger of the oblivion of our Being and the peril of an endless descent into a void where every meaning is relative and even truth can no longer be the ground of beings since the question and the seeking of Being has long been forgotten.

Martin Heidegger, especially during the later stages of his thought, raised many concerns regarding the calculative and instrumental character of our society. Human being, as the omnipotent Cartesian subject, has cast all around him a web of objects whose only center is the human being and his thought. Everything has been calculated for centuries through these lenses of the subject-object distinction. Beings around us, even gods, are objects that can be physically or mentally grasped by the human being who then will attribute to them the meaning and the values they have, till the time is ripe for a revaluation of all values and for the inevitable repetition of the same process. Being, as well, has not escaped the fate of beings, becoming a concept whose evidence can never be cast in doubt, nor, unfortunately, properly understood. Quoting Heidegger:

> It is said that 'Being' is the most universal and the emptiest of concepts. As such it resists every attempt at definition. Nor does this most universal and

[4] The above is expounded at length in Heidegger's *Being and Time*.

> hence indefinable concept require any definition, for everyone uses it constantly and already understands what he means by it. In this way, that which the ancient philosophers found continually disturbing as something obscure and hidden has taken on a clarity and self-evidence such that if anyone continues to ask about it he is charged with an error of method. (Heidegger 2001, 21)

Clarity and self-evidence is the way modern human being lives, acts and works. Everything has to be clear, detailed, predictable, and replaceable. Human being as the subject has to be capable of controlling and steering the realm of his objects, through the production of beings or ideas. The world hence becomes a realm of objects waiting for the guidance of the human being to structure them, put them into order, and, finally, give them the meaning he considers appropriate. This unilateral and essential way of existing and thinking brings forth barriers between the human being, nature and the world since there is no space for interaction, relationship and recognition. Capitalism and technology have granted powerful tools to an already powerful mind whose goal is not to produce things wherein he would reach self-consciousness, as was the case with Marx; the goal of the modern capitalist human being is to tame the world, make it bend to his rules and make of the whole world a creation of the human beings image. While for Marx, as we have seen before, the worker separates himself from the world due to the alienation taking place during and after the productive activity, according to Heidegger the modern capitalist human being, thanks to the limitless capacities offered to him by technology, separates himself from the world through his desire for utter domination and control. The beings no longer stand against us as the unsurmountable objects, as the enemy that has to be overcome[5], but now become mere resources and the entire world an enormous warehouse always ready-at-hand to satisfy our incessant needs and desires. Even the distinction between subject and object disappears in this vortex where everything, human being included, becomes resources and raw material; everything becomes “standing-reserve”. Quoting Heidegger:

> Everywhere everything is ordered to stand by, to be immediately at hand, indeed to stand there just so that it may be on call for a further ordering. Whatever is ordered about in this way has its own standing. We call it the standing-reserve [Bestand]. The word expresses here something more, and something more essential, than mere "stock." The name "standing-reserve"

[5] For an ontological explanation of human being’s constant struggle against nature and the beings surrounding him see Heidegger’s interpretation of Antigone’s Ode to Man in his work *Introduction to Metaphysics.*

> assumes the rank of an inclusive rubric(…) Whatever stands by in the sense of standing-reserve no longer stands over against us as object. (Heidegger 1977, 17)

The emergence of beings as standing-reserve is one of the most radical changes modernity, technology and capitalism have brought upon our societies. The vanishing of the object and its dissolution into mere raw material standing there and waiting for its exploitation also disintegrates the idea of the subject as we have known it so far. The human being, the worker, becomes now an automatized conscious(?) machine whose only task is the gathering, ordering and replacing of beings. The productive activity is now a machinelike process and nature is no longer the mediator through which our being is reflected on the world; labor is automatization and nature is a gigantic warehouse. The modern worker of the capitalist society is immersed in a faceless and soulless productive process where there is no place for joy, happiness or tranquility. No longer does the worker feel at home at work since the concept of home itself has been violently altered. If nature is a warehouse and the world is the sum of beings standing and waiting to be properly ordered and ordained, then the idea of the abode becomes blurrier and more artificial than ever. The modern human being throughout his productive activity is getting more and more alienated from himself, no longer seeking to see his being reflected on the world and on beings. This decision of the human being to unconceal the world and beings as mere resources and standing-reserve is the aftermath of the domination of technology's essence as "Positionality". Following Heidegger:

> We now name the self-gathered collection of positioning [des Stellens], wherein everything orderable essences in the standing reserve, positionality [das Ge-Stell](…) Positionality names the universal ordering, gathered of itself, of the complete orderability of what presences as a whole. The circuit of ordering takes place in positionality and as positionality. In positionality the presencing of all that presences becomes standing reserve. Positionality constantly draws what is orderable into the circuit of requisitioning, establishes it therein, and thus assigns it as something constant in the standing reserve. The assignment does not place what is constant outside of the circuit of positioning. It only assigns it, but off and away into a subsequent orderability, i.e., back and forth into a requisitioning. (Heidegger 2012, 31)

The modern worker in the capitalist society alienates himself from his own self and the world as a whole in the crudest way: through transforming beings into standing-reserve and through the ordering and the requisitioning of every single being. There is no longer reflection of the self through labor, only the necessity to maintain positionality intact, through the deprivation of every being from its most essential characteristics, even its own objectification! Beings are no longer objects because their objectification is not important during the process of positionality. Things are stored, packed, used and replaced. Labor is now totally defined by the utility and the maximization of speed. There can be nothing or no one irreplaceable because that would alter the efficiency of the whole process. Modern capitalist society does not need unique works or unique products: it needs massive production, speed light replaceability and constant renovation of needs so that the process does not stop. Positionality is permeating the worker, demanding of him to be fast, efficient and resourceful. The labor is no longer the expression of the worker's personality because there is no space for expression and personal touch. The whole world must bear the stamp of positionality and the worker and his labor become the press of this higher and more powerful impersonal will. The whole event of positionality is so massive, fast and overwhelming that we should ask ourselves whether workers are actually conscious of the automatization and mechanization that is now dominating their labor. Are we actually conscious of what our labor has become or has necessity deprived us of every possibility to (re)consider the significance of our labor? In other words, is there still any barrier protecting us from becoming standing-reserve just like the rest of beings or have we finally succumbed to positionality's and alienation's demands? Following Heidegger the control of the situation has slipped from our hands:

> Men and women must place themselves in a work service. They are ordered. They are met by a positioning that places them, i.e., commandeers them. One places the other. He retains him. He positions him. He requires information and an accounting from him. He challenges him forth. Let us now enter into the meaning of this word "to position, place, set" so as to experience what comes to pass in that requisitioning through which an inventory arises [der Bestand steht] and is thus a standing reserve. (ibid. 26)

4) Work as joy: piecing together worker's fragmented self

So far I have focused my attention on the ontological and existential dead ends workers are facing in their labor. We have seen how capitalism and the use of technology are alienating the worker from his product and from his productive activity, blocking thus the path for a more genuine and fruitful relationship with labor as productive activity and the product. I have dedicated a considerable part of this chapter to the analysis of alienation in some of its forms because it is through our awareness and detection of the ontological problems that modern workers are facing that we can actually react, deconstruct and refound. Quoting Hölderlin, “But where danger is, grows, the saving power also. (Heidegger 1977, 28)” A radical change in labor in the modern capitalist society cannot take place through small steps that will eventually slightly ameliorate the workers’ conditions. What is needed is a radical and thoughtful redefinition of the relationship between the worker and his productive activity, a redefinition that will dare to set forth the necessity of joy in labor.

But how can joy enter once again in the field of labor? Should we suppose that it is directly related to a high wage and good working conditions? That, of course, could improve the situation but would also lead us farther away from work’s essential core, namely, the worker’s becoming self-conscious of his own self through his productive activity and creations. Work, as we have seen before, is a world-forming activity and it is the way we shape beings so as to reflect our being and personality. Heidegger, as well, when speaking about the works of art, sees work as “setting up a world”. Following Heidegger:

> The work as work sets up a world. The work holds open the Open of the world(…)The work as work, in its presencing, is a setting forth, a making(…)To work-being there belongs the setting up of a world. (Heidegger 1975, 45)

Through work we open the Open of the world, that is, we open the possibility of relationality and disclosure in the world. Through labor we should be able to relate to nature and to our product and through our product genuinely relate to ourselves. The product is not something alien, it is the worker’s struggle to find himself in what is outside of him, to find himself in the world and as part of the world. Alienation deprives us from the possibility of relationality blocking our way to the products of our activity, converting them into standing-reserve, thus blocking our own possibility of genuinely relating to ourselves through labor. Labor hence becomes an activity of automatic and meaningless production, aiming at the satisfaction of the incessant needs of modern capitalist society. The real joy is when we manage, through our labor, to become part of the open that we have opened, to open and consciously expose ourselves to the whole matrix of relationships the world creates and maintains. When Heidegger makes a reference to the creation of a temple in his “Origin of the work of art” he says that the temple “is a work that lets the god himself be present and thus *is* the god himself. (Heidegger 1975, 42)” The same happens during the act of the creation of a jug as a sacrificial vessel in Heidegger’s essay “The Thing”. Namely the jug is the vessel through which the wine may be offered to the gods uniting the rain that nourished it, the earth where the vinery emerged from, the mortals who as a community offer to the gods recognizing their godhood and the gods that accept the offering letting their divinity shine by means of a mortal-made jug. This simple product of labor, a jug, becomes the core of a whole matrix of relationships where the human being is able to relate with nature, with his fellow citizens and with the spirit of his community as a whole. Thus labor becomes a productive activity that gathers, unites and attunes the workers with the world and the rest of the people. In this act the worker feels joy because his work is not exclusively utility-driven but aims at something higher and nobler: at the gathering of himself, of nature and of the rest of his community in a product that enables all of them to freely and consciously relate. Labor and each product become then small spots of relationality; small openings wherein the worker sets free the possibility of relating to the others and to his own creation as well. It is the exact opposite of alienation whose goal is to sink the worker into a relationless misery, converting him into a massive machine of ceaseless production. The goal of the alienation is the impossibility of relating, the imposition of an ingenuine utility-based relationship that would never halt the progress of the production. While the alienation fragments and scatters the worker’s self in an alien world where the products cannot relate back to their creator, the labor as gathering helps the worker find himself again in a world that is full of his own meaningful creations. The worker finds joy in this act of gathering because he can see the continuity and the sense of his own labor. Like a temple or a jug that bring together the communal spirit letting each thing shine, each work of labor should be able to open different and various ways of relationality among the people and nature. The joy of the worker is the joy that we feel when someone says to us that what we do matters and that our own productive activity matters as well. But most importantly joy comes when we understand and sincerely believe that what we do matters and is significant. If we limit labor to the strict necessity of profits and gains then we may become richer but, at the same time, we are entering anew into the vicious circle of necessity that urges us to produce more, to gain more, to offer more and to scatter ourselves more.

Furthermore, feeling joy in our labor is not an addition, an accessory to the main act of producing, in order to make it sound or look more attractive. Companies and the economic systems cannot offer us happiness and joy because seeking and achieving them is our own personal quest. Companies may offer us a space wherein necessity’s chains might be looser and the working conditions better. Still labor as self-realization and self-completion can only happen when labor recovers its lost ontological significance and importance, that is labor as joy and as creation. Joy in the labor is more than a feeling; it is an existential state that reaffirms our own being in our creation. When feeling joy we feel at home and at work we no longer feel enchained. Through labor as joy we gather ourselves in the world and we start to see our being and personality reflected on our creations. We shape the world and we let it shine through our own shining in and on it.

Concluding, trying to find joy in our labor is not a simple option among many others; it is the only option that will not let the whole world become an enemy in the eyes of the workers. We have seen before that through alienation the worker feels miserable during his productive activity and regards his own products alien to him, like things that stand against him as a constant reminder of his own exploitation and fragmentation. If the workers do not find joy and meaning soon in their work then the risk arises for the whole world to become an enemy for them whose different aspects would be: the alienated product made by the workers, the bosses and their demands, the companies with their gigantic bureaucratic and ice-cold systems, the whole society that cannot stop demanding new things in order to create and fill ever emergent needs. Still, not having joy as the essence of labor, does not mean that a matrix of relationships may not arise or develop; nonetheless, while through labor as gathering those relationships were gathered and attuned to the satisfaction of a creative production, in the meaninglessness of labor as endless production the workers' relationship with the rest of the world is one: despise, anger and frustration. The injustice of not being able to relate to our products and the despair of feeling homeless at work are only some of the possible dangers that could eventually spark an explosion inside the capitalist system. The shackles of necessity are still strong and tight but living constantly under the obligation of producing, as well as underestimating the importance of the workers' joy and well-being during their labor are dead ends that could bring workers to their extremes. Work should not be felt like a prison but as a place of creation and self-completion. Dragging those two elements away from the sphere of work is the proof that the way we understand labor should be totally and radically redefined. If work gets utterly limited to production and automatized action, if work has nothing more to offer to workers than a monthly salary then something has gone terribly wrong during the decades. Work as joy is our right to self-completion and self-realization. The joy we feel at work is the joy of a creator that (re)finds himself in his creations. Through work the world becomes hospitable, closer and more familiar to us. Each society and each political and economic system that does not comprehend workers' necessity to be joyful and feel homely at work is doomed to be considered the obstacle to the workers' right to feel complete and fulfilled. Finally, although labor alienation deprives workers from any possibility of relating to their productive activity and products, the eventual identification of the capitalist system with the alienation and the misery of the workers can only lead to one possible relationship: conflict.

References

Heidegger, Martin. 1975. "The Origin of the Work of Art" in *Poetry, Language, Thought.* Translated by Albert Hofstadter. New York: Harper & Row Publishers

Heidegger, Martin. 1977. *The Question concerning Technology*. Translated by William Lovitt. New York: Harper & Row Publishers

Heidegger, Martin. 2001. *Being and Time*. Translated by John Macquarrie and Edward Robinson. Oxford: Blackwell

Heidegger, Martin. 2012. *Bremen and Freiburg Lectures.* Translated by Andrew Mitchell. Indiana: Indiana University Press

Heidegger, Martin. 2014. *Introduction to Metaphysics.* Translated by Gregory Fried and Richard Polt. Yale: Yale University Press

Hemming, Laurence Paul. 2013. *Heidegger and Marx: A Productive Dialogue over the Language of Humanism*. Illinois: Northwestern University Press

Honneth, Axel. 2007. *Reification: A New Look at an Old Idea*. Oxford: Oxford University Press

Horkheimer, Max. 2004. *The Eclipse of Reason.* New York: Continuum Publishing Company.

Junger, Ernst. 2017. *The Worker*. Edited by Laurence Paul Hemming and translated by Bogdan Costea and Laurence Paul Hemming. Illinois: Northwestern University Press

Khan, Nasir. 1995. *Development of the Concept and Theory of Alienation in Marx's Writings*. Oslo: Forlum Sorlag

Mandel Ernest and Novack George. 1977. *The Marxist Theory of Alienation: Three Essays*. Atlanta: Pathfinder Press

Marx, Karl. 1988. *Economic and philosophic manuscripts of 1844*. Translated by Martin Milligan. New York: Prometheus Books

Mészáros, István. 2006. *Marx's theory of alienation*. London: Merlin Press

Ollman, Bertell. 1996. *Alienation: Marx's conception of man in capitalist society*. Cambridge: Cambridge University Press

Sayers, Sean. 2011. *Marx and Alienation: Essays on Hegelian Themes*. London: Palgrave Macmillan

Wallimann, Isidor. 1981. *Estrangement: Marx's Conception of Human Nature and the Division of Labor*. Connecticut: Greenwood Press

Wendling, Amy. 2011. *Karl Marx on Technology and Alienation*. London: Palgrave Macmillan

Cynical Reason in the Academe

Anton Heinrich Rennesland

Peter Sloterdijk mocks the Enlightenment project and unveils contemporary reason's own discontent as the enlightened false consciousness evident today through society's grey areas of populism, the Anthropocene, Big Data, and, for this essay, the domination of Capital's language. These ambiguous occurrences in society are not without critical reflection, even as similar trends happen within the academe. Never have Higher Education Institutions (HEIs) "been so numerous or so important" while at the same time "suffer[ing] from such a disabling lack of confidence and loss of identity."[1] The academe now faces its *becoming-ambiguous* notwithstanding the declaration some 42 years ago that the "university is an autonomous institution at the heart of societies" and that its teaching ought to remain "independent of all political authority and economic power."[2] What we witness today is a crisis in the humanities,[3] and I narrow my scope to the academician's vexed selfhood vis-à-vis the academe's ambiguity. In this essay, I draw affinities between Sloterdijk's enlightened false consciousness and today's academician to render the academician's vulnerable condition bare. Doing such an unmasking of society's greater discontent of Capital, I prompt a reconsideration of the academician's loneliness from a mere existential offshoot to her magnifying lens when engaging with society.

1

The "enlightened false consciousness" is an oxymoron of 'enlightened' and 'false' together, showing how today's reason "has learned its lessons in enlightenment, but it has not, and probably was not able to, put them into

---

[1] Stefan Collini, *What are Universities For?* (London: Penguin Books, 2012), §1.
[2] *Magna Charta Universitatum* (18 September 1988), http://www.magna-charta.org/resources/files/the-magna-charta/english.
[3] See Yehuda Elkana and Hannes Klöpper, *The University in the Twenty-first Century: Teaching the New Enlightenment in the Digital Age*, ed. Marvin Lazerson (Budapest: Central European University Press, 2016), 120ff.

practice."[4] This accentuates Kant's distinction between enlightenment as the current time (*in einem Zeitalter der Aufklärung*) and as an approach to life (*in einem aufgeklärten Zeitalter*) which ultimate reveals enlightenment's paradoxical character.[5] Living through the Enlightenment ought to have meant a clarification of our experiences but turned out to itself require explanation especially since humanity's history may be surmised as the development from the slingshot to the atom bomb.[6] We witness today the development of ideology from Marx to Žižek, from "not knowing and doing" to "knowing and yet still doing[,]"or how Sloterdijk characterizes it as when people "know the truth about themselves and, in spite of this, 'go on as before[.]'"[7] In this peculiar (pseudo-)enlightenment, reason emerges as cynical, falling short of actual enlightenment and embracing false consciousness. Enlightenment once sought to dispel myth and possibly religion, yet in its failure operated under the mask of its opposition.[8] Today, we witness the resurrection of religion but as that of Capital.[9] The world confesses a blind faith that should cause an alarming discontent as we transcended ourselves at the expense of life's immanence to embrace the speed of society's progression. In context of the academe, the contemporary university is forced open to address society's needs and numerous "irrelevant" departments have shut down due to a dwindling number of enrollees since the market economy has become "impatient" with these

---

[4] Peter Sloterdijk, *Critique of Cynical Reason*, trans. Michael Eldred (Minneapolis: University of Minnesota Press, 1987), 5.

[5] See Immanuel Kant, "Beantwortung der Frage: Was ist Aufklärung?" (1784), https://www.projekt-gutenberg.org/kant/aufklae/aufkl001.html and Geoffrey Galt Harpham, "So... What Is Enlightenment? An Inquisition into Modernity," *Critical Inquiry* 20, no. 3 (Spring 1994): 531, https://www.jstor.org/stable/1343868.

[6] See Katerina Deligiorgi, *Kant and the Culture of Enlightenment* (New York: State University of New York Press, 2005), 6, and Theodor W. Adorno, *Negative Dialectics*, trans. E. B. Ashton (New York: Continuum Press), 320.

[7] Cf. Karl Marx, *Das Kapital: Kritik der politischen Ökonomie*, in *Karl Marx-Friedrich Engels-Werke, Band 23* (Dietz Verlag: Berlin[/DDR], 1962), I.1.88, http://www.mlwerke.de/me/me23/me23_049.htm, and Slavoj Žižek, *The Sublime Object of Ideology* (London: Verso, 1989), 30, and Sloterdijk, *Critique of Cynical Reason*, 102.

[8] See Neil Wilson, "Punching out the Enlightenment: A Discussion of Peter Sloterdijk's Kritik der zynischen Vernunft," *New German Critique* 41, Special Issue on the Critiques of the Enlightenment (Spring - Summer, 1987): 54, https://www.jstor.org/stable/488275.

[9] See Walter Benjamin, "Capitalism as Religion," in *Selected Writings, Vol. 1: 1913-1926*, ed. Marcus Bullock, Michael W. Jennings (Belknap Press, 1996), and Peter Sloterdijk, *You Must Change Your Life*, trans. Wieland Hoban (Cambridge: Polity Press, 2013), 1.

departments' "traditions of open-ended enquiry[.]"[10] What backs this move is "the 'commonsense', and unprovable, catchphrase: 'the jobs of the future don't exist yet.'"[11] The neatly identified outcomes (courses, lessons, programs) of yesteryears are rapidly considered inessential for tomorrow's world. The academe today welcomes Capital's frenzied and deterritorialized investments of desire.[12] The academe must keep with society's pacing in hope for its continuous sustenance as Capital offers the academe's future, a shift from mole to snake, from disciplinarity to control. This transition to a business model resounds buzzwords of motivation, optimization, and standardization that pervert "excellence" into a maximization of possibilities veiled behind the soothing invitation that we *can* become excellent. Enlightenment today means an attempt at or an ideology of excellence.

The incalculable prospects offered by Capital and the serene invitation of the word *can* must not mislead us. The transition from disciplinarity to control evokes the shift of *should* to *can.*[13] We lay ourselves bare not to strict requirements but to today's infinite possibilities. Capital fast-tracked development to a state in which horizons are filled with *can*, expanding while merging, and the academe is left to reckon with this. With this vista, Capital has branded the academe as the "University of Excellence."[14] The

---

[10] See Byung-Chul Han, *Psychopolitics: Neoliberalism and New Technologies of Power*, trans. Erik Butler (London: Verso, 2017), 86, and Collini, *What are Universities For?*, §1.Concrete instances have been reported around the work: Alex Dean, "Japan's humanities chop sends shivers down academic spines," *The Guardian*, September 26, 2015, https://www.theguardian.com/higher-education-network/2015/sep/25/japans-humanities-chop-sends-shivers-down-academic-spines; Justin Weinberg, "Liberty University Jettisons Entire Philosophy Department," *Daily Nous*, May 12, 2020, https://dailynous.com/2020/05/12/liberty-university-jettisons-entire-philosophy-department/, or quite recently Australia-based Philosophers, "An Open Letter on the Importance of Protecting Philosophy," *ABC* (3 August 2020), https://www.abc.net.au/religion/open-letter-on-the-importance-of-protecting-philosophy/12517642?fbclid=IwAR1gvNJ6UN7NCqufz Wz2Rfke1g3 0J4Wey1aTdtl_1YxUJ3A5nd6ySs3qgww.

[11] See Greg Thompson and Ian Cook, "The Lack of Work and the Contemporary University," *Education and Technological Unemployment*, ed. Michael A. Peters, Petar Jandrić, Alexander J. Means (Singapore: Springer Nature, 2019), 30.

[12] See Han, *Psychopolitics*, 18 and Gilles Deleuze and Félix Guattari, *Anti-Oedipus: Capitalism and Schizophrenia* (Minneapolis: University of Minnesota Press, 1983), 373.

[13] See Byung-Chul Han, *The Burnout Society*, trans. Erik Butler (Stanford, CA: Stanford University Press, 2015), 9ff.

[14] See Bill Readings, *The University in Ruins* (Cambridge: Harvard University Press, 1996), 152.

university has—mind the pun—*canned* itself as a commodity. It is only through its canning that it preserves itself for tomorrow's possibilities. HEIs transitioned from mole to snake, concerning itself not with spaces of enclosure but with specializations, services, and control.[15] In this effort to remain relevant, we should notice certain obvious dysfunctionalities as the textbook assumes the role of an instructional manual, equating excellence to maximization.[16] George Riter considers this as Capital's McDonaldization, the attempt at total quality management (TQM) that wipes the messiness out of learning to focus on efficiency.[17] Teaching has become an assembly line of educational management in which *perpetual training* replaces learning and foresight simply as crisis management.[18] Amidst these, the academician bears the toll in delivering "quality" education as she shifts from teacher-educator to teacher-administrator.[19] Through the serenity of *can*, education has been enticed into a commodity and is capitalized on to maximize efficiency. It is gamified and the academician-administrator is compelled to play this exhausting game.

Amusingly, HEIs around the world are all quantified into ranks, seemingly taunting all academicians to secure their spot in the competition.[20] Yet, we

---

[15] See Gilles Deleuze, "Postscript on the Societies of Control," *October* 59 (Winter, 1992): 6, http://links.jstor.org/sici?sici=0162-2870%28199224%2959%3C3%3APOTSOC%3E2.0.CO%3B2-T

[16] See Readings, *The University in Ruins*, 151ff.

[17] See George Riter, *The McDonaldization Thesis: Explorations and Extensions* (London: Sage Publications, 1998).

[18] See Deleuze, "Postscript on the Societies of Control," 5.

[19] See Readings, *The University in Ruins*, 152.

[20] University rankings are published by three companies with their own methodologies: Quacquarelli Symonds (QS), Times Higher Education (THE), and Shianghai Jiao Tong University.

QS: Academic reputation (40%), Student-to-Faculty Ration (20%), Citations per Faculty (20%), Employer reputation (10%), and International Faculty Ratio (5%) and International Student Ratio (5%)

Shanghai Jiao Tong University: Quality of Faculty (40%: Staff of an institution winning Nobel Prizes and Fields Medals [20%] and Highly cited researchers in 21 broad subject categories [20%]), Research Output (40%: Papers published in Nature and Science* [20%] and Papers indexed in Science Citation Index-expanded and Social Science Citation Index [20%]), Per Capita Performance (10%), and Quality of Education (10% [Alumni of an institution winning Nobel Prizes and Fields Medals]).

Times Higher Education: Teaching (30% Reputation survey [15%], Doctorates-awarded-to-academic-staff ratio [6%], Staff-to-student ratio [4.5%], Doctorate-to-bachelor's ratio [2.25%], Institutional income [2.25%]), Research (30%: Reputation

must be critical of these because, save for the top universities, "rankings are essentially not much more than a gloried guessing game[,]"[21] instigated by Capital's dominating language. The market language is understood only by its speakers as it is realized within a plane of immanence peculiar to Capital;[22] the academe has shifted its mother tongue, evident in words such as TQM, outcomes, and teacher-administrator. Today's narrative is dominated by that single language that determines which components should be improved to secure a higher spot the following year. Tangible aspects such as the number of PhD graduates, foreign students, and syllabi are assessed and considered more than the student-teacher interaction which is impossible to fully quantify in the semester-end evaluation. The quantifiable aspects form a checklist for excellence, and so a university's own cultivation, developed through hundreds of years, can simply be discounted as not part of today's metrics of excellence substantiated in the assembly line's manual.

Academic capitalism is induced by the outward-oriented administration that caters to the global market.[23] The McDonaldized University of Excellence is a knowledge-producing corporation, playing a ranking game created by equally competitive institutions. This game churns out knowledge conformed to market needs which in turn brands universities "to attract fee-paying students as well as philanthropic and government grants and subsidies"[24] because they are market relevant. This singular language is straightforward in saying that all faculties and departments *can* become excellent and *can* gain immediate returns. This ramifies the university into a neoliberal stronghold: learning is convenient, teachers, efficient, and courses, important.

---

survey [18%], Research income [6%], Research productivity [6%]), Citations (30%), International Outlook (7.5%: Proportion of international students [2.5%], Proportion of international staff [2.5%], International collaboration [2.5%]), and Industry Income (2.5%).

See "Methodology," QS World University Rankings, QS Quacquarelli Symonds, updated 10 June 2020, http://www.topuniversities.com/qs-world-university-rankings/methodology; "Methodology," Shanghai Ranking Consultancy, http://www.shanghairanking.com/ARWU-Methodology-2016.html; and "World University Rankings 2019: methodology," Times Higher Education World University Rankings, https://www.timeshighereducation.com/world-university-rankings/world-university-rankings-2019-methodology.

[21] Elkana and Klöpper, *The University in the Twenty-first Century*, 161.

[22] See Deleuze and Guattari, *Anti-Oedipus*, 240.

[23] See Thompson and Cook, "The Lack of Work and the Contemporary University," 35-36.

[24] Elkana and Klöpper, *The University in the Twenty-first Century*, 161.

This is the promise of excellence, i.e. producing docile bodies for the workforce. Capital dictates what is essential for tomorrow's success and the liberal arts' struggle is just a farce, an exaggerated feat, as per the market's consideration.

We though must be critical of this Capital's gamification. What happens is that we are drawn into a vicious cycle, a game authorized by the administrators and played by the faculty. *The academician is a player in this rigged competition.* We have to see that "gamification is destroying play's potential to set free. Play should make it possible to use things in wholly different way; it should liberate them from the theology and teleology of Capital."[25] The slow loss of freedom and creativity—the unsurety of the liberal arts—reflects the pathological element of this game. The game's rules are kept to a minimum for the least amount of order protects society from chaos:[26] follow the assembly line, nothing more, nothing less. It is either one plays and is fully engrossed or is left out and easily substituted by another. Capital perverts play into an eerie seriousness that increasingly plagues society's playground.[27] One is left to realize that these rules constitute the thin line between order and barbarism; in the university's own enlightenment, freedom does not mean self-autonomy as the academician is only free to become the administrator. A shift in lexicon reveals our current state, from "publish or perish" to "play or perish." Enlightenment boils down today as an invitation we cannot refuse, to play the game of Capital.

2

From this consideration, I concentrate on the academician as the enlightened false consciousness. As I have sought to illustrate, Enlightenment's development ironed the wriggles out of thinking, yet the "more modern society appears to be without alternatives, the more it will allow itself to be cynical. In the end it is ironical about its own legitimation."[28] Our progress is simultaneous to our rationalization of it. We justify the steps we take in progressing for excellence. What is cynical about this is that one's ideology is both its idealism and masquerading.[29] On the one hand, reason legitimizes excellence through rankings and other quantifiable elements, while on the

---

[25] Han, *Psychopolitics*, 52.

[26] See Gilles Deleuze and Félix Guattari, *What is Philosophy?,* trans. Hugh Tomlinson and Graham Burchell (New York: Columbia University Press, 1994), 201.

[27] See Sloterdijk, *Critique of Cynical Reason*, 118.

[28] Sloterdijk, *Critique of Cynical Reason*, 112.

[29] See ibid., 111.

other acknowledges the system's deficiencies. Enlightenment entailed diffused cynicism as one is both controller and controlled, administrator and administered, speaker and listener, teacher and taught, at the same time. Ideology is a necessary false consciousness.[30] It is antithetical to its very self—yet existence continues.

The academician lives through this cynical fate and, despite signs of dysfunctionality, persists to work. She is the enlightened false consciousness. She has become *Anybody* (*Das Man*), homogeneous to other cogs in the gamified customer satisfaction. She dons the crew cap of the McDonaldized University of Excellence and hides her face behind the cap's stiffed bill. She is pseudo-enlightened, antithetically cynical using language merely aligned to Capital. The academician is *Anybody*, nearly tantamount to citations, published articles, and students' evaluations. Upon deeper reflection, we opine a peculiar loneliness under this veil of anonymity. *Becoming-Anyone* disburdens us of the more serious questions of life. It is easier to ride the wave than to be its riptide. One gets to hide behind the crew cap's stiffed bill of memo, order, and meeting for the sake of tenurial and promotion. However, it is at these ambiguous moments of everyday life, that we slip into mindlessness and *Anyone*'s real dictatorship is unfolded.[31] *Anyone* stands as the mask of the public sphere that disburdens us of the heaviness of living, of choosing which principles to uphold. It is easier to just follow the Market's language than to create disruptions. Through this obedience, we experience an assimilation by growing nearly identical to each other with the same dreams, goals, and even causes of suffering. Unknowingly, we have accepted today's mask of nihilism: the sight of humanity, the sight of thought, makes us weary.[32] This lukewarm-ness leads us to understand Heidegger's association that *Anyone* is no one.[33] *Anyone* stands among all of us yet is no one in particular. *Anyone* lives in ambiguity. *Anyone* is a fake.[34] We are alone in Capital's vicious game; the academe's taunt is a

---

[30] See Theodor W. Adorno and Max Horkheimer, *Towards a New Manifesto*, trans. Rodney Livingstone, Ian Macdonald, and Martin Shuster (London: Verso, 2019), 17.

[31] See Martin Heidegger, *Being and Time*, trans. John Macquarrie and Edward Robinson (New York: Harper Perennial Modern Thought, 2008), 164.

[32] See Friedrich Nietzsche, *The Genealogy of Morality*, in *The Genealogy of Morality and Other Writings*, ed. Keith Ansell-Pearson, trans. Carol Diethe (Cambridge: Cambridge University Press, 2006), I:12.

[33] See Heidegger, *Being and Time*, 165.

[34] Cf. Romualdo Abulad, "Filipino Postmodernity: Quo Vadis?," *Kritike* 13, no. 2 (December 2019): 44,

transcendental movement away from oneself, leaving us bereft of our individuality in face of Capital's decrees. We are left with this peculiar loneliness within the academe in *becoming-Anyone*, in a doubling of subjectivity.

In face of Capital's dominating language, the academician vexes between the fear of non-compliance and a dedication to one's discipline. Subjectivity is doubled as the academician pledges allegiance to splitting paths of Capital and Academe. She persists to write but have yet to realize that *writing is dead; you and I are its murderers.*[35] We have condoned the killing of writing outside Capital's language: more demands for publication are made for faculty and student and impact factor determines quality. What matters in the University of Excellence is not how hard the academician plays Capital's game but her behavior in playing. She may distract herself when she rejoices in a superb student evaluation, but the discomfort she experiences within her unholy family of Capital, Academe, and herself, is not without qualification. In a figurative sense and in a bold move, I recognize our protagonist as an illegitimate child, the family's black sheep, who despite her status still endeavors to tend to her parents with devotional faith. This is her double life; she endeavors to please her parents while subjecting herself to a worry, an anxiety, and ultimately a discontent with herself. She does the academe's bidding yet ramifies Capital's influence. In this process, she eventually forgets for what she endeavors.[36] It is a life in ambiguity, of *becoming-Anyone* through the academe's gamification. Ironically, "Enlightenment means to affirm all antischizophrenic movements" but "universities are scarcely the place where this happens."[37] The academician is tugged between both parents, overworked in the gamified McDonaldized University because of "overproduction, overachievement, and overcommunication" which become an immanent violence to the system.[38] The tantalizing effects of Capital's language is that it simplifies lexicons, abridges thought, yet bombards the grammatical structure with the same elements, a maximization through the use of *can*. This is the violence of today's *Newspeak*, the language of Capital.[39] The academician has honed her language skills yet is required to simply use the basic details, more

---

https://www.kritike.org/journal/issue_25/abulad2_december2019.pdf, and Heidegger, *Being and Time*, 217-219.

[35] See Deleuze and Guattari, *Anti-Oedipus*, 240.

[36] See Sloterdijk, *Critique of Cynical Reason*, 114.

[37] Ibid. 120.

[38] Han, *The Burnout Society*, 5-6.

[39] Referencing *Newspeak* in George Orwell's *1984*.

numbers and figures, the better. This is the violence in the academe today, a crisis not just in embracing Capital's language but by *becoming-Anyone* in face of it.

A *becoming-Anyone* in enlightened society is a numbing or a doubling of subjectivity. A parody of Hegel's unhappy consciousness, reason after engaging with society ultimately becomes cynically apathetic, a schizoid consciousness.[40] Cynicism is "enlightenment turned sour" that results from a "self-survival in a society dominated by instrumental rationality[.]"[41] What makes cynicism indiscernible today is that enlightenment incorporated its adversaries. This causes a diffused discontent, growing while simultaneously abating itself; reason is cynical: "the cynic orients himself in a demystified world by focusing his energies on self-preservation and self-advancement" and any form of critique is not for "implementing social change but with the aim of getting ahead in the world."[42] This cynicism today is far different from its roots. Sloterdijk recognizes this dichotomy and differentiates *Kynismus* (kynicism), in reference to the Greek origin, from *Zynismus* (cynicism), to signify today's indifference. The latter is indifference that modernity makes our protagonist feel frighteningly alone. Loneliness creeps in when the bastard child confronts her true position within the unholy family: she is just a cog in the machine, working as *Anyone* behind the crew cap's stiffened bill in hope of getting by.

Becoming-Anyone existentially eradicates identity and uniqueness, and in theory leaves each alone to fend for herself. Enlightenment's bigotry is our cynically blind religious dedication to Capital's language. The system reinforces itself by providing the same images and expressions that numb consciousness. It prompts a paranoia in each to outdo the other, to be cunning in playing the rigged game, because without enough performance one is easily replaced. A tacit dedication is given to this dominating language since despite objective dysfunctionalities, one persists to play. One becomes solitary through this level of competition, fearing that the other might outdo her. This theoretical isolation is supplemented by an abundance of tasks from a practical consideration: from educator to administrator, from teaching and grading students to attending meetings, accomplishing forms, and pleasing accreditation-assessment criteria. The difficulty of suggesting hope in face of objective dysfunctionalities is partly

[40] See Louisa Shea, *The Cynic Enlightenment: Diogenes in the Salon* (Baltimore, ML: The Johns Hopkins University Press, 2010), 149.

[41] "Wilson, "Punching out the Enlightenment, "55.

[42] Shea, *The Cynic Enlightenment*, 147 and 152.

due to, following Sloterdijk, its heavy theological underpinning that has left us with only a dreary unhappiness.[43] We have bastardized the idea of hope by associating it with utopia and an eternal redemption to anticipate. Instead of treading this path, a sense of optimism may be sourced from alternatives. What Sloterdijk suggests is a reconsideration of kynicism as a search for a lost innocence we cannot regain, after society's lambasting of repetition's eccentricity.[44] It is an attempt at peering at society with difference in face of repetition. What would be providential to argue is a reassertion of critical space in Capital's plane of one-dimensionality. A reconsideration of alternatives affords us an understanding of one's loneliness in this cynical state.

3

For the last part of this essay, I glance at alternatives to our protagonist's cynical reason. With alternatives, we see multiple dimensions, intersections of planes, and the ability to transverse or interfere with other planes of immanence. The solitude of the academician's existential state makes the form's error the content; loneliness in fact stands as our protagonist's vantage. To exhibit an alternative understanding of her vexed solitude, I present three images of this weary optimism:

Any sense of radical emancipation would be futile considering factors surrounding the advent of today's cynicism. No department could unreservedly go against the university-administration, for a simple memo of the latter could dismantle any oppression; one cannot choose not to collect publications or earn degrees lest certain positions or opportunities would not be available. Enlightenment earnestly confronted ambiguity yet was subsumed by its adversary. Our academic pathology in its atypical certainty resounds a cheeky idealism. Our first image of a bleak alternative is Descartes's Cartesian Doubt that resembles our enlightened false consciousness: "I am deceived, therefore I am. And: I unmask deceptions, I myself deceive; therefore, I preserve myself."[45] This ironic deception is a mark of today's cynicality. From his quasi-enlightened position in face of unsurety, Descartes' solitude afforded him a kynical laugh. He is remembered for his value of solitude, sleeping for hours, lingering in bed,

---

[43] Sloterdijk, *You Must Change Your Life*, 32.

[44] See ibid., 404ff.

[45] Sloterdijk, *Critique of Cynical Reason*, 331.

pondering and writing until 11 in the morning.[46] He ridicules his friends who make fun of his lifestyle, reproaching them for their irreligious contemplation of isolation. We today cannot match this level reverence but only mimic it. "Thoughts now become internalized forms of work, and the life of the mind itself is put on the path toward the production of useful things."[47] Descartes wallows in his solitude and perceives his loneliness, idleness, and seclusion as an alternative plane for the critical mind.

This solitude is theoretically identical to what others experience yet in reality unique to each person, and from this particular solitude are one's views fundamentally formed. Our second image is Adorno's parodic rendition of the biblical image, "The splinter in your eye is the best magnifying-glass."[48] Capital dominates society however not by punishment but by enticement, and because of its serenity we are lured: *conformity has replaced consciousness*.[49] This is the domination of reason. He points us to a twin reality of how thoughts are materially conditioned which then in turn condition our actions. Since ideology dominates Capital's logic, Adorno is pessimistic to accentuate subjectivity because "popular thinking" or, put fittingly, *unenlightened consciousness* creates pseudo-individuality.[50] Popular thought conjures a sense of forgetfulness of civility, deliberation, and even of our very selves and presupposes the "violent, hard-hitting, unresting jerkiness of Fascist maltreatment."[51] Reason's authoritarian dominion is the reign of pseudo-individuality, ratified by Capital's overabundance. Everyone, despite the differences in occupation or place, experiences the domination of totalitarian consumerism in the Culture Industry. We though may be different, but the Culture Industry subsumes each as the *same*. What makes one different from another is the exact locale where she is subsumed. Her baggage in approaching Capital is her magnifying lens in exposing social pathologies. For Adorno, one's locale provides the *a priori pain*, a remaining sensitivity in face of hardening, and a maturity to burst negativity

---

[46] See Mason Currey, *Daily Rituals: How Artists Work* (New York: Alfred Knopf, 2013), §René Descartes.

[47] Peter Sloterdijk, *Philosophical Temperaments: From Plato to Foucault*, trans. Thomas Dunlap (New York: Columbia University Press, 2013), 30.

[48] Theodor Adorno, *Minima Moralia* (London: Verso Press, 2005), 50.

[49] Theodor Adorno, *The Culture Industry: Selected Essays on Mass Culture*, ed. J. M. Bernstein (London: Routledge, 1991), 104.

[50] See Theodor Adorno and Max Horkheimer, *Dialectic of Enlightenment: Philosophical Fragments*, ed. Gunzelin Schmid Noerr, trans. Edmund Jephcott (Stanford, CA: Stanford University Press, 2002), 125.

[51] Adorno, *Minima Moralia*, 40.

open.[52] Cynicism is when one simply allows this fascist domination to violate the locale; kynicism is when one lives through the system from a critical viewpoint.

Lastly, we observe Diogenes who continued living an irreverent life of free speech (*parrhêsia*) in abject poverty that "exchanged the false effigies of socially created wants and desires" with a life attuned to nature.[53] He stands as a solitary social irritant, a reminder that thought ought to remain free. He barges into the *polis* and lashes out unsolicited opinions and impolite remarks. He masturbates in public and pees against the wind, but "wiry and tough as he may be, [he] is no Hercules and pissing, like spitting, into the wind is messy."[54] He embraces the mess and laughs at this tomfoolery, while we, observing him with our perverted gaze, chuckle along. Diogenes stands as language's grammatical error, a gadfly to Socrates' rational system. He willfully stands at society's margins, alone and reveling in his barrel. He orders Alexander the Great to move away and not block his sun, which leaves the latter at awe at this boldness: a confrontation between rational order in "Alexander, the King" and cheekiness in "Diogenes, the Dog."[55] Diogenes stands as an opposition to social and political training, an alternative, a difference to life lived according to repetitive rational (and cynical) reason.[56]

In reviewing these glimpses of optimism and in light of cynical reason's objective dysfunctionalities, we are drawn to reflect on loneliness that traverses several planes of immanence. In spite of how Capital "compromised academic life and sped up the clock" we must be mindful how the academe "should be cultivating deep thought" and not merely swayed by the industry's "time crunch and making those of us subjected to it feel powerless."[57] Within the unholy family, cynical reason should once again be mindful of play's ability to liberate than dominate, as a resistance against the rigged game of domination and rationality.[58] This reveals a certain dialectics, a violence within the family, for her to overcome. She may be

---

[52] See Sloterdijk, *Critique of Cynical Reason*, xxxiii-xxxv.
[53] Shea, *The Cynic Enlightenment*, 8.
[54] Babette Babich "Sloterdijk's Cynicism: Diogenes in the Marketplace" *Sloterdijk Now*, ed. Stuart Elden (Cambridge: Polity Press, 2012), 23.
[55] See Diogenes the Cynic, *Sayings and Anecdotes*, trans. Robin Hard (Oxford: Oxford University Press, 2012), §236-238, 242.
[56] See Sloterdijk, *Critique of Cynical Reason*, 168.
[57] Maggie Berg and Barbara K. Seeber, *The Slow Professor: Challenging the Culture of Speed in the Academy* (Toronto: University of Toronto Press, 2016), x.
[58] See Sloterdijk, *Critique of Cynical Reason*, 102.

secured in her deception, though what remains is her peculiar disposition. "I am deceived therefore I am" must be turned into "I am deceived therefore I can," a parody of the enticing *can*, reclaiming it from society's enticement prompted by Capital to a fundamental part of subjectivity. It is a shift from Capital's *can* to one's capacity and will to do things. *I am deceived but I know that I am, and I know that I can look beyond.* The academician's current state offers her the premium of disclosure. Her isolation is her own baggage in thought, her magnifying glass to read the fine prints of Capital's language. Her vulnerability within the academe allows her to express the condition fully, to write and to discourse about it to like minds. As the kynic positioned himself at societal margins, so too must our protagonist recognize an intersection of planes at the borders of thought to regain this sense of difference. Difference, and not simply a reiteration, is found along the way of a creative struggle as satire replaces conversation;[59] the violence in the unholy family is today's academician's dialectic in thought. This type of thought-difference counters *Anyone*'s indifference. Kynicism is the adulteration of the currency of (what is accepted as the) truth without prompting actual violent confrontation. It is a satirical insubordination—not a whitewashing of the superficial orderliness which wipes genuine chaos away—that reasserts lost subjectivity in face of today's language.

Loneliness as a divergence ought to be reckoned as a reminder of nature lost. Being the kynic is a deliberate attempt to be cheeky with meditation afforded by one's solitary standpoint and should not be confused with mere childish behavior.[60] It is an attempt at changing the grammar of our behavior within Capital's dominating language.[61] What Sloterdijk does in exposing cynical reason as the enlightened false consciousness is " a self-confident, watchful miming of critique and a 'bodily' disclosure of truth that ultimately [...] 'provokes' a living stage on which are comprehensible, but only secondarily, the discourses of abstract critique and rationalist idealizations."[62] In a sense, we are brought to notice a (possibility for a) genuine philosophical event in the eventless barrel of Diogenes and the *canned* university of the academician. What loneliness offers is a recognition of

---

[59] See Shea, *The Cynic Enlightenment*, 151,

[60] See Shea, *The Cynic Enlightenment*, 153-54.

[61] See "Changing the Grammar of our Behavior," the fifth episode in the second season of DW's *On the Green Fence*, a podcast hosted by Neil King and Gabriel Borrud with guest Peter Sloterdijk for the episode, https://www.dw.com/en/se-02-episode-5-changing-the-grammar-of-our-behavior/av-53432043.

[62] Sjoerd van Tuinen, "Critique Beyond Resentment: An Introduction to Peter Sloterdijk's Jovial Modernity" *Cultural Politics* 3, no. 3 (November 2007): 277, doi:10.2752/175174307X226861.

critical space for thought, a self-reflexivity and a realization of the ability to be cheeky. As Diogenes looks at Alexander with a kynical face, so too can our protagonist gaze at the simplification of Capital's language with resolute determination to laugh at this pseudo-authority. Her loneliness provides silence amidst Capital's hubbub, a release from *Anyone*'s tyrannical overabundance. From this lonely state, she realizes how thinking is at work in solitude; there exist no insular thoughts for these are fundamentally materially conditioned—there is no degree of discourse without that degree of loneliness. Her isolation stands as a stimulus of thought, a slowness in contrary to Capital's speed. Despite an abundance and a repetition of the *same* (memo, meeting, form), her moments of despair and frustration at these within the academe cause her a release from diffused discontent. They cause the latter to saturate. Her magnifying lens affords her a seriousness not at what Capital provides, but ironically a seriousness of not taking things too seriously, a humor that releases us from our emotional comfort zones and affords us a shift to another plane, a cultivation not of diffused emotions but rage within this novel economy of garrulous discontent and resentment.[63] The authenticity of the kynic thus is the divergence from Capital's normalcy, and the academician's loneliness is not just a divergence but is in itself the difference, the opportunity to traverse to other planes for a reassertion of critical thought.

Bibliography

Abulad, Romualdo. "Filipino Postmodernity: Quo Vadis?." *Kritike* 13, no. 2. (December 2019): 37-59. https://www.kritike.org/journal/issue_25/abulad2_december2019.pdf.

Adorno, Theodor W. *The Culture Industry: Selected Essays on Mass Culture*. Edited by J. M. Bernstein. London: Routledge, 1991.

—. *Minima Moralia*. London: Verso Press, 2005.

—. *Negative Dialectics*. Translated by E. B. Ashton. New York: Continuum Press.

Adorno, Theodor W. and Max Horkheimer. *Dialectic of Enlightenment: Philosophical Fragments*. Edited by Gunzelin Schmid Noerr. Translated by Edmund Jephcott. Stanford, CA: Stanford University Press, 2002.

—. *Towards a New Manifesto*. Translated by Rodney Livingstone, Ian Macdonald, and Martin Shuster. London: Verso, 2019.

[63] See Peter Sloterdijk, *Rage and Time: A Psychopolitical Investigation*, trans. Mario Wenning (New York: Columbia University Press, 2010), 26.

Benjamin, Walter. “Capitalism as Religion.” In *Selected Writings. Volume 1: 1913-1926*. Edited by Marcus Bullock and Michael W. Jennings. Belknap Press, 1996.

Berg, Maggie and Barbara K. Seeber. *The Slow Professor: Challenging the Culture of Speed in the Academy*. Toronto: University of Toronto Press, 2016.

Collini, Stefan. *What are Universities For?*. London: Penguin Books, 2012.

Currey, Mason. *Daily Rituals: How Artists Work*. New York: Alfred Knopf, 2013.

Deleuze, Gilles. “Postscript on the Societies of Control.” *October* 59 (Winter, 1992): 3-7, http://links.jstor.org/sici?sici=0162-2870%28199224%2959%3C3%3APOTSOC%3E2.0.CO%3B2-T

Deleuze, Gilles, and Félix Guattari. *Anti-oedipus: Capitalism and Schizophrenia*. Minneapolis: University of Minnesota Press, 1983.

—. *What is Philosophy?*. Translated by Hugh Tomlinson and Graham Burchell. New York: Columbia University Press, 1994.

Deligiorgi, Katerina. *Kant and the Culture of Enlightenment*. New York: State University of New York Press, 2005.

Diogenes the Cynic. *Sayings and Anecdotes*. Translated by Robin Hard. Oxford: Oxford University Press, 2012.

Elden, Stuart, ed. *Sloterdijk Now*. Cambridge: Polity Press, 2012.

Han, Byung-Chul. *Psychopolitics: Neoliberalism and New Technologies of Power*. Translated by Erik Butler. London: Verso, 2017.

—. *The Burnout Society*. Translated by Erik Butler. Stanford, CA: Stanford University Press, 2015.

Harpham, Geoffrey Galt. “So... What Is Enlightenment? An Inquisition into Modernity.” *Critical Inquiry* 20, number 3. Spring 1994524-556. https://www.jstor.org/stable/1343868.

Heidegger, Martin. *Being and Time*. Translated by John Macquarrie and Edward Robinson. New York: Harper Perennial Modern Thought, 2008.

Kant, Immanuel. “Beantwortung der Frage: Was ist Aufklärung?.” 1784. https://www.projekt-gutenberg.org/kant/aufklae/aufkl001.html.

Magna Charta Universitatum. 18 September 1988. http://www.magna-charta.org/resources/files/the-magna-charta/english.

Marx, Karl. *Das Kapital: Kritik der politischen Ökonomie*, in *Karl Marx - Friedrich Engels - Werke, Band 23*. Dietz Verlag: Berlin(/DDR), 1962. http://www.mlwerke.de/me/me23/me23_049.htm.

Nietzsche, Friedrich. *The Genealogy of Morality*. In *The Genealogy of Morality and Other Writings*. Edited by Keith Ansell-Pearson. Translated by Carol Diethe. Cambridge: Cambridge University Press, 2006.

Peters, Michael A., Petar Jandrić, Alexander J. Means, ed. *Education and Technological Unemployment*. Singapore: Springer Nature, 2019.

Readings, Bill. *The University in Ruins*. Cambridge: Harvard University Press, 1996.

Riter, George. *The McDonaldization Thesis: Explorations and Extensions*. London: Sage Publications, 1998.

Shea, Louisa. *The Cynic Enlightenment: Diogenes in the Salon*. Baltimore, ML: The Johns Hopkins University Press, 2010.

Sloterdijk, Peter. *Critique of Cynical Reason*. Translated by Michael Eldred. Minneapolis: University of Minnesota Press, 1987.

—. *Philosophical Temperaments: From Plato to Foucault*. Translated by Thomas Dunlap. New York: Columbia University Press, 2013.

—. *You Must Change Your Life*. Translated by Wieland Hoban. Cambridge: Polity Press, 2013.

Tam, Maureen. "Outcomes-Based Approach to Quality Assessment and Curriculum Improvement in Higher Education." *Quality Assurance in Education* 22, no. 2 (2014). http://dx.doi.org/10.1108/QAE-09-2011-0059.

van Tuinen, Sjoerd. "Critique Beyond Resentment: An Introduction to Peter Sloterdijk's Jovial Modernity." *Cultural Politics* 3, no. 3 (November 2007): 275-306. doi:10.2752/175174307X226861.

Wilson, Neil. "Punching out the Enlightenment: A Discussion of Peter Sloterdijk's Kritik der zynischen Vernunft." *New German Critique* 41. Special Issue on the Critiques of the Enlightenment (Spring-Summer, 1987): 53-70. https://www.jstor.org/stable/488275

Žižek, Slavoj. *The Sublime Object of Ideology*. London: Verso, 1989.

On the Peculiar Nature of Work Crisis in Academia

Navjot Kaur

Introduction

In this chapter, I intend to develop the idea as to how the problem of loneliness and crisis related to work in Academy are the symptoms of a deep routed, routinized and unfortunately normalized work ethics where, as Aristotle would have us identify, the act of work is not performed for the sake of its own self (i.e., in and for itself) but for purposes often alien to it. Not to dismiss the need for an economic and social convenience to be derived from work, the situation becomes tragic and indicates something like a crisis when the work involves intellectual activity. I identify the root of the problem as a sustained training of the human mind and body to serve the needs of the capitalistic set up with the pursuit of the thing for its own self being lost. This becomes terrible when it creeps into the structure and working of the academic system which asks of us to lead an intellectual life, practicing a domination of the rational part of the soul which alone can free oneself of the mundane and routine that threatens to overtake the major part of one's life and thought. Unfortunately, the system of education right from the beginning is aimed at pushing the student to produce measureable outcomes. The subtle leanings of the 'self' find little space for recognition. By the time one enters the University system this aberration becomes normalized. This reflects in the systems and procedures adopted right from the entry level to further stages of career advancement.

I intend to showcase through my reading of Aristotle how only a pure pursuit of wisdom holds scope for any deliverance from the state of affairs that capitalism has silently created around us which gently whisper their dictates that we have been so customized to as identifying our own voice. Only genuine intellectual exercise, even if on the part of a few, can free the thought imbued minds and the many similar minds which find their inspiration there. I have at the back of my analysis a training fostered by

Aristotle. In the modern debates around loneliness, I find my voice in the works of Berdyaev.

This chapter is divided into two parts- the first is a discussion of loneliness and the related concepts of alienation and solitude. I propose here a continuum of experience with faint lines of demarcation delineated by the intensity of personal engagement with the task at hand; the second is a discussion of the nature of work-narrowed down to an academic exercise. We then follow up with a discussion of how a crisis situation is precipitated in an academic sphere which is contrary to the nature of what an academic environment is actually supposed to foster and hence the situation becomes all the more tragic.

Understanding Capitalism

What does capitalism signify when it acts as a perversion to what should be man's most natural desire-the appreciation of the wonders of Being? Capitalism exercises its influence through the multitude of structures (formal, informal) it creates around us which have the overpowering tendency to assign as primary the sustenance issues, conveniently transformed into created needs for vulgar luxury. Capitalism is the work structure, environment and ethics that afford to man as urgent, activities which quickly engross him and provide justification to divorce oneself from that which would best nourish him. Nourishing oneself is a painful process. Reversing the distance that the routine has created for us, within ourselves; to pick up oneself from the endless abyss of material desire; to re-claim oneself, one's authentic existence is a task too demanding for the body and mind. One requires preparedness on one's part to firstly recognize and then deal with the silent conditioning capitalism ordains. An individual is not just a silent spectator to the whims of capitalism. In fact one chooses to stay ignorant and cherishes the laziness of mind it creates. One derives pleasure, though far from an authentic one for one's base desires and conveniently creates for himself the issue to be addressed as the dictates of capitalism and chooses to respond to those alone.

An important insertion of Capitalism into the routine lives through which it secures man's alienation is of a culture of propagation and preference for populism. To a mind that has yet not cultivated for itself an eager eye to watch over what lies behind the seemingly regular; popular cinema, music, art, literature, media to just name a few influences of a routine character, all acquire a nature that prods one to wishful thinking, creating for oneself a veil that blinds one's vision of any tendency towards thoughtful habituation and insightful living. Man finds it convenient to visit things and occurrences on the surface level without any need felt to look beyond for that which is actually creating an influence and what part of it is affecting his psyche conditioning the creation of his world. The world that man creates for himself, that which his ego considers as real is the point of intervention of capitalism and hence a problem according to our present analysis. Academy thus influenced by the dictates, methods and procedures of capitalism fails to foster an authentic quest, the seed for an informed living and hence the crisis.

Part I: Loneliness

Loneliness is a moment in time when an individual is called upon to engage with one's own self. It is the recluse that he is called to inhabit. The call being an internal one is inescapable; it can only vary in the response it receives. However hard one's inclination to escape, one has to address it. In the effort to analyze the problem at hand philosophically, to untangle it from the sociological tone which often threatens to overpower one's concerns due to their proximity to the anthropological aspect of man's existence, I divide the study of loneliness into two parts. Loneliness as occurring in the midst of:

(1) Our own search for meaning of life. This is the call asking for attention towards the nature of Being. Based on an individual's reciprocity to this call, loneliness can transform into:
   a) Alienation
      This is fostered by the capitalist structure.
   b) Solitude
      This works as an antidote to the pressures of capitalism at work on reducing man to a cog in the wheel

(2) Our encounter with the world.
   It is on both that the capitalist structure has an influence.

(3) Loneliness as occurring in the midst of our own search for meaning of life

Loneliness is one of the fundamental experiences of every human life. It is the feeling of a sense of aloofness. This aloofness is not the same as being alone. In fact, it can be quite the contrary. Loneliness arises in oneself as a painful seclusion while being amongst others. Loneliness is the feeling of an absence, an absence the causes of which can be multiple. Psychology identifies the reasons as manifold, the discussion of which is beyond the scope of our present study. What is important for us philosophically is the point at which it appears as an intervention in the routine seemingly normalized life pattern. The recognition of this absence is a task of inwardness. In most cases the individual is responding in some or the other manner to the felt deficiency without actually having the necessary personal preparedness to deal with it. The preparedness to deal comes from the constant endeavor by an individual to enrich oneself, of developing one's creative faculties which allow his smooth transition into a thinking being. The absence of such preparedness is assured by the slew of onslaughts by the capitalist mode of ordering of things which delegates the responsibility of self cultivation on external entities-external in the sense of non-involvement of an individual in the processes of their influence, non control over the extent of their influence due to the seemingly innocent routinization of their onslaught and hence reducing an individual to the position of passivity.

The response of an individual to capitalism can be understood as one's response to one's conception of the capitalism- created world. Tuning into the subtleties of human mind and attitudes, capitalism silently responds to those aspects of one's psyche which are most prone to finding escape from one's active watch. The elements of one's consciousness which are constantly involved in making and breaking of attitudes are the ones in the process of growth. This process of creation is often lost in the typification caused by the fixed definitions dictated by the surplus that capitalism preserves. What an individual is often responding to is not to the correct dimension of an occasion but to its perverted form, which is colored with the preferences of capitalism. Unable to find solace in one's response to the onslaught of affections the nature of which is not clear to oneself, one becomes a victim of the structures of manipulation working to keep one ignorant and passive. Amongst the noise that capitalism fosters, loneliness is a genuine response of an individual to the manipulative structures. It signifies one's discontentment with the affairs around. An individual's true self is unable to find its expression and mode of intervention in the often disturbing way of things around. What thus emerges within the depths of one's existence is alienation. The concept of alienation became important in Hegel. Alienation was a result of man's inability to look beyond the objectification of the world, and realize the entirety as a facet of his own self-consciousness. Marx develops this concept in the economic sphere of participation of man. What the spirit of preserving capital does to an individual is that it deprives the event of the recognition of loneliness of its relevance, depth, sincerity and urgency. It overpowers it with the call for urgency of the necessary and routine, depriving the individual of the pause needed to meaningfully tap into this resource. It subverts the journey towards solitude- an essential requisite for his personal enrichment.

> "The sense of solitude springs from man's endeavor to develop his personality regardless of the life of the species. Only when man is alone, when he is overwhelmed by a distressing sense of his isolation, does he become aware of his personality, of his originality, of his singularity and uniqueness, of his distinctness from everywhere and everything else." (Berdyaev.1938. 68,69.)

Solitude affords to oneself a pause, a pause within the rushes of necessity, urgency. It is the interception of the flow of the routine. The pressures of the routine convince man to relinquish himself of his most important need-the need to contemplate. In Aristotle every individual is cajoled to perform the best that is in correspondence with his own particular state of intellectual development. It is only for a few that contemplation - the highest form of activity and the peculiarity of human existence becomes a natural disposition. Contemplation and wisdom pervades the realms of the theoretical as well as practical. It creates for man a particular posture which allows him to gauge the universal. The universal is that the knowledge of which affords to an individual a glimpse behind the urgencies posed by the routine and comprehend the entire picture. In the present context, this focus on self cultivation towards wisdom is important because the sense of the universal is extremely necessary to avoid falling into the trap of ideology-one of the ways of lure of capitalism.

> "Human life is in the process of constantly transcending itself; but the fact of man's materialization, however partial, in the objective world makes his existence a torture and torment to him. The ego's reality has in its endeavor to transcend itself. It perishes as soon as it can find no further outlet for itself. That constitutes the ego's fundamental enigma." (Berdyaev, 1938, 68)

Capitalism pressurizes through its control on not only the economic convenience available to man but also correspondingly to his social positioning. It frames you, conditions you and seeks you to respond accordingly. Only a personal intellectual endeavor can alleviate from this bondage.

(2). Loneliness as occurring in the midst of our encounter with the world

An individual's interaction with the world is the second point of contact of oneself with the manifestations of the system in place having as their primacy the manipulation of genuine intellectual pursuit; though this time in a new form. Here man has a genuine choice. To wake up from the slumber of ease, convenience and conformity; or, to remain fooled by its urgency at the cost of addressing that which really troubles him. That which will continue to resurface amongst all that which was to ensure its disappearance.

> "Man has a choice of two attitudes in every creative and intellectual act; he can confront the mystery of Being, the Divine mystery; or he can restrict his relationships to a purely social plane. In the first case, he attains to an authentic philosophy by means of intuition and revelation; in the second, he is forced to adapt his philosophical knowledge as well as his revealed truth to the needs of a particular society. But in return for social security thus granted, he has to falsify his conscience and help to propagate socially useful falsehoods. In society, in the company of the other men, man tends to become an actor; he is one also when he becomes an author. He is obliged to play a part because of his social position; like an actor, he depends on other people, on the public, and on the police to protect him in case of need. The man who sets out in quest of truth, and who finds himself face to face with the Divine mystery, not only often cries in the wilderness, but also leaves himself open to attack by the pontiffs of both religion and science. This situation is implicit in the very nature of philosophy and constitutes its inherent tragedy" (Berdyaev 1938, 17)

The event of loneliness when it becomes visible in the social sphere becomes a space for onslaught by non-sensitive responses which traumatize one's experiencing and inner turmoil, the way out of which the individual sees in confirmation to the patterns which were the initial cost paid for silencing of the inner upheaval so as to convince oneself of one's sanity and conformity to the social norms. Academy is I believe a sacred space where such internal engagement could be channeled out to elicit a genuine response and interaction. In the present scenario when the universities too are dependent on funding that prioritizes research of the nature of which would produce more economic abundance, the genuine quest of an academician finds no voice. The place for the coming together of insightful ideas has become, owing to the overtaking of university structures by the needs of the capitalist, a factory to turn out research which aids the proliferation of surplus for a few. I will discuss this further in the second part of this chapter.

Part II: Work

All definitions of work agree on two aspects - an effort on the individual's part and a deliverable outcome resulting thereof. As a noun, the word is ambiguous with respect to process/ product. As a verb it refers to an active engagement, an *actus*. As a process, it is at the same time both a noun and a verb. The uniqueness of this aspect is well evident in the history of philosophy with marked changes in focus from Aristotle's *energeia* to the self-referential movement of Spirit in Hegel. In the present context of our effort to study the crisis situation arising in work of an intellectual nature, focus is drawn towards the nature of outcome sought. Outcome is of two sorts. First, as an external deliverable. This has a social, economic or a political recognition arising from it. The other has the nature of an initiation, propagation, keeping in process of an internal engagement. The engagement is two-sided from perception to intellection and vice versa. While it is easy to understand that perception provides material for the intellect to work upon, it is important to acknowledge that the quality of intellection does in turn affect and beautify perception. The intensity of one's inner self-enriching exercise, the rigor with which one engages with one's own perceptions of the world and tries to free those from the onslaught of emotions, biases and ideology determines one's ability to create in oneself the space for free expression and enunciation of knowledge. The inner exercise is a result of the creative aspect that an individual through his effort against the ever seeming necessities and traps of his economic and social determination by capitalism fosters within as a preserve; a preserve for all that is sacred and beautiful. This is a resource with which he is in constant companionship and determines the form of his responses to the external world.

The burden of capitalism on academic spaces lies in its tendency to feed the researcher's weaknesses, to free oneself of the burden of one's spiritual responsibility and facilitation to reside and feel satisfied at a level of intellectual enrichment which is not only poor but also conveniently disguises the slumber it cajoles an individual into.

> "Even the university will only admit him (philosopher) on condition that he keeps discreetly silent about his own philosophy and devote his attention primarily to the history of philosophy and doctrines of other philosophers." (Berdyaev 1938, 9)

Berdyaev here well catches the sad state of affairs of an academic environment where a genuine attitude of contemplation finds no appreciation. I propose that this change in attitude and expectations from the overall work, nature and environment of the University owes to the change in the understanding and execution of academic work from what is in Aristotle *praxis* to *poiesis* form of activity. Aristotle himself does not contrast these concepts, as is usually held to be. He is discussing these in the light of tradition. What I intend to demonstrate here is the use of these terms as he enunciates.

Poiesis is understood as an activity which has the end distinct to the activity. In Aristotle, this is subordinate to the realm of *praxis*. *Praxis* as an activity is complete in itself. It is an activity that has no end outside it. It is an end in itself. In it the end, the seeking of a *telos* is a process involving its own enriching. It is at every moment, at every now, not the same but its own perfected state. The movement is towards the realization of its own Being. It is a movement of the self, having in sight the illumination of the Being. The sense of *poiesis* converts into that of *techne*, while that of *praxis* has a leaning towards *phronesis*, commonly translated as practical wisdom.

In Aristotle there is a clear hierarchy of the relevance of these activities for the expression of an individual's true nature. Nichomachean Ethics begins with a search for what is truly a characteristic human nature. What is that which an individual seeks as an end? In production, end is the product, an external entity. In action however producer and user are the same, for good action is the end. (Eth Nic VI2, 1139b3-4; 1140b70). Action has no end outside itself (Pol VII3, 1325b15ff). *Praxis* or action is a complete activity (Met Theta6, 1048b18ff) which gives a determinate meaning to individual existence. The preference for *praxis* lies in it being its own end. An end that is chosen for its own sake is a complete and perfect end in an absolute sense. (Eth. Nic I5, 1097a30). Intellectual activity in Aristotle belongs to the realm of *praxis*. What *praxis* affords to an individual is a timeless-ness.

The externality of the product should not only simply be regarded as a physical externality, but also depicts its severance from the role the creative aspect involved in its production had with it.

There are two important things here in context of our present discussion:

i) The producer's creative relationship with the object of his making.
ii) The severance of the bond, not as aloofness but as non-affection and an endeavor to view it critically once the product has been created.

Poiesis is the foreground for *techne*. *Techne* has become the tool in hand for capitalism to create an abundance of products, all suited to create and respond to a market of profitable goods in ample amounts. The Aristotelian *praxis* however refuses to succumb to work and its pressures. It is an activity free in itself, for itself. I propose that it is precisely in this shift into *poiesis* from *praxis* that resulted in the diminishing of the Academy's own relevance by its participants that aggravated the schism between what has now become an academic 'work' and what should have been a general posture of quest of a scholar.

It was Hegel who ultimately dissolved the differentiation between *praxis* and *poiesis*. For him, production and activity became two sides of spirit's self-objectification. This historical progression gets unified in the concept of work. Man's participation in time is evaluated from the product of his activity as a tangible. What is happening here is that political economy makes a space in the sphere of exercise of practical knowledge. This is a decisive point of intervention. This affords to man another avenue-work, labor to externalize with the possibility of this externalization being the outreach of its own self-consciousness to itself. Marx who takes on further the elaboration of Hegel in the social-political realm hence encounters alienation for the worker.

In Hegel, "work is the double negativity transforming both the object and our desire; it is formative, and not just lacking in freedom like Aristotelian production. Work is formative precisely because we objectify our will in a product that will be consigned to externality and lead a life of its own, independent and beyond the power of its originator. At the same time, we are not bound to identify ourselves once and for all with the product". (Ferrarin 2001, 97). The relinquishment from nature of the control over the product to man's own will does appear as a very encouraging prospect for the actor. But we need to note that this is deemed to be acting in a sphere which is not actually conducive for the spirit's own quest.

Once the nature of academic exercise is fixed as *poiesis*, an Academician enters a sphere of intense social engagement which is often not very close to the sublime needs of his intellectual pursuit. The academic endeavor, like any other cannot be free from the calls of society. An academician faces pressures from the sides of the students as well as the administrative structure of the University. The student coming with his own set of anxiety for being able to become a part of the workforce impinges on the teacher's focus on the primacy of knowledge. The student is to be nourished on multiple levels. Once both the student and the teacher adapt to a consumption mode of exercise, none of the two are able to achieve a consensus on keeping knowledge primary. The administration too demands of the academician endeavors and a posture which might not have much to do with the bringing forth of the true spirit and knowledge of the subject at hand. There is lost in the pressures of performance appraisals, the time and peace required for the roots of knowledge to grow. The ad-hoc nature of teaching appointments has made the University an avenue for exchange of benefits and mutual adjustments.

The protestant work ethics which feeds capitalism creates a fundamental discrepancy between the genuine expression of the self and the work-culture. One's self almost always fails to prosper fully. The conditions of work in the academic sphere are sadly not conducive to its flourishing. The work then is removed from its being undertaken for its own self. It no longer remains *praxis* which is the true nature of an intellectual exercise. It's shift into *phronesis* is subverted. *Phronesis* as the exercise of wisdom of the earthly sphere is what is necessary to provide a work-self balance and foster creative activity. Work as a refinement of one's own self, as one's constant endeavor at self-beautification is lost in the urgencies of the capital driven academic structures. As Aristotle would explain, the quest for final good which is self-sufficient is replaced by focus on transitory goods which create an unsurpassable gap between the individual's worldly pursuit and one's inner drives creating an unfortunate crisis.

Bibliography

Aristotle. *The Nicomachean Ethics*. Translated with commentaries and glossary by Hippocrates G. Apostle. 1975. Dordrecht, Holland. D. Reidel Publishing Company.

Aristotle. The Complete works of Aristotle. The revised Oxford translation, edited by Jonathan Barnes. 1984. Princeton.

Arendt, Hannah. *The Human Condition*. 1958. Chicago. The University of Chicago Press.

Arendt, Hannah. *The Origins of Totalitarianism*. 1973. New York. Harcourt Brace and Company.

Berdyaev, Nicolas. *Solitude and Society*. 1938. London. Geoffrey Bles: The Centenary Press.

Berdyaev, Nicolas. *The destiny of Man*. 1960. New York. Harper and Brothers.

Ferrarin, Alfredo. *Hegel and Aristotle*. 2001. Cambridge University Press.

PART II.

LONELINESS AND THE CRISIS OF WORK UNDER CAPITALISM

THE INVISIBLE FRAME: AN EMPIRICAL PHILOSOPHICAL STUDY OF THE PRODUCTION OF LONELINESS IN "RESPONSIBLE CAPITALISM"

CHRISTOPH JEDAN, HEIDI JANSEN AND HANNEKE MUTHERT

Philosophy has trivialised loneliness for too long. We need to acknowledge that loneliness is not an inexorable ingredient of the human condition that can be veiled with a romantic rhetoric, claiming an ulterior purpose for it. Here, we study loneliness from the perspective that we, collectively, *produce* loneliness by the ways in which we allow work to be organised.

The present chapter addresses the connection of loneliness and work by tracing an apparent paradox: Over the last decades, there have been more and more calls for a "responsible" or "sustainable" capitalism. As business magazine *Fortune* has it, this is a form of capitalism in which "companies have a clear purpose to serve society, their customers, and their employees as well as their investors. When they do so, they create the most sustainable long-term value for their shareholders" (George 2019). Businesses have followed suit, vying with one another for better reputation as employers, offering programs that focus on the wellbeing of their workforce, and so forth. In this context it may seem surprising that there could ever be a "crisis of work", that employees feel in fact "burned out", overwhelmed and lonely in and due to their work. And yet, a host of HR managers, job coaches, cultural pundits as well as, indeed, individual introspection can inform us that this is in fact the case. How is this even possible? To answer this question, we analyse the nexus of loneliness and work in the context of today's "responsible capitalism" in an empirical-philosophical way, combining conceptual insights and interview data. We suggest that the employee-facing side of "responsible capitalism" is the combination of two potent ideologies, neoliberalism and the human potential movement in management studies. Combined, they provide a "frame" that structures policies, programs and perceptions, yet—and this is crucial—without the individual even noticing this. To all intents and purposes, the frame is "invisible".

The structure of the chapter is as follows. (1) We introduce the problems of the modern workplace through a short discussion of Zygmund Bauman's *Liquid Times*. (2) We then analyse responsible capitalism into its constituent elements. (3) We demonstrate the invisibility of the framework with an interview conducted with "Ellen", HR manager in a multinational energy company, and (4) end with a short conclusion on the implications of our argument.

1. Liquid Times?

In his book *Liquid Times*, the Polish-British philosopher and sociologist Zygmunt Bauman analyses *inter alia* work in contemporary society. He states that work used to give security and connectedness, but is now a place where employees have to prove their use and are in constant competition with each other:

> Interhuman bonds, once woven into a security net worthy of a large and continuous investment of time and effort, and worth the sacrifice of immediate individual interests (…), become increasingly frail and admitted to be temporary. Individual exposure to the vagaries of commodity-and-labour markets inspires and promotes division, not unity; it puts a premium on competitive attitudes while degrading collaboration and teamwork to the rank of temporary stratagems that need to be suspended or terminated the moment their benefits have been used up. (Bauman 2007, 2-3)

Employees have to act as entrepreneurs, managing and promoting their skills and knowledge. They continuously have to decide and plan how to develop themselves and learn about future possibilities that match their knowledge and experience. To do this, they have to know what sort of work will be required and how they can compete for these jobs with other (younger) workers. The competition is complicated by the fact that companies do not have fixed career paths anymore, and they do not know what will be the requirements of future jobs. This uncertainty turns each and every worker into a "hunter" (Bauman 2007, 104), a hunter for possibilities and chances. Who cannot keep up, becomes the prey. However, life as a hunter does not produce meaning, Bauman states:

> Having reshaped the course of life into an unending series of self-focused pursuits, each episode lived through as an overture to the next, it offers no

> occasion for reflection about the direction and sense of it all." (Bauman 2007, 109)

Bauman tells us how everyone is left alone, trying to "make it":

> In a world, (…) in which each individual is left on his or her own while most individuals are tools of each other's promotion. The solitary life of such individuals may be joyous and likely to be busy—but it is bound to be risky and fearful as well. In such a world there are not many rocks left on which struggling individuals can build their hopes of rescue and on which they can rely in case of personal failure. Human bonds are comfortably loose, but for that same reason frightfully unreliable, and solidarity is as difficult to practice as its benefits, and even more its moral virtues, are difficult to comprehend. (Bauman 2007, 24)

Bauman's analysis of work and loneliness today is an odd mixture of acute observations and a disturbing undertone of quiet resignation. The resignation seems tied to the generality of his analysis. It seems a matter of necessity that our "liquid" time leads to such scenes, attitudes and practices; Bauman may or may not wish himself beyond their reach, towards a utopian future that resembles a paradisiac past. Arguably the best use of Bauman's analysis is, therefore, twofold: first, we ought to acknowledge that Bauman has correctly identified large-scale and largely unrecognised loneliness that forms the backdrop to a vast variety of practices we see around us today. The metaphor of the "hunter" is valuable in this regard, conjuring up social contract theorists' imageries of the pre-social condition. Clearly, Bauman shows no inclination to glorify this status in a Rousseauian fashion. Second, however, we ought to move forward, beyond Bauman's generalities towards a more specific analysis. Which ideological constructs inform the structure of modern work to produce this omnipresent loneliness? In the next section, we offer a suggestion.

2. Moving beyond generalities: Neoliberalism, Human Potential Movement and Responsible Capitalism

The contemporary *homo economicus* (or *femina economica*) sketched by Bauman is clearly the representative of a recent stage of capitalism. The individual job (and life) hunter, we hear, has temporary, insecure bonds to employers or organisations and temporary, fragile bonds with colleagues through teamwork and cooperation. None of these aspects, however, marks an entirely new situation. What places our hunters firmly in the present is their being cast as "entrepreneurs", who are ultimately responsible for their own lot. The individual job and life hunter is given key divine attributes of premodern metaphysics and theology; the imagery of an unmoved mover is held up to us: an unmoved mover who should live unaffected and invulnerable through those "liquid" times.

We suggest that this specific constellation should be seen as a combination of two ideological forces: the neoliberal world view and the human potential movement. In what follows we shall begin with a brief discussion of neoliberalism, since this has become a well-known concept and a focus of political contention. For our analysis here, the exact history of neoliberalism—whether or not we can trace its principles backwards beyond the Reagan and Thatcher era to the early twentieth century—is hardly relevant. We follow Bal and Dóci's definition that focuses firmly on a contemporary understanding of neoliberalism:

> The core principle of neoliberalism is that human welfare will be maximised when individuals have the ultimate economic freedom to act. (…) in neoliberalism, the meaning of work is reduced to a mere transaction between two parties, thereby neglecting the intrinsic meaning of work and employment relationships for people. (Bal en Dóci 2018)

It is this ideology that is ubiquitous in our society and workplaces today. Its view of the individual is largely that of an independent, self-governing male, who must take care of himself to make his life a success. Bal and Dóci (2018) state that the main goal of organisations is to achieve high organisational performance, profit and shareholder value. The value of employees is instrumental and they must, therefore, continually prove their worth in competition with other employees or applicants. "Neoliberalism presents all human skills as simple commodities with a price tag. Skills used at work are separated from social relations and are presented simply as individuals putting them to use for the rewards—or wage 'premiums'—that they can bring" (Holborow 2015, 20). Neoliberalism has become a background assumption that we rarely recognise as such due to its pervasiveness (Monbiot 2016): "We appear to accept the proposition that this utopian, millenarian faith describes a neutral force; a kind of biological law, like Darwin's theory of evolution. But the philosophy arose as a conscious attempt to reshape human life and shift the locus of power" (Monbiot 2016). Neoliberalism shifted the locus of power from governments to the market because "neoliberalism sees competition as the defining characteristic of human relations. It redefines citizens as consumers, whose democratic choices are best exercised by buying and selling, a process that rewards merit and punishes inefficiency. It maintains that "the market" delivers benefits that could never be achieved by planning" (Monbiot 2016). As a result, workers are also part of this market, and employers expect entrepreneurialism from their employees. This "entrepreneurialism theorem" requires people to stand up for themselves, perceive opportunities and actively work on their career, while at the same time clear and lasting career paths are increasingly disappearing from organisations, due to their shorter-term orientation towards profit.

At first sight, it might seem surprising that the entrepreneurialism theorem that is inherent in neoliberalism did not lead to protests, since it does present a major change in the status of the workforce, who are credited with key attributes of the capitalist entrepreneur, yet without the concomitant financial benefits. The reason for this seems to be that entrepreneurialism had begun to be perceived as a normality, something rightfully expected of every employee, of every human being. The massive mentality change has been the effect of the human potential movement. To our knowledge, the Canadian philosopher Charles Taylor has been the first to highlight that the movement is a key indicator of large-scale cultural change. In Taylor's analysis, the human potential movement only values behaviour aimed at self-expression, self-realisation and the discovery of authenticity. The way of life promoted by these goals tends to be superficially consumerist, according to Taylor, because nothing is allowed to trump the value of self-realisation as a subjective construct. Ideas such as community spirit and togetherness come second (Taylor 1989, 507). The human potential movement perfectly undergirds neoliberalism, since it presents a normative anthropology that universalises and thus devalues entrepreneurial capacities and attitudes. One cannot expect extra protection or remuneration for what is a mere normality, a universal human trait.

The emphasis on self-realisation began to take hold in the 1960s.[1] It achieved large-scale cultural penetration in the 1980s, parallel with Reagan and Thatcher-style neoliberalism. Today, the movement's basic principles are a staple of management books, employee programs, training curricula, and so forth, at an international scale. The (self)management book market is replete with titles from the perspective of the human potential movement.[2] In terms of self-management programs, the activities of organisations such

[1] The emphasis on realising the potential of the individual human being is certainly older; the beginning of the human potential movement is often dated to the founding of the Esalen Institute in 1962 (see e.g. the Wikipedia entry "Human Potential Movement", https://en.wikipedia.org/wiki/Human_Potential_Movement, last accessed 15 November 2020)

[2] Examples include Coley 1989; Robbins 1991; Eaton and Johnson 2001; Beck 2002; Brown 2010; Pink 2011.

as Scientology and *est* (which was later called Landmark) are well-known examples (Chryssides 1999). In this type of activity, participants learn to set and achieve personal goals. Those goals often have to do with performing better and acquiring wealth and success in business and personal life. The core of this type of training and coaching is that by "flushing out" limiting beliefs and learning new behaviour, people can achieve whatever they want and be more successful at work. Indeed, self-realisation is also credited with being a key dimension of "meaning" of the modern worker to give meaning to their working life (Martela en Pessi 2018).

Against the background of the prevalence of human potential thinking, it is evident how organisations today—priding themselves to be representatives of a "responsible" and "sustainable" capitalism—conceive of, approach, and manage their personnel: Employees are attributed entrepreneurship, the linchpin of human potential thinking and neoliberalism. "Responsible" or "sustainable" organisations thus continue a tradition of normative anthropology that derives from those two ideologies. And due to their prevalence, those (twin) ideologies act as an invisible frame that informs the thinking of participants to an astonishing degree.

3. "Ellen" and the invisible frame

The present chapter builds on interviews with CEOs and senior HR managers in the Netherlands, conducted in 2019 and 2020. The interviews are part of ongoing research about the future of work, and the way people find meaning through their work. In this article, we will focus on one of those interviews, conducted with a senior female HR manager ("Ellen") of an international energy company also operating in the Netherlands ("Ellen's company"). What this interview illustrates is the incredible, unrecognised hold that the ideological framework of entrepreneurialism in neoliberalism and human potential movement exerts over the thinking of a conscientious, empathetic and well-meaning senior manager. When asked about the role of her company concerning the meaning of work and the wellbeing of employees, Ellen is confronted with numerous instances of the darker side of work: way beyond being instrumentally necessary for maintaining one's economic status, work is claimed to be key to the self-realisation of individuals. From this perspective, the vulnerability of workers has increased, yet workers are on their own when it comes to performing and keeping their job. They should of course feel a connectedness with the purpose of the organisation and with colleagues, but they cannot count on reciprocity from the organisation. Yet, confronted with all of this, Ellen's replies are nothing short of remarkable. In what follows, readers should stay alert to the ideological work that Ellen is performing, making light of or glossing over the evident darker sides of work. In fact, the only thing Ellen will not be seen doing is to turn round to question the ideological framework itself.

We do not want to pretend that anything about this situation is unusual, on the contrary. The international energy company is a "model citizen" in the economic landscape of today, having very much the interest of their employees at heart. Ellen is—and we would like to stress that again—a "model employee" whose thoughtful answers could inform more analyses than the one conducted at present. What is interesting about this specific interview is the extent to which Ellen's replies are characteristic of the larger current of "responsible" capitalism today. In this sense, our interview with Ellen illustrates the role of the ideological framework for the analysis of work and loneliness way beyond the specific case. We structure Ellen's replies according to five key issues.

3.1. Individualisation and social isolation

In the interview,[3] Ellen outlines the environment in which employees must do their jobs. They work in a matrix organisation, where an employee can have several managers because of different projects. One manager may ask to give priority to assignment *x*, while another asks for assignment *y*. How the employees deal with this, depends on empowerment and the ability to understand the purpose beyond the projects. Add to this the fact that Ellen's organisation works across borders and that employees must therefore be able to deal with cultural differences. Moreover, this multinational cooperation requires personal independence because employees do not see their supervisors every day. "Individual responsibility is part of the culture", Ellen says.

Social isolation may be an effect for members of teams that work across different countries; for them, it is not possible to walk into the office of a manager or meet team members during a coffee break. They can only be reached online. Ellen tells us that in order to have the opportunity of meeting (new) employees, there is a quarterly drink at the office and a monthly information session where employees talk about how business is going. The management team takes care to plan meetings at different locations each time. They plan an "ask & share" hour with employees, where employees

[3] The interview was conducted in Dutch, in what follows we provide our translation.

can learn how the business is going and where they can share their own experiences. These meetings are meant to organise connectedness, but we wonder if an hour now and then really gives enough room for discussing personal questions. The onus to perform is on the individual employee. Perform the best you can, cooperate with national and international colleagues, manage work and private life, take care of being noticed by superiors, follow training programs, take care of relaxation through sport or yoga (all provided by the company), is key. Working in an international organisation means working with different time zones, which forces people to work outside office hours. The company thus swallows up its employees.

It is not the case that Ellen is blind to disadvantages the company culture may have, but at the same time, company culture is a convenient shorthand for placing choices beyond individual control. So, even if Ellen thinks that the responsibility for managing careers rests sometimes too much on the individual employee, this is not held against the corporate culture. The way Ellen talks, no unfairness is more than an instance of a specific regard in which the corporate culture may be a "little bit unbalanced". People who fail, who fall through the net, as it were, fall in Ellen's parlance "a little bit through the net". In this vein, Ellen talks, for instance, about "people who just stand still": "they do not know exactly where to start, and if you don't have a manager who also takes them along and guides them, (…) that leads to (…), slower growth or stagnation. So, yes, I think that sometimes we place the responsibility a bit too much on the employee for that." There is no clear direction for employees to manage their careers and that creates frustration, she says. If there are real possibilities for managing careers that would not have to be a problem, but there are no fixed career paths. Ellen: "We also have the policy within our company that (…) all vacancies are advertised (…). So there is always an open process, which of course is very much in line with our culture. But the downside of that is that (…) succession planning is hard to do. So, it is complicated to say to a talented person: '(…) if you just do well these next two years, we'll have an opening (…).' You can't really promise that because you always have to go external, I mean not external, but in the group. You have to; there must be a procedure (…), so you cannot promise people much perspective, in that sense and for many people this is a barrier (…)." With these words, Ellen demonstrates the working of the internal job market in her organisation. She does see the lack of commitment to employees' continued career, but she does not question the organisational culture.

Ellen recognises the problem of self-management as we ask about other training programs for employees. Ellen: "that's where that whole self-management problem comes into play again, if you don't have a manager who is somewhat active in that, and you're not very resolute yourself, then it may just be that you fall a bit through the net."

3.2. Open plan office

Ellen also mentions the burden of working in an open-plan office. The idea behind this spatial arrangement was to create workplaces where people could work together effectively—and, of course, to cut costs—, but this has caused new problems, she says. Since nobody has their own room anymore, not even Ellen herself, everybody has to find a place to work each day, in an environment that is noisy (at least most of the time). It might seem as if being together in an open plan office were an antidote to loneliness, but that is not in fact the case. Workers do not have a permanent spatial anchor in all of this anyh more. The result is what might be described euphemistically as a "healthy struggle" for the best places. The massiveness of (and lack of private space in) an open office plan makes people smaller, a mass product. That can increase feelings of loneliness amid the hustle and bustle. Those who want to consult with colleagues must strategically plan to occupy the needed space. This daily necessity of searching for one's work place is an extra burden. In fact, more and more employees ask for the opportunity to work at home, alone. Ellen, therefore, wonders aloud whether a smaller and more local organisation would not better for the wellbeing of people. Ellen describes the energy it costs to work in such a flexible environment and wonders how it would be: "people wonder: is it still worth it, you know, to allow this energy drain." She notices that people even leave the company for that reason. "I now see quite a few people leaving, who (…) go to entirely local companies, who opt for: 'I just want everyone in one location again, and it is all manageable, and I have, say, the whole scope of responsibilities in one place (…).' Those are reasons why people say they are leaving."

3.3. Self-improvement

Today, organisations state proudly that they offer employees possibilities to develop themselves. Ellen has started setting up four different talent programs for employees who show great potential and/or leadership qualities. In these training programs emphasis is laid on "making an impact", Ellen tells us. The programs focus on the question "where do you want to make an impact?" She explains this with the choices people (have to) make for different roles in their lives. As young parents, for example, employees make different choices about working long hours than their peers without children.

All of this is very well meant, of course, and one might see in this the company's intention to support employees in difficult times of their life. However, Ellen tells us, as a matter of course, that in those programs the ideas of Franklin Covey (1989, see above) are key, obviously adjusted to the European context. The core of Covey's ideas is personal responsibility in every situation and attention to self-growth. The individual takes centre stage, and much less attention is directed at the importance of team efforts. Employees who can take part in the company's self-improvement programs are the ones that are seen as "high potentials". In that respect, the mere fact of being invited to the programs is some sort of reward. Even at this level, the company makes visible a difference between two constituencies, those with promise, and those without, increasing the pressure on those who want to keep their place at or near the top. Just being "good enough" is no option. Employees who put family first, however, will put less effort in their careers, and the question is, of course, what impact this will have on their careers. Thus, inviting young parents to take part in the programs amounts to contradictory signalling. The overt goal is to support employees in making choices that are best for themselves, even if that might reduce their "output", at the same time the very way of organising the programs pre-empts the possibility of actually choosing that route. In effect, the company has offered no more than a rhetorical blanket to employees, increasing instead of lowering the pressure on them.

3.4. Flexible workers and employee rights

In the Netherlands, 40 per cent of the workforce work flexibly, and this is a situation that leads to several problems, as the Work Regulation Committee's (2020) report "In what country do we want to work?" has concluded at the behest of the Dutch government. The flexible Dutch workforce consists of self-employed workers, temporary workers and workers on short-term contracts. The problem identified in the report is the emergence of a class of workers with almost no rights, no insurance and no pension; and a growing gap between people with secure work and people with precarious work. Of course, there is a big difference between highly-educated self-employed consultants and the mail delivery men and women, but both are vulnerable to (economic) crises. Working on short-term contracts or being self-employed means extra pressure to perform. Labour laws can add to the pressure: a temporary contract can only be renewed for a small number of times, otherwise, the employer is obliged to enter into a permanent working contract. Trade unions have lost their influence and are therefore not in a position to negotiate good working conditions for flexible workers. Employees and employers are, therefore, continually assessing their positions and are looking for better opportunities. This assessment affects commitment. Why should one commit to an organisation if employment contracts can be dissolved at any time, and if it is a matter of uncertainty whether a contract will be renewed? In addition to this, the broader cultural trend and public rhetoric amount to a wide-ranging "expectation management" vis-à-vis work. It has become an article of public religion that lifelong employment does not exist anymore. Employees should rejoice in this, because it is bad for one's career to commit oneself to a single employer for too long. To all intents and purposes employees and organisations are thus trained to see flexibility, the scarcity of legal protections and a low commitment of employers towards their employees as the cultural norm. And it shows: in the Netherlands, employees change employers on average every ten years (Dekker 2018). Many organisations, including Ellen's company, still have "permanent" employees, in the attenuated sense of the word that we have explained above: in the case of Ellen's company, more than a thousand employees fall into that category.

In our present context, another group of employees is even more interesting: Ellen's company has, as so many others, a sizeable "flexible" layer. Ellen's favoured term for this "layer" is the Dutch word *schil* that primarily refers to the skin of fruits and vegetables. Ellen talks about the "flexible peel", as if it was a matter of course and of no concern to "peel off" those employees should circumstances make this desirable. For Ellen it is also a matter of course that her company's primary responsibility lies with the "permanent" staff. There are even different kinds of "flexible peel"; next to staff on flexible contracts, there is a host of contractors, with even lower standards of protection. In the Ellen's company, little is known about the latter, even about something so elementary as whether and how employment standards are being complied with. Ellen recognises that fact, and accepts as a matter of course that her company has only an attenuated responsibility for them: "so we have the internal employees, then we have a flexible peel of temporary contracts who are still directly employed by us, and on top of that there is the contractor peel. So those are contracts that we put out to tender, right? So then … a company that will, for example, lay the foundations of wind turbines for us. Yes, they will arrange it all again with subcontractors and personnel, and of course, we have standards for this, about human rights, equal pay, health and safety, things like that, but they are of course a good bit further down the line."

The "flexible peel" is not really connected to the company, and Ellen notices some dilemmas around this: "So we have always been cautious not to become too big too fast because then you no longer control it, but because of that you now see that we have a relatively large number of external parties, say, who are less involved. The mission of your company, the values of your company (…) um, that sometimes makes it difficult. For example, we had, which is a foolish dilemma, but last Christmas (…), we actually always had a drink before [Christmas]. But we wanted to do something nicer for once, so we made a deliberate decision only to invite the internal people, because there were already 200. And we went to The Cooking Factory, a cooking workshop for large groups. But yes, if you had to invite all those external parties as well, we would have had another 150. And that becomes too much, but you don't really want to make a distinction. (…) Somehow you turn them into second-class employees, and somehow that's (…), yes, of course, they aren't, but they're not really internal either. (…) So I have to say that I myself have mixed feelings about it."

Ellen's company offers a permanent contract for positions for which the work has been proven to be structural, but even then, Ellen adds, laying off employees is not too difficult. Here, too, the employer benefits from the increased flexibility. According to Ellen this is advantageous for both parties. After all, it also becomes easier to hire someone if the employer knows that a dismissal will be not too complicated. One might wonder whether this is a rather one-sided advantage for the employer, but Ellen argues that this reduction of workers' rights is a good thing after all: "I do think that people realise that (…) internal people also have more and more flexibility, of course, so in that respect, the laws and regulations around this are of course also changing and if I am honest, we also have a large activity in Denmark, where this is very flexible, so it is relatively easy to get rid of the employee as an employer, but that also makes the entire market much more liquid. So, (…) at first, that seems a disadvantage for employees, but on the other hand, companies are also hiring people much faster." Asking her for confirmation on this point, she continues: "Yes, you can clearly see that, so because (…) what employees initially think to be a disadvantage, is actually ultimately an advantage for the entire economy and also for the employee, because it is therefore much easier to go elsewhere. And (…) um, well, you see that happening more and more in the Netherlands, so I think the fear of really helping employees to get a (permanent) contract is just gone. So, we hardly ever make annual contracts anymore. Because then I think, 'why would you do that, a contract for a year?' (…) I mean, a permanent contract under the current regulations …, if it doesn't work out after six months or a year, you know, you can, then the difference is not that big compared to what you must do with an annual contract."

We ask if the point of a permanent contract is to give employees the confidence they can stay for a longer time. Ellen answers: "We actually only do it (offer short-term contracts) with roles that we really are not sure if they are still there. For example, we are setting up our solar business now, and we just have to see if that will work. So, yes, there we give an annual contract. (…) how do you treat people who are connected to the organisation in different ways and where the internal employee is of course very purpose-driven, it is (…) not always the same for the external employees, I mean, there are also plenty of them who just want to grab an hourly rate. They are all happy, whether it is a project about wind energy or a project at the tobacco industry, they don't really care."

3.5. Workload

In all the interviews we have conducted in our project, workload was an important issue. This is also the case with Ellen: "it's just always busy. So, yes, it's not like it used to be, then you just had a peak, and then you recover. It is simply continuous performance under high pressure." She tells us how this is reinforced by digitalisation, the pressure of being available all the time. Employees are thus consumed by their work. Officially, there is a "culture" at her company, that allows employees not to work outside regulated working hours, but Ellen also has some doubts about the extent to which that culture actually conveys rights: "So people do feel that they have to explain that (they leave early). I think the culture is indeed not like that at all. Think that at around 5:30 PM people go home, we don't have a company culture where everybody stays till seven. But I do think that, because you are always connected, that you (…) still have work input all the time (…) do you have the discipline to just turn off your mail? That will not always work, and that is why I thought about it when you asked about the possibility of taking time for informal care. Look, it is, of course, one thing for you to arrange this contractually. But it is another thing that if you want to spend every Friday with your sick father, that you really have that time, or feel that you have it, you know; is your workload really reduced by 20 per cent, or are you just expected to work a bit more efficiently in the four days that you are at work. You can therefore delete all meeting requests, but are you still expected to comment? I'm not entirely sure about the latter." This is an interesting and revealing admission from a senior HR manager, whose job it is to know this sort of thing and to offer guidance in such cases.

We ask how employees deal with this high pressure, and she answers with great composure: "That depends. There are people out there who are just pretty good at drawing a line, saying: 'okay, if I have to do this, then this should be taken off my plate. Manager, tell me what to prioritize, then.' What we see among our specialists, and what is very difficult for them, is that they often work on multiple projects. Their line manager is not in those projects, so they are in a challenging situation, where all kinds of projects want to prioritise all kinds of things, their line manager actually does not fully oversee it, and they themselves have the feeling that they are out of control. And that is also what we place a lot of emphasis on in [our] training program for specialists. We say: 'okay, how can you, looking ahead in your agenda and in the planning of those projects, how can you already see where things will soon go wrong? If you have a deadline there in May, and also another project has, then you already know that you will have a huge problem in May. What can you do about it now?' So we try to teach people (…) also to look ahead a bit more structurally and (…) um, yes and a week has 40 hours, but you should not plan them full, because there are always unforeseen things. Some can handle it better than others. Some are a bit more assertive about this than others. What makes it difficult in our international organisation, is that you do not always realise in time if someone is having a hard time. So for us, it is really normal, potential burnouts or people who really, uh, well (…) get a bit overworked. And yes, that is just a big risk, or sometimes difficult to see in time."

Ellen tells us that "the management" tries to set a good example, showcasing how to deal with situations such as these. She tells that she herself had gone on a sabbatical in the past and communicated to the employees about it on the company's intranet. Officially, this possibility is open to all employees, but how likely is it that employees outside the smaller circle of "the management" will actually make use of it? It depends on financial reserves, and also on experienced job pressure. In a competitive environment, it is not convenient to disappear from the radar for a longer time. So it may well be that we see here the parading of privilege rather than a scheme that actually helps employees.

4. Conclusion: Towards a new perspective?

Organisations feel the obligation to take care of the wellbeing of their employees, to be "responsible" citizens in the land of the globalised economy—or so we hear in our interviews. What do they mean by this? In practice, it seems to boil down to "opportunities for self-improvement"—in effect, highly selective training programs for “high potentials” that only serve to increase competition and pressure—and courses that teach those stressed-out employees “how to relax”.

Remarkable is the amount of intellectual energy that our interviewee Ellen expends at glossing over the cracks in the system, and the composure with which she integrates obvious injustices into larger ideological constructs that make her company, ultimately, the best of all possible worlds: a benevolent company culture; individual, “bit-sized” shortcomings that represent no more than slight unbalances in the overall advantageous scheme of things, for the greatest mutual advantage for employer and employee.

In his book *The Thought of Work*, John Budd states that “the pull to translate personal fulfilment and positive affective states into productivity, job performance, and competitiveness is a powerful one. (…) The overarching question in the academic and practitioner field, therefore, is what set of human resource management practices optimises employee performance” (Budd 2011, 96). In the all-pervasive managerial discourse of today, there seems to be no room for another view. Just as any other brand of capitalism, “responsible capitalism” focuses on return on investment, shareholder value and maximisation of profit, created through disadvantages for workers. In a market, where every worker is a competitor for the best jobs, the highest salary and the best opportunities, many fall short and are seen as losers, especially in their own eyes. Workers have nothing to expect from employers other than pointers to their (the employees’) responsibilities: “People are obliged to sell their potential to work in the labour market because this is the only way to earn a living and to pay for things that they need; however, once they enter the work system, their creative potential becomes something over which they have little or no control” (Holborow 2015, 15). The result is an atomised workforce consisting of lonely monads involved in a constant struggle to reach optimum performance.

Could this ever change? Bal and Dóci point out that we require new theories concerning the workplace. They write about “workplace dignity”. This theory postulates that everything in the workplace, including people, animals and resources have an intrinsic value, and should be treated accordingly (Bal en Dóci 2018). Arguably, such attempts are destined to become the latest fad in managerial jargon, but no more than that—comparable to the darling projects in Ellen’s company, increasing rather than reducing the stronghold that the organisation exerts over its employees.

Perhaps, we need to rethink work altogether and associate it more with play. Dutch political philosopher Govert Buijs, for one, has described in an interview the kind of workplace he would like to see emerge: "It would be nice not only to design work processes from an efficiency point of view but in such a way that everyone feels they are doing something valuable. Work is not just a cost item; it is also a consumer good: we derive a great deal from it. How come we continue to put enormous pressure on something that can also be in the sphere of relaxation and creativity?" (De Jong 2019). We cannot even begin to spell out what sort of changes would be needed to realise such a vision, but it is evident that the direction in which we are collectively headed today is a cul-de-sac.

Bibliography

Bal, P. Matthijs, and Edina Dóci. 2018. "Neoliberal Ideology in Work and Organizational Psychology." *European Journal of Work and Organizational Psychology* 27(5), 536-48.

Bauman, Zygmunt. 2007. *Liquid Times: Living in an Age of Uncertainty*, Cambridge/Malden: Polity Press.

Beck, Martha. 2002. *Finding Your Own North Star: Claiming the Life You Were Meant to Live*, Random House: New York.

Brown, Brené. 2010. *The Gifts of Imperfection: Let Go of Who You Think You're Supposed to Be and Embrace Who You Are*, Hazelden Publishing: Center City, MN.

Budd, John W. 2011. *The Thought of Work*, New York: Cornell University Press.

Covey, Stephen R. 1989. *7 Habits of highly effective people: Powerful lessons in personal change*, Simon & Schuster, New York.

De Jong, Marjolein. 2019. "Waarom werken we zo hard?" ["Why do we work so hard?"] *VU magazine*, 8 augustus 2019. https://www.vumagazine.vu.nl/waarom-werken-we-zo-hard (last accessed 15 November 2020)

Dekker, Fabian. 2018. "Arbeidsmobiliteit in Nederland: probleem of oplossing?" ["Work mobility in the Netherlands: Problem or Solution?"] De Burcht—Wetenschappelijk Bureau voor de Vakbeweging: Amsterdam.

Eaton, John and Roy Johnson. 2001. *Coaching successfully*, DK Publishing: London.

George, Bill. 2019. "Forget Socialism: The U.S. needs Responsible Capitalism." *Fortune*, 6 May 2019, https://fortune.com/2019/05/06/socialism-ceo-leadership-responsible-capitalism/ (last accessed 15 November 2020)

Holborow, Marnie. 2015. *Language and Neoliberalism: Language, Society and Political Economy*, New York: Routledge.

Martela, Frank, en Anne B. Pessi. 2018. "Significant Work Is about Self-Realization and Broader Purpose: Defining the Key Dimensions of Meaningful Work". *Frontiers in Psychology* 9, 363. https://doi.org/10.3389/fpsyg.2018.00363.

Monbiot, George. 2016. "Neoliberalism – the Ideology at the Root of All Our Problems." The Guardian, 15 April 2016. https://www.theguardian.com/books/2016/apr/15/neoliberalism-ideology-problem-george-monbiot (last accessed 15 November 2020).

Pink, Daniel H. 2011. *Drive: The surprising truth about what motivates us*, Canongate Books, Edinburgh.

Robbins, Anthony. 1991. *Awaken the Giant within: Take immediate control of your mental, emotional, physical and financial destiny*, Simon & Schuster, New York

Taylor, Charles. 1989, *Sources of the Self: The Making of Modern Identity*. Twelfth edition. Cambridge University Press, Cambridge

Work Regulation Committee [Commissie Regulering van Werk]. 2020. "In wat voor land willen wij werken? Naar een nieuw ontwerp voor de regulering van werk. Eindrapport van de Commissie Regulering van Werk" ["In what country do we want to work? Towards a new blueprint for regulating work"] Policy Report. Ministry of Social Afairs and Employment: The Hague.

COOPERATIVES, MENTAL HEALTH AND THE CRITIQUE OF WAGE LABOR

CHRISTOPHER MORALIS BONILA

Introduction

Affirming that wage labor is in crisis, is both a problem and a demand. First, it is a problem for critical thinking because the main means of survival in current social conditions passes, almost necessarily, through wage-earning work, i.e the sale of time in exchange for a salary. But it is also the claim that this scheme is beginning to show signs of exhaustion, and of restructuring. The reason is that, for decades now, one of the most important foundations that makes wage labor the most important social activity of our daily lives has begun to break down: the equalization between work and guaranteed survival. In other words, what is beginning to break is the connection between exercising a wage-earning activity and obtaining a salary in return with which to have all the elements of a guaranteed dignified life.

Without a doubt, this crisis begins with a shift in international politics that is, at the same time, a paradigm shift in hegemonic social thought. As a consequence of the loss of strength in both Soviet influence, as a threat to the hegemony of Western capitalism, and as well as the collapse of the welfare state, a model of management of the social that has been called neoliberalism appeared (Harvey, 2007); which consisted mainly of constantly degrading working conditions in order to adjust as much as possible the relationship between wages and survival, so that profits on the business side could be increased. In more recent years, this trend has been reinforced by the new logic of precariousness, through which what neoliberalism understood as a process that was still in its infancy, and before which it still had to face what was left of the combative impulse of the labor movement, in recent years has become the normal condition of work (Graeber, 2018; Standing, 2016).

However, the disconnection between work and survival has a very important aspect that has not been studied in sufficient depth and that is partially a feature of social conflict different from the classic scheme in which the struggle for the right to decent work is established, since at least the time of Marx. This new logic has led to the appearance of a whole series of psychological and physiological effects in the world of work which, to a large extent, implies a whole new social dimension. If in the classical scheme, the conflict in relation to work involved the struggle for waged work with decent pay and conditions; today this struggle is nuanced by the various mental illnesses produced by everything related to the world of work.

Thus, paid work appears as a pole of production of mental illness. Depression, anxiety, sleep disorders, etc., begin to be more normal consequences of work. But, and this is a great novelty, not only of the own wage-earning activity, but of its absence. On the one hand, the ever-increasing degradation of working conditions and, on the other, the exclusion from the circuit of work and exploitation, have very serious consequences for the mental health of workers. It is no longer a question of a series of isolated cases in relation to particularly stressful jobs in which there is a great deal of pressure; today, and thanks to this logic of precariousness, the consequences of work, and of its absence, for mental health are already beginning to be a very important problem for public and private health systems in industrialized countries.

In this way, what could be called the "therapeutic society" emerges. This is the whole set of techniques, procedures, knowledge, strategies and practices with which to manage the consequences of the organization of work from the point of view of the mental health of workers. This includes the new fashions on *wishful thinking*, *positive thinking, coaching, the* increasing need for psychological and psychiatric help, self-help books, more or less natural therapies to achieve well-being and health and, most importantly, the exponential increase in the consumption of antidepressants and anxiolytics in industrialized countries. In this way, a different perspective is opened up in the way of understanding the struggle for work: if in the previous model, everything revolved around demands for justice (fair work, fair pay, fair working conditions, etc.), today this struggle is joined by that of healthy work that does not produce a radical malaise that leads to some kind of mental illness.

In recent years, there has been an increasing amount of research trying to establish ways in which this crisis can be solved. Surprisingly, most of the studies that have attempted to address this issue make a very close connection between the way the world of work is organized and mental illness. To wit, there is growing evidence that a large part of mental illness is caused by work that is organized in a hierarchical way, that is, where the worker is a piece of a gear completely alien to him. There his or her work consists of carrying out a series of very specific tasks that cannot be questioned in terms of their usefulness or how they fit into the rest of collective work. In short: hierarchical work, and the authoritarian organization of work, begins to reveal itself as a source, in the long run, of a radical psychological malaise that leads to mental illness.

Therefore, these investigations begin to work with a hypothesis that has to be empirically proven in much greater depth: the reorganization of work, where possible, in favor of more democratic, horizontal, self-managed and cooperative forms seems to be a really effective way of overcoming all the psychological consequences that traditional salaried work has. Far from assuming something similar to the utopian visions of work formulated by Marx or Fourier, these are forms of work organization that sometimes involve longer working hours, greater responsibility and involvement in the collective management of a given enterprise, etc., but which have the positive aspect of producing a sense of belonging, identity and connection that, by the empirical results, completely eliminates all work-related mental illness.

Crisis and Disconnections of the Wage Labour

To understand more accurately what is the psychological aspect of waged work, both its activity and its absence, it is necessary to understand in depth what is the crisis of waged work, in what sense it is possible to say that waged work is in crisis, since it is not a type of statement that is absolutely evident. Of all aspects of the crisis of labor, it is necessary to understand in depth what is the overcoming and destruction of the equation between work and survival. Only in this way will it be possible to understand what role the appearance of mental illness plays in this problem.

The disappearance of the equation between wage labor and survival must be understood as the overcoming of one of the fundamental elements of the labor movement. From the very beginning of the industrial era, wage labor was understood as the means through which the worker can obtain enough money with which to ensure their survival. For its part, the socialist movement understands that wages must always be adjusted to maximize the employer's profit, allowing the workforce to simply survive. In contrast, the conception of socialist society is understood not as the overcoming of work as such, but the reorientation of the product of work towards the socialization of the wealth produced.

In the context of the defeat of the revolutionary movements of the early 1980s, both Margaret Thatcher and Ronald Reagan introduced a change in labor practices. The relationship of the workforce to survival is again transformed after decades in which the labor movement, along with the Soviet threat, had achieved more or less guaranteed security of labor rights. Neoliberalism, the doctrine of the new stage of capitalism at the end of the twentieth century operates in a very concrete way: the state intervenes in the economy to turn every element of social life into a commodity.

But it is necessary to understand the role of the state in order to grasp the contemporary crisis of labor. As opposed to what a certain hegemonic discourse has tried to establish, neoliberalism is not the absolute withdrawal of the State from the sphere of the market, becoming a neutral actor in relation to the private contract between individuals. Rather, it puts all the institutions, including the military, in place to *produce* a market; so that it truly becomes a sphere of freedom in which everything can become a commodity. The most extreme case is found in the military operations of the Reagan administration in South America to eliminate those models of government that endangered the freedom of U.S. companies in those countries (Chomsky, 1991).

After the beginning of the 21st century, what was called "neoliberal globalization" became the new theoretical configuration of capitalism; the financial crisis of 2009 has opened a new era of international capitalism that today receives a new impulse since the crisis of COVID-19. In relation to wage labor, the period that opens with the bankruptcy of Lehmann Brothers is another opportunity to tighten the belt of workers, increasingly reducing the possibility of having a life beyond mere survival. In other words, with the financial crisis and the current crisis of the pandemic, the world of work shows its main trend, which is none other than that of necessarily reducing the profit of the worker in relation to the profit of the company, reconfiguring the distribution of wealth produced by work.

However, up to this point it could be understood that the more or less classic diagnosis of the anti-globalist left in relation to the hardening of working conditions is true, and that it is sufficient to understand the crisis of wage labor. The realization that today a job does not necessarily guarantee access to the means to a guaranteed life is a diagnosis accepted by almost any critics of capitalism. But the relationship between wage labor and survival is much more complex than that diagnosis of the left. The main problem that exists between these two elements is that, unlike what happened some decades ago, we find ourselves at a moment in which everything points to the fact that the impoverishment of the relationship between work and survival is no longer a tendency that can be reversed, but rather appears as the essential logic of the world of work.

The logic of precariousness is that from which it is no longer possible to glimpse a previous future like that of certain previous generations, in which at the end of the labor career there was stability, the possibility of having the security that not only guaranteed survival, but that the salary allowed, at last, the worker to become bourgeois. This is, perhaps, one of the most important elements that the tradition of the left coming from Marxism has not understood: in a certain sense, and taking as valid the two social categories of the class struggle, the proletariat does not seem to want to become that type of subject that is lost in workers' assemblies and who seeks to have a determining role in all aspects of its life. Rather, he tends to want to become a bourgeois, in the sense of enjoying a level of wealth similar to that of someone who steals his working time.

For this reason, the logic of precariousness as the irreversible logic of labor displaces to some extent the interpretation of social conflict in classical Marxist terms. What sense does it make today to vindicate the workers' movement when it no longer exists either ideologically or sociologically? The phenomena of the new right-wing populism is supported, fundamentally, by what some time ago were the forces of the workers' movement. Today, the world of labor does not produce class-conscious subjects in the traditional sense of the term, but creates new subjectivities in which the problem of survival is at the center, that is, in which the most important thing is a kind of return to a social Darwinism in which everyone must fend for themselves. Without a doubt, this is the triumph of ideological neoliberalism, but only in the sense that it has managed to materially transform the labor market in such a way that there is no room left for classic elements of the labor movement such as solidarity or mutual aid.

When work and the struggle for its conditions are no longer at the center of the problem, survival appears as the element that, in large part, reorders the social conflict. In this sense, if work no longer seems to be a type of social activity that always appears on the horizon of the worker, then other elements appear in the equation. Thus, for example, unemployment appears as an important factor in the ordering of work. Although Marx already intuited this logic when he spoke in *Das Kapital about the* i*ndustrielle*

Reservearmee (Marx, 1991: 564 ff.) today we can understand that this logic has become much more acute. Today we can speak of a *necropolitical logic* (Mbembe, 2019) in which it is no longer only necessary for a part of the population to be unemployed in order to regulate wages according to the supply of labor, but in this new logic there is a determined effort to let certain parts of the population die whose care can no longer be maintained by the state. The COVID-19 crisis highlights this logic, in the sense that certain vulnerable layers of the populations in Western countries are abandoned to their fate insofar as the State has to focus on those layers of workers who can become productive. The elderly, disabled or poor in general are more likely to die from the pandemic than sectors of the population with value-added occupations.

But, in addition, this necropolitical logic is based on a sociological fact, which is also new in relation to the classic ways of understanding wage labor: there is no work for the whole population. More and more studies show the growing inability of the labor market to absorb the whole set of individuals who are of an age to produce. Thus, the logic of letting people die does not appear as a Machiavellian effort on the part of national and international institutions, but as an immanent consequence of the very dynamics of the labor market, regulated precisely by those same institutions. Processes such as the automation of labor contribute decisively to the increasing number of unemployed worldwide whose situation seems to be becoming chronic and irreversible (Aronowitz & Difazio, 1996; Caffentzis, 2013; Dinerstein & Neary, 2001; Doogan, 2009; Friedmann, 1964).

In short, the sense in which we can talk about a crisis of wage labor is different from that which could be understood from a Marxist tradition. It is no longer a question of the struggle for dignified working conditions, but for the possibility that having a job does not guarantee the minimum conditions of a dignified life; of understanding unemployment not as an undesirable consequence of the labor market but as a consequence of the limits of that market, precisely because of its internal logic. For this reason, new elements arise with which to understand, and propose solutions, to this crisis. Thus, new ways of understanding the organization of work as the cooperative model, new ways of proposing solutions to the problem of survival such as basic income, etc., emerge. However, before being able to understand these new elements of the labor market, it is necessary to grasp one of the main consequences of this restructuring of work: the appearance of mental illnesses as a result of the new forms of exploitation.

Mental Health, Work Organization and Therapeutic Society

The emergence of mental illness in relation to the organization of wage-earning work is a new field of study of the consequences of new labor practices for subjectivity. It is no coincidence that the conviction of the harmful effects on mental health of everything related to work is related to the history of the degradation of working conditions and the emergence of new logics that not only eliminate the main and historical objective of the movement, but also make the main objective disappear, which was none other than to fight for a form of activity that, today, is in danger of becoming something increasingly strange. Thus, the emergence of all kinds of work-related illnesses already implies placing oneself in a framework of knowledge different from that of social theory with Marxist roots.

There are two distinct areas in which the work ends up producing some kind of psychological discomfort. Both spheres are, however, deeply connected, complementing each other. Firstly, there is the whole set of disorders produced by the wage-earning activity itself. Here, anxiety appears as a result of the growing pressure to meet objectives, the increase in working hours, the instability of work contracts or the loss of social life related to this increase in working time. If in the model of the *Welfare State* the worker seemed to have gained a space of life outside of work, from the logic of neoliberalism and precariousness, that time tends to disappear in an increasingly evident way. The time of life ends up being completely equalized with the time of work. There is no rest, no disconnection of the worker from his job. The emergence of new technologies such as smartphones has helped to make the connection with work permanent. It is never possible to leave the workplace because it always accompanies the worker.

In this way, what could be called the *therapeutic society* emerges. It is the set of practices, institutions and knowledge that are oriented to solve and manage the effects that contemporary transformations of work have on workers. This includes the medicalization of workers, i.e. the increasing use of antidepressants and relaxants in order to alleviate the effects of anxiety and depression or the increasing assistance to psychologists and psychiatrists for disorders related to salaried activity. The *therapeutic society* is the way in which the social organization seeks to keep the whole workforce ready for production, offering partial solutions to problems that have to do with the organization of work (Espai en Blanc, 2007).

However, here a question arises: what is happening in the new forms of work so that the appearance of this type of disorder is becoming more and more frequent? The answer has to do with the fact that some psychological trends have been studied for some decades and they are now being applied to the world of work. This question is that of *meaning*. The subject needs to have a dimension of meaning in the activity he or she carries out. Not only on the level of his work activity, but on the level of his own daily life as a whole, more and more psychological and psycho-sociological studies are beginning to demonstrate the need to carry out meaningful activities, activities that have an important meaning for the person who carries them out (Hari, 2018: 110 ff.). Thus, carrying out a salaried activity for the sole purpose of obtaining a salary does not seem to be sufficient to produce lasting psychological well-being.

The current organization of work described above finds its direct connection to the proliferation of mental disorders here. If the world of work is increasingly precarious, increasingly oriented to the achievement of absolutely meaningless tasks, increasingly disconnected from the attribution of meaning to the subjects, then we understand clearly the relationship between work organization and mental disorder. The appearance of anxiety or depression is nothing more than the necessary consequence of a logic of salaried work in which meaningful activities are increasingly difficult to find, in which the worker, in general, is limited to forms of work in which he does not find an essential meaning for himself. Work becomes an activity in which one acts and obeys, but in which the element of search for meaning that seems to be reproduced in human psychology is completely eliminated (Almond & Healey, 2003; Layard, 2013; Markowe & Barber, 1953; Schofield, Kelly, Shrestha, Callander, Percival & Passey, 2011).

The process that is occurring in this logic of work, and that seems to be demonstrated as the essential element that triggers mental disorder, is that of disconnection (Hari, 2018: 99 ff.). The worker, before becoming a patient, finds himself disconnected from that which he considers to be a framework of meaning within which to order his own daily life. The reproduction of labor activities in which no type of creativity, participation or expectation of progress is put into play ends up completely eliminating the sense of connection with a meaning, with a frame of reference. Although this element may seem a kind of sign of weakness of character (especially if we compare it with the form of organization of work that existed 50 or 100 years ago, in which work was basically industrial work) the truth is that the objective increase of mental disorders in relation to work shows that something is happening between human psychology and the form of organization of wage labor.

The second area in which the relationship between work and mental disorder is found is in the absence of work. This problem has a first classic version in Marx through the already mentioned *industrielle Reservearmee*. In this first approach, unemployment is a product of the organization of work, that is, it is the result of a way of managing the workforce through which to establish a certain limit to the number of workers occupying a job. The limitation of the activity of the productive force has the advantage of being able to establish low wages by promoting competition, always downwards, between several workers for the same job (Marx, 1991: 564 ff.).

However, unemployment works differently in the current reorganization of work. The production of layers of the population that are outside the labor market no longer responds to the need for wage regulation. The capacity of capital to establish wages increasingly adjusted to mere survival now responds to a triumph of its hegemony, to the disappearance of those forces which historically served as a counterweight. On the basis of the neoliberal logic and precariousness, wage labor does not need that reserve army of workers ready to work for a wage always downwards.

Thus, exclusion appears as a process with no turning back. More and more, sectors of the population are appearing whose exclusion from the world of work is becoming chronic. There is no longer the perspective of a job, of some type of salaried activity. Exclusion becomes a perpetual logic that is absolutely irreversible. It is no longer a question of artificially keeping a certain number of workers out of the circuit of work in order to organize and regulate it, but now it is simply a question of the number of workers left over. And they are surplus in the sense that the labour market neither wants to, nor can, absorb them, introduce them, manage them within that world. This includes growing sectors of the black and immigrant population in the United States, the inhabitants of the French *banlieus* and slums cities, etc. (Benanav, 2015).

Thus, unemployment appears as the other side of the destructive logic of work. If salaried activity has as one of its consequences all sorts of mental illness, the exclusion of that possibility produces similar effects. The impossibility of establishing a future of meaning, the impossibility of projecting one's life, the impossibility of being able to get out of poverty, etc., are elements that also produce all types of mental illnesses. This kind of *laisser mourir* is related to the same harmful effects of the current organization of work, only by different means.

Therefore, paid work seems to be deeply related to the exponential increase in mental illness. Not only its possession but also its dispossession, are related to the appearance of all kinds of disorders, in which the worker ends up being inserted in a therapeutic society that is in charge of being able to continue moving through the circuit of salaried work. The first consequence of this new configuration of labor is that it supposes a change in the way of understanding the struggle for labor exposed by critical Marxist theory. The new configuration of work is situated before that, in the sense that it understands that what is in question is the very possibility of being able to access a type of wage-earning activity which allows one to have a dignified life without paying the toll of the appearance of mental illness. For its part, that Marxist theory could only understand unemployment as an artificial creation of capital; today we can see that it is a direct consequence of the fact that capital needs less and less labor to be able to increase its profit margin.

With this understanding of the problem, it seems that there is no alternative. Both paid work and its absence are intimately related to mental illness and all kinds of related disorders. However, understanding the current organization of work in this way implies grasping the contemporary capitalist organization of work as a kind of immovable historical fact, along with its consequences for mental health. However, there is a whole set of alternatives that have been tested through many experiences of reorganization of work that not only involve new ways of overcoming the organization of waged work, but the whole of the consequences for the mental health of workers.

The Cooperativization of Work

However, the current organization of paid work does not imply any form of fixed and immovable structure. The way in which wage labor is ordered in our contemporaneity is nothing more than the result of a whole series of forces, practices, institutions and historical struggles that have shaped wage labor activity in the way we can experience it today (Postone, 2005). For this reason, and from a theoretical point of view, it is possible to think of different ways of organizing productive activity that, among other consequences, does not lead to the appearance of mental disorders. In this sense, it is necessary to study in a theoretical and practical way the different forms in which, both in the past and in the present, different forms of wage-earning activity have been tried out from the capitalist forms.

There is an element that is essential in this organization of work and that takes on special importance when it comes to thinking about the possibility of new work organizations. This element is the hierarchical arrangement of production, in other words, the model through which the worker is always within a vertical organization, where all aspects of production are outside his decision. Thus, in this model the worker is limited to carrying out orders, just as in the structure of an army. However, Marx's own critique in the *Manuskripte of* 1844 emphasizes precisely this element, not so much in denouncing the hierarchization of labor as the alienating effects of such organization on the worker. This is the meaning of the famous category of *Entfremdung* (Marx, 2009: 656 ff.).

What models can we extract from the history of the labor movement that could serve as an alternative to this hierarchical structure of labor? The model of cooperative work appears as an effective possibility of ordering production. This model has two main advantages: the first is that it does not fall into the utopian traits of other models of work, such as those of Fourier or Lafargue. The second characteristic is that the cooperative model is on the border between social transformation and the traditional form of wage labor: it respects the essential elements of capitalist production (production oriented towards surplus value, free market, etc.), but at the same time, it introduces the possibility of decision making, control and self-management of the workers in the whole of their activity.

Especially since the crisis of 2009, the cooperative model has become an effective, pragmatic and plausible alternative for reordering work. Where many small businesses have had to close, their workers, equipped with real knowledge of how to run the business, have decided to carry out the same type of work they had before the crisis but now under a cooperative model. Thus, the advantage of being able to exercise direct control over all production matters has the advantage of being able to be responsible for their own productive life. In addition to this, another improvement is that they can run the same type of business without making the mistakes that led to the closure of so many companies. Thus, the reappropriation of production and democratic control over it has become a growing trend within developed capitalist economies.

However this democratization of work is joined by another advantage, which is most interesting in relation to the problem of the proliferation of mental illnesses. When this democratic process of recovery of control of production takes place, a kind of "reconnection" is reproduced between the worker and his productive activity. One only has to listen to workers who have lived through this process:

> "I can certainly see depression and anxiety being related to the fact that people feel really, really confused and helpless ... I think it's hard for people to live in a society where you have got no control over anything ... You don't control your economic life, from the standpoint that it's precarious whether you've got work at all, and then if you do have a job, you walk into the place, spend forty, fifty, sixty, eighty hours a week in this place. You don't have free speech. You don't have any sort of voting." Anxiety and depression seem to him, he says, "rational reactions to the situation, as opposed to some kind of biological break." (Hari, 2018: 113)

By being able to influence all aspects of the activity they carry out, by feeling that their creativity and their opinion count in their productive life as a whole, the worker finds that element which is essential for the absence of mental disorder: a job with meaning. There are many experiences of workers throughout different countries that begin to demonstrate the direct relationship between democratization of work and the disappearance of mental disorders:

> "It's not the work itself that makes you sick. It's three other things. It's the feeling of being controlled-of being a meaningless cog in a system. It's the feeling that no matter how hard you work, you'll be treated just the same and nobody will notice an imbalance, as he puts it, between efforts and rewards. And it's the feeling of being low on the hierarchy of being a low status person who doesn't matter compared to the Big Man in the corner office" (Hari, 2018:112).

Thus, the cooperative model is beginning to show that it can serve as a means of introducing a certain dissonance into the hegemonic organization of capitalism. While it does not pose a direct threat to their survival, it does introduce different elements that widen the possibilities for workers to have much more democratic control over their productive lives. Moreover, the cooperative model seems to be an effective remedy against the crises of meaning that lead directly to the emergence of a multitude of mental disorders. Whether this model can become a truly effective and lasting alternative at the global level of the hierarchical structure of labor will be seen in the decades following this millennium.

Bibliography

Almond, Stephen and Healey, Andrew. "Mental Health and Absence from Work: New Evidence from the UK Quarterly Labour Force Survey". *Work, Employment and Society*, no. 17(4) (2003): 731-742.

Aronowitz, Stanley and Difazio, William. *The Jobless Future. Sci-Tech and the Dogma of Work*. Minneapolis and London: University of Minnesota Press, 1996.

Bakaikoa, Baleren, Errasti, Anjel and Begiristain, Agurtzane. "Governance of the Mondragon Corporación Cooperativa". *Annals of Public and Cooperative Economics*, 75(1) (2004): 61-87.

Benanav, Aaron Seth. *A Global History of Unemployment: Surplus Populations in the World Economy, 1949-2010*. Los Angeles: University of California, 2015. Unpublished Dissertation.

Caffentzis, George. *In Letters of Blood and Fire. Work, Machines, and the Crisis of Capitalism*. Dexter (Michigan): PM Press, 2013.

Chomsky, Noam. *Deterring Democracy*. London & New York: Verso, 1991.

Dinerstein, Ana C. and Pitts, Frederick H. "From Post-Work to Post-Capitalism? Discussing the Basic Income and Struggles for Alternative Forms of Social Reproduction". *Labor and Society*, 2018. DOI: 10.1111/lands.12359

Dinerstein, Ana C. and Neary, Michael (eds.). *The Labour Debate: An Investigation into the Theory and Reality of Capitalist Work*. Hants/Vermont: Ashgate, 2001.

Doogan, Kevin. *New Capitalism? The Tranformation of Work*. Malden (MA): Polity Press, 2009.

Espai en Blanc. *The therapeutic society*. Barcelona: Bellaterra, 2007.

Fleming, Peter. *The Mythology of Work. How Capitalism Persists Despite Itself*. London: Pluto Press, 2015.

Frayne, David. *The Refusal of Work. The Theory and Practice of Resistance to Work*. London: Zed Books, 2015.

Friedmann, Georges. *The Anatomy of Work. Labor, Leisure and the Implications of Automation*. Translated by Wyatt Rawson. New York: The Free Press of Glencoe, 1964.

Graeber, David. *Bullshit Jobs*. London: Simon & Schuster: 2018.

Hari, Johann. *Lost Connections: Why You're Depressed and How to Find Hope*. London: Bloomsbury, 2018. EPUB Version.

Harvey, David. *A Brief History of Neoliberalism*. Oxford: Oxford University Press, 2007.

Layard, Richard. "Mental Health: The New Frontier for Labour Economics". *IZA Journal of Labour Policy*, 2(2) (2013): 1-16.

Livingston, James. *No More Work. Why Full Employment Is a Bad Idea.* Chapel Hill: The University of North Carolina Press, 2016.

Mckay, Alisa. *The Future of Social Security Policy. Women, Work and a Citizens' Basic Income.* London and New York: Routledge, 2005.

Markowe, Morris and Barber, Leslie E. D. "Mental Health in Relation to the Labour Turnover of Unskilled Workers in a Large Industrial Establishment". *Brit. J. prev. soc. Med.* 7, (1953): 205-210.

Marx, Karl. *Das Kapital. Kritik der politischen Ökonomie. Erster Band. Hamburg 1890.* Berlin: Dietz Verlag: 1991.

—. *Gesamtausgabe (MEGA), I. Abteil, Band 2.* Berlin: Dietz Verlag, 2009.

Mbembe, Achille. *Necropolitics. Theory in Forms*. Durham: Duke University Press, 2019.

Postone, Moishe. *Time, Labour and Social Domination: A Reinterpretation of Marx's Critical Theory.* Cambridge: Cambridge University Press, 2005.

Schofield, Deborah J, Kelly, Simon J., Shrestha, Rupendra N., Callander, Emily J., Percival, Richard and Passey, Megan E. "How Depression and Other Mental Health Problems Can Affect Future Living Standards of Those Out of the Labour Force". *Aging & Mental Health, 15*(5) (2011): 654-662. DOI: 10.1080/13607863.2011.556599.

Standing, Guy. *The Precariat: The New Dangerous Class*. Bloomsbury: Bloomsbury Academic, 2016.

Wall, Derek. *Elinor Ostrom's Rules for Radicals. Cooperative Alternatives Beyond Markets and States*. London: Pluto Press, 2017.

Weeks, Kathi. *The Problem With Work. Feminism, Marxism, Antiwork Politics, and Postwork Imaginaries*. Durham and London: Duke University Press, 2011.

BARE LIFE AND WORK: MECHANISMS OF EXCLUSION

IRENE ORTIZ

Introduction

What are the mechanisms through which people are forced to unemployment and loneliness? In this chapter I examine what role work plays and, consequently, the lack of work and unemployment in societies that tend to prioritize social recognition through wages and the type of work. The chapter is divided into four sections: the first, entitled "Working Time" where some problems related to the relationship between working time and living time are presented. The second, under the name "The Unemployment" focuses on the peculiarities of the population that do not have work. The third, titled "An example of empowerment", analyzes some social movements that try to revoke the situation of loneliness and ostracism through collective mobilization and the resignification of precariousness. Finally, some conclusions are presented that allow the debate to be broadened beyond the limits of individual responsibility for unemployment, and an examination is proposed that does not forget the important role that the capitalist system plays in the tacit condemnation of precarious people.

Working time

The conciliation between time of life and working time is presented as a dilemma that is difficult to solve. The work-life balance refers to the optimal balance between the time dedicated to work and the time dedicated to the personal life of an individual. As Jorge Moruno has pointed out, time comes to be understood under a new social regime of time, "a way of living time dominated by the regulation of the clock and the temporalization of space"[1]. According to this rigid division of time between working time and time of

---

[1] Jorge Moruno, *La fábrica del emprendedor. Trabajo y política en la empresa-mundo.* (Madrid: Akal, 2015), 62.

life, time does not pass, it is wasted. Time is included in the market as another good. In order to support individual property rights as natural rights, Locke underlined how the fruit of one's labor are one's own because one worked for it. If goods are produced through work, they belong to those who have dedicated their time to produce them.

In this scenario, the division between working time and living time is established through a strictly economic distinction. Time is distinguished according to its usefulness and the products it can generate, so that time that is not productive, that cannot be exchanged for goods, is almost wasted time. Of course, this division privileges the time dedicated to producing goods over the time that does not participate in the market logic. In Moruno's words:

> "Ending the refusal of workers and peasants to carry out routine and rationalized working hours entailed arduous cultural and not only economic work, in which the company transforms what was previously felt as a stone and a shame into an object of pride and the axis that vertebrates society. From now on, the ideology of work will place work as a social obligation and the path to personal success, thereby achieving a double effect: the effort printed at work -carrying the cross of Christ- and its hostile reverse towards who does not work, perceived as an outcast and a burden for society."[2]

Only under the premise that work is a source of pride can the concession of sacrificing time of life in working time be made. However, this logic has some implicit ones that should be pointed out: work is a source of pride because it participates in the economic system. Working time is exchanged for goods, and it is thanks to this exchange that working time becomes more valuable than time of life. In this sense, working time, by being exchanged for a salary established between the employer and the employee, actively participates in the economic system, by allowing the worker to accumulate more goods. Pride, derived from the improvement in the quality of life, makes the sacrifice of time of life for time of work carried out with the approval of the collective imagination. Since success is measured through standard of living, dedication of life to work is understood as one of the greatest forms of success.

---

[2] Jorge Moruno, *La fábrica del emprendedor. Trabajo y política en la empresa-mundo.* (Madrid: Akal, 2015), 63.

However, it is mandatory ask: "Why is it accepted as fair, equitable, and just, in many contexts, that the pursuit of profit should be considered more important than people and families?"[3].

None of this can be understood without the complicity of the work system, which has reinforced some behaviors through pay as a reward and has punished others with sanctions and fines. The capitalist system privileges those forms of life that participate in the economic system while expelling to the margins those lives that do not produce goods. Furthermore, the work centers have assumed the hierarchy derived from the institution of the family. Thus, the figure of the employer assumes the role of father, who is responsible for reinforcing appropriate behaviors and punishing mistakes. As Moruno recalls: "The image of the notebook that needed the employer's signature to mark the worker for his good or bad behavior is a clear example of an employer's paternalism that helps the city be ordered and cleansed itself of false poor people, even at the cost of treating the worker as a socially childlike being"[4]. The infantilization of the worker, therefore, is carried out through the system of rewards and punishments that, as we will see, has consequences in the location in the social hierarchy. In fact, "workplace cultures influence the way workers experience their jobs and perceive their options. The culture is likely to be shaped most forcefully by those at the top of an organization, thus forcing workers at the middle and lower rungs of the hierarchy to adjust as best they can"[5].

In this context, we must ask ourselves about the autonomy that the worker has to participate in the world of work. Of course, the articulation between private life and work life plays an important role when looking for a job. In a scenario such as that of the free choice of the individual, the tendency will be to think that the choice of the type of work is the consequence of a premeditated decision by an individual. Thus, it will be said that the types of work, as well as their working conditions (hours, salary) are the result of a dialogue between employers and employees. In this way, the precariousness of certain jobs is justifiable thanks to the argument that the

---

[3] Suzan Lewis and Linda Haas, "Work-Life Integration and Social Policy: A Social Justice Theory and Gender Equity Approach to Work and Family" In *Work and life Integration. Organizational, Cultural and Individual Perspectives*, ed. Ellen Ernst Kossek and Susan J. Lambert (New Jersey: Lawrence Erlbaum Associates, 2005), 349.

[4] Jorge Moruno, *La fábrica del emprendedor. Trabajo y política en la empresa-mundo.* (Madrid: Akal, 2015), 66.

[5] Jerry A. Jacobs and Kathleen Gerson, *The Time Divide. Work, Family, and Gender Inequality*. (Cambridge: Harvard University Press, 2004), 61.

workers have accepted these conditions and that, therefore, there is not much more to discuss. However, we must approach the question of work precisely by doubting this statement to deduce whether this analysis offers us tools to analyze our principal issue.

> Certainly, we cannot assume that workers' choices are merely a reflection of their own personal preferences. In a myriad of ways, the world of work is organized and structured by forces far beyond any individual worker's control. It is thus not enough to know how the behavior of workers has changed. We also need to ask whether, and to what extent, contemporary work patterns reflect the preferences of workers or the demands and constraints of the options they are offered[6].

Thus, the first thing we must question is the mantra that the world of work is the result of a dialogue between the two parties involved. Is the labor market a reflection of the demands of the workers? Are workers the result of the labor supply? This is not a minor question, since the answer we owe to these questions will lead to the answer to the most important question we can ask ourselves as a community: What aspect privileges our social value system: life or the economy? This question, of course, has been shown with all its violence in recent months as a result of the coronavirus pandemic. Many citizens have been perplexed at the speeches of our presidents, who posed with an unprecedented naivety this question: what is more important, the economy or life?

This crisis has revealed the extent to which not only our leaders, but also ourselves, the citizens, have internalized the mantra that puts the needs of the market before the needs of life. In several European countries, during the peak of the pandemic, you could see deserted streets in which only some *riders* who were going to deliver their packages circulated. They, the precarious workers, continued to work during the pandemic. How was it justified? Once again, appealing to the freedom of the individual in economic matters. The *riders*, it was said, could have chosen not to work, but they *freely* chose to. However, the question is a bit more complex:

> Freedom is not the obligation to adapt to an environment that is not discussed and that is imposed on the population. Freedom is not submitting to the needs of the market. It is the other way around; the market has to submit and relate to the benefit of people's needs. The first model of the world-company

[6] Jerry A. Jacobs and Kathleen Gerson, *The Time Divide. Work, Family, and Gender Inequality*. (Cambridge: Harvard University Press, 2004), 59.

> builds servants; the second, free people who decide in common the how and what of their life[7].

We must ask this question as many times as necessary because life depends on it. Continuing to repeat the mantra that working conditions are established on an equal footing between the employer and the employee does not seem to make any sense, especially if we review what has happened during the COVID-19 crisis. As I pointed out before, the situation of the riders has been particularly scandalous and has exemplified in all its harshness how there are some lives that are susceptible to being sacrificed. Claiming that the most precarious people, with worse working conditions and lower wages, choose these jobs is a fallacy that we must denounce.

There can be no freedom of choice when the dichotomy is between working under the conditions set by the employer and not being able to pay where you live. In this sense, it is important to recognize the abyss that separates this reading from that which only underlines the meritocratic system, where wealth is the result of effort. However, in a system where what is presented is the imposition of working to survive, free choice is a chimera.

> The fear of marginalization or forced exclusion, of being left out of the consumer system, pushes those who are at risk, to submit to the harsh rules of being inside. The economic order uses exclusion as a ghost that frightens those inside and as a reality that keeps a pool of available workers at its doors. I could not do without it at the risk of losing a labor market fully adaptable to any type of conditions. Exclusion is an externality, that is, an unavoidable and unaccounted for damage to our economic system. Work is presented as an element of integration, although this is fragile in the case of precarious work[8].

In the case of unemployed people, it becomes even more evident how their freedom of choice is denied. It is unreasonable, we are told, not to take a job. It's as if the only thing that could be more humiliating than having a precarious job is precisely not having it. The absence of work, especially if an unemployment benefit is being collected, is understood as an individual failure. Despite the fact that there are millions of people in a precarious situation, who lack sufficient income to live with dignity and, in many cases,

---

[7] Jorge Moruno, *La fábrica del emprendedor. Trabajo y política en la empresa-mundo.* (Madrid: Akal, 2015), 95.

[8] Yayo Herrero, Fernando Cembranos and Marta Pascual. *Cambiar las gafas para mirar el mundo. Una nueva cultura de la sostenibilidad.* (Madrid: Libros en Acción, 2011), 210.

to survive, the phenomenon of unemployment is analyzed from a strictly individual perspective, as a result of personal choices.

The Unemployed

Not working not only has the economic consequences derived from the deprivation of wages, but also negative effects that the community has on people who do not participate in economic activity. In this sense, the social imaginary tends to punish those unemployed because it is understood that, if the labor market develops within the limits of individual freedom to accept and reject the job offer, the person who does not work is because it does so has decided.

> Contempt for the pariah does not come from the popular sectors; On the contrary, it can be manifested among them, but it is a discourse that always emerges from the elites and that is inoculated from top to bottom in defense of their interests. In Hungary, the extreme right that governs that is already setting up work camps to fill them with unemployed and enacts laws to criminalize and penalize begging. In England, without going so far but on the same sidewalk, multiple cases have already come to light where the unemployed are used to clean houses and offices of companies and supermarkets for free. In Spain the way is being processed for the unemployed to carry out social activities, as if they were guilty of something, as if they owed something[9].

The responsibility, therefore, falls on the unemployed person, who not only has economic problems but also lack of social recognition. The question arises about him as to why he does not work, why he prefers to be an outcast rather than a very precarious job (because it is understood that these are always available). In fact, one of the things that the so-called "collaborative economy" has favored is that one can sign up for a delivery service and automatically start to have a job (even if legally they do not have an employer, since they employ themselves). The responsibility of the precarious situation is experienced as the exclusive result of individual decisions. Thus, we avoid thinking about the labor market, the work system and, ultimately, the economic system. By accepting that the situation unemployed find themselves in is solely the result of their choices, it is produced an ostracization of those individuals who do not meet a certain standard of living.

---

[9] Jorge Moruno, *La fábrica del emprendedor. Trabajo y política en la empresa-mundo.* (Madrid: Akal, 2015), 90.

As several studies have pointed out, the unemployment situation not only has dramatic economic effects on people's lives but also psychological ones:

> Since the 1930s, social scientists have been demonstrating that unemployment is it stressor for workers and their families. Unemployment is considered a highly stressful, negative life event, with good reason: Studies of both general unemployment and plant closings show that unemployment is associated with a significant increase in symptoms such as perceived physical illness, hostility, paranoia, drinking problems, family conflict, and demoralization, as well as depression, anxiety, and somatic symptoms[10].

In this way, it is important, when talking about unemployed people, not to forget the psychological effects that this condition causes on them. It is not only a situation of economic precariousness but also an emotional one. Among the symptoms that are often identified as products of unemployment depression are: "loss of sexual interest or pleasure, trouble getting to sleep or staying asleep, thoughts of ending your life, poor appetite, crying easily, a feeling of being trapped or caught, blaming yourself for things, feeling lonely, feeling blue, worrying or stewing about things, feeling no interest in things and feeling hopeless about the future"[11]. Of course, the economic issue cannot be left aside when analyzing the situation of the unemployed, but it is important not to forget to pay attention to the strong impact that lack of work has on the mental health of the unemployed. Work has a role in social hierarchy and that is why the lack of work has consequences in mental health.

> The central plank of this argument revolves around the idea that there are several latent functions of paid employment, what might be called 'categories of experience', to which the unemployed are denied access. These latent functions are distinct from the manifest functions of employment to earn money and include: a structured experience of time; regular social contacts; participation in collective purposes; social status which provides personal identity and regular physical activity[12].

---

[10] Clifford L. Broman, V. Lee Hamilton and William S. Hoffman, *Stress and Distress among the Unemployed. Hard Times and Vulnerable People*. (New York: Springer Science+Business Media, 2001), 13.

[11] Clifford L. Broman, V. Lee Hamilton and William S. Hoffman, *Stress and Distress among the Unemployed. Hard Times and Vulnerable People*. (New York: Springer Science+Business Media, 2001), 69.

[12] Paul Bagguley, *From Protest to Acquiescence? Political Movements of the Unemployed*. (London: Macmillan Education, 1991), 15.

For our analysis, it is essential to understand what are the causes that cause these symptoms in unemployed people.

Once again, we must avoid falling into the sole responsibility of the unemployed. If depression and the rest of the symptoms associated with unemployment occur in a generalized way in the population that does not have work, it is unlikely that this is the result of the individual psychology of everyone. On the contrary, we should examine whether there are social conditions that favor these types of symptoms. When we say that unemployed people are stigmatized in the collective imagination, we must justify how this process occurs. Thus, in the first place, it is important to look at the institutional narratives that are made of the unemployed population. If we take the example of Spain, it is easy to see how the representation of the unemployed as lazy or weak occurs at institutional headquarters. In Moruno's words:

> Temporary work agencies (TWA) that comply with current regulations will be in charge of locating the unemployed in any way and in any garbage. I say "whatever" because the words of José Bono, a baron of the PSOE (Socialist Party), who was scandalized when an unemployed person rejected a job, are made official and, therefore, that could not be allowed. "Unemployment cannot be more attractive than a job," Bono declared (…) It works the same with the unemployed; If the employment that exists degrades the person, enjoying unemployment benefit must be even worse - less time, less quantity, more difficult access- for this principle to be fulfilled. It seems that the problem is not the job, but the unemployed, so if you earn € 850 unemployment and reject three offers of bullshit jobs -that's what the temporary employment agencies do- where they pay you less than what you receive with the benefit, they take it away from you. The worse the working conditions, the more the entitlement to unemployment benefit must be adjusted. It is the contemporary neo-servitude, one is free to support oneself, but in the absence of a minimum guarantee to be able to do so[13].

The speeches that are made from the political tribunes have a great impact on the collective imagination of a certain community. The stigmatizing capacity of political speeches should not be underestimated. Therefore, "not only is the debate on unemployment monopolized by different types of expert and excludes the unemployed themselves, but in addition, the media broadcast strongly stigmatizing material about the jobless, concentrating on

[13] Jorge Moruno, *La fábrica del emprendedor. Trabajo y política en la empresa-mundo.* (Madrid: Akal, 2015), 91-92.

the responsibilities of the individuals themselves and not on the profound changes suffered by the country in a very short space of time"[14].

Trying to make an analysis of the unemployment situation without considering technological changes within the capitalist system, as well as the impact of globalization, is an error that can only lead us to think that unemployment is the product of individual decisions. It is precisely this responsibility assumed by the unemployed as a result of the stigmatization suffered that makes their mobilizations appear delegitimized and devoid of force. In this sense, "the aim was to better understand the mechanisms of precarization so as to confer on the unemployed a collective dimension and thus fight different forms of stigmatization and prevent them from being victimized as the guilty"[15]. Thus, it seems that the suppression of the individual's working life extends to his personal life. The unemployed person is reduced to a bare life that participates in the socio-political context only because he is excluded from it. It is as if the unemployed, being stripped of his working life, also lost all his qualities as an individual. Stigmatization reduces the particularities of the unemployed to a homogeneous mass made up of lazy individuals unable to participate in the economic system. Its individual characteristics are erased, its peculiarities are eliminated, and the phenomenon is analyzed as an endemic disease of some people. As it has been underlined: "in a society that increasingly highlights the (in)capacities of the individual. The task is not simple and supposes the distancing of values currently widespread. It is a question not only of overcoming stigmatizing representations often attached to the unemployed, but also of struggling against the depersonalization to which this statute contributes"[16].

The biopolitical constitution of the individual as a citizen is also determined through their ability to participate in not only political but also economic aspects. Thus, through the situation of unemployment, a mass of men is relegated to an indefinite spectrum that does not manage to retain their status as citizens. When Giorgio Agamben points out that "rights are attributed to man (or originate in him) solely to the extent that man is the immediately

[14] Paul Bagguley, *From Protest to Acquiescence? Political Movements of the Unemployed*. (London: Macmillan Education, 1991), 20.
[15] Paul Bagguley, *From Protest to Acquiescence? Political Movements of the Unemployed*. (London: Macmillan Education, 1991), 37.
[16] Paul Bagguley, *From Protest to Acquiescence? Political Movements of the Unemployed*. (London: Macmillan Education, 1991), 42.

vanishing ground (who must never come to light as such) of the citizen"[17], we feel the need to extend that it is not just a political problem. Man, in order to be recognized as a legitimate participant in a certain community, must also meet economic and status requirements that are denied to unemployed people. Indeed, their life is always under the suspicion of not being good enough to integrate into the community, since they do not have a job.

> It is as if every valorization and every "politicization" of life (which, after all, is implicit in the sovereignty of the individual over his own existence) necessarily implies a new decision concerning the threshold beyond which life ceases to be politically relevant, becomes only "sacred life," and can as such be eliminated without punishment. Every society sets this limit; every society – even the most modern – decides who its "sacred men" will be. It is even possible that this limit, on which the politicization and the *exceptio* of natural life in the juridical order of the state depends, has done nothing but extend itself in the history of the West and has now – in the new biopolitical horizon of states with national sovereignty – moved inside every human life and every citizen. Bare life is no longer confined to a particular place or a definite category. It now dwells in the biological body of every living being[18].

The border between a life worth living and an easily suppressible life, as Agamben recalls, is not a clear and delimited line. Our contemporary biopolitical societies tend to shift the border based on their needs. Thus, the lives of migrants, who lack the rights granted through citizenship status, are always suspended at the mercy of political will. On the other hand, the lives of unemployed people are also found, for economic reasons and for social recognition, under the suspicion of being unproductive lives and of little value to the economic system. In this way, the process of depersonalization of those excluded from the world of work has consequences on their own psyche and on the way, they connect with their environment.

If certain rights are systematically taken away from some individuals, it is because there is an explicit declaration that "they are not considered as other members of society, equally responsible."[19]. This form of contempt sends a clear and evident message to people in exclusion, and it is none other than

---

[17] Giorgio Agamben, *Homo sacer. Sovereign power and bare life.* (Stanford: Stanford University Press, 1998), 76.

[18] Giorgio Agamben, *Homo sacer. Sovereign power and bare life.* (Stanford: Stanford University Press, 1998), 82.

[19] Axel Honnet, *La lucha por el reconocimiento*. (Barcelona: Mondadori, 1997), 162.

to highlight the lack of the status of being a subject of equal and fully valuable moral interaction. Precisely due to the processes of discrimination, stigmatization and depersonalization suffered by unemployed people, it is important to end our analysis with the example of how collective action can restore dignity to a group that has been unjustly mistreated.

An example of empowerment

One of the first consequences of the 2008 crisis was the rise in evictions. The growth in unemployment meant that unemployed people were unable to pay their mortgages and eventually had to face losing their homes. In this way, the housing problem arose, which until then had been relegated to what were thought to be marginal groups. With the outbreak of evictions due to non-payment of mortgages, the great problem of the precariousness of employment and, finally, of unemployment became visible.

> Beyond the organizational context in which the mobilization of the unemployed develops, the cultural, ideological, and cognitive environment of a society also plays an essential role in the conditions for emergence of a movement of the unemployed. The political invisibility to which the unemployed are generally confined is inseparable from a certain number of misconceptions, of stereotypes, stigmas even, which are opposed to their mobilization, or which tend to discredit them when they do manage to organize themselves collectively[20].

In this context, the Platform for People Affected by Mortgages (PAH, for its acronym in Spanish) was born. Ada Colau, who was the spokesperson of the PAH before becoming mayor of Barcelona, explained how the Platform has a transformative character for people facing eviction: they go from victim to activist. The first thing an affected person hears when he arrives at the PAH assembly is: this is not an NGO, here we need your collaboration, and from now on your case is ours and ours are yours. It is an exercise in empowerment and a struggle that questions existing power relations[21]. Faced with the passive treatment that "users" receive in NGOs, the platform offers recognition of the name and history of the affected person. In the words of her former spokesperson: "Each affected person has a name, a story, a journey. Exists. Appears. You are not a number, but a person and as such you are recognized (…). The PAH offers roots and

---

[20] Didier Chabanet and Jean Faniel, ed., *The Mobilization of the Unemployed in Europe. From Acquiescence to Protest?* (New York: Macmillan, 2012), 19.

[21] Ada Colau and Adrià Alemany, *¡Sí se puede!* (Barcelona: Ediciones Destino, 2013).

belonging"[22]. This space offered by social movements is decisive for improving the quality of life of the affected people. In the specific case of the PAH, for those who are facing eviction, it is essential to generate new stories about the mortgage processes that redistribute responsibilities and recognize bad banking practices. That the PAH has transformed the social reality of tens of thousands of families is an undoubted fact, but not only that. It has transformed, and continues to do so, the collective imagination that criminalized the evicted, has introduced notions such as abusive clauses or legitimate recovery, making familiar a reality that seemed to always be resolved in the private sphere. Experience confirms that when this personal reality has been opened to the public, it has been proven that it was a problem that responded to a perverse logic on which housing has been managed.

In this way, families affected by the 2008 economic crisis, with one or more of their members unemployed, managed to convey to public opinion that their situation was more complex than a sum of bullets decisions. As Colau writes: "Families feel guilty of the situation they are going through and attribute it to personal failure. Surely, the society in which we live, which values what we are for what we have, and tells us that we have what we deserve, has a lot to do with it"[23].

Conclusions

In the case of unemployed people, it is crucial to modify the individualistic narratives that lead to their exclusion. Facing the economic crises and the unemployment situation from the collective and not as individual problems becomes a moral imperative to leave no one behind. For all this, a new sociology of work is necessary to address the problems facing our societies. Given that "only through the labor mechanism can the person obtain the means of employment to meet their needs, and these means are not always insured, because productive needs do not always require it, becoming poor and staying out is possible"[24]. The precariousness of employment and, finally, unemployment, is one of the most serious problems that our societies face. And if we must be clear about something to tackle this

[22] Ada Colau and Adrià Alemany, *¡Sí se puede!* (Barcelona: Ediciones Destino, 2013), 48.
[23] Ada Colau and Adrià Alemany, *Vidas Hipotecadas. De la Burbuja Inmobiliaria al Derecho a la Vivienda.* (Barcelona: Cuadrilátero de libros, 2012), 94.
[24] Jorge Moruno, *La fábrica del emprendedor. Trabajo y política en la empresa-mundo.* (Madrid: Akal, 2015), 121.

problem, it is that a collective problem requires collective solutions, but also analysis from a collective point of view. We cannot expect solutions that have a collective impact if the analysis from which they start is that the unemployment problem is a strictly individual issue. Narratives about failure must emerge from the solipsism to which they are reduced by their eagerness to approach problems from an individualistic perspective.

In this way, the stigma of unemployed people can be eliminated and solutions to something that is an economic problem can be sought. We do not know what the solution is, but what does seem to be clear is that the stigmatization of the unemployed population and the precariousness of working conditions are events that occur at the same time. Therefore, instead of giving responsibility solely and exclusively to the unemployed person, we must think about the conditions that the labor market offers, its constant precariousness and the growth of inequality.

Bibliography

A. Jacobs, Jerry and Gerson, Kathleen. *The Time Divide. Work, Family, and Gender Inequality*. Cambridge: Harvard University Press, 2004.

Agamben, Giorgio. *Homo sacer. Sovereign power and bare life*. Stanford: Stanford University Press, 1998.

Bagguley, Paul. *From Protest to Acquiescence? Political Movements of the Unemployed*. London: Macmillan Education, 1991.

Broman, Clifford, Hamilton, V. Lee and Hoffman, William S. *Stress and Distress among the Unemployed. Hard Times and Vulnerable People.* New York: Springer Science+Business Media, 2001.

Colau, Ada and Alemany, Adrià, *¡Sí se puede!* Barcelona: Ediciones Destino, 2013.

Colau, Ada and Alemany, Adrià. *Vidas Hipotecadas. De la Burbuja Inmobiliaria al Derecho a la Vivienda*. Barcelona: Cuadrilátero de libros, 2012.

Didier Chabanet, Didier and Faniel, Jean, ed., *The Mobilization of the Unemployed in Europe. From Acquiescence to Protest?* New York: Macmillan, 2012.

Herrero, Yayo, Cembranos, Fernando and Pascual, Marta. *Cambiar las gafas para mirar el mundo. Una nueva cultura de la sostenibilidad.* Madrid: Libros en Acción, 2011.

Honnet, Axel. *La lucha por el reconocimiento*. Barcelona: Mondadori, 1997.

Kossek, Ellen Ernst and Lambert, Susan J., ed., *Work and life Integration. Organizational, Cultural and Individual Perspectives*. New Jersey: Lawrence Erlbaum Associates, 2005.

Moruno, Jorge. *La fábrica del emprendedor. Trabajo y política en la empresa-mundo*. Madrid: Akal, 2015.

PART III.

CONCERNS FROM THE PANDEMIC

Migration and Subjectivity: Conditions of Existence and the Right to Desire

Somyabrata Chowdhury

Introduction: Who is the subject of migration?

Let us start with a seemingly trivial question: Who is the subject of migration? At first glance the question seems trivial because the answer is apparently contained in the question itself: The subject of migration is the migrant. The migrant is understood as someone who, under specific circumstances, is either unintentionally dislocated from one spatial or territorial site to another or she, out of her will and desire, moves from one place to another on a relatively stable or even permanent basis.

This above description is more or less the common understanding and image of migration. In so far as the question of the subject of migration is concerned, it is analysed to be the form or agent which bears the objective description of the spatial movement on its particular "body". In this sense the migrant is fundamentally the bearer of her *body* which moves through a certain distance and between sites to condense within itself the very experience of this movement. So the common image of the migrant as the self-evident subject of migration already demands a certain subjective depth — the depth of a migratory experience.

While the empirical and descriptive part of the ordinary definition of the migrant clearly requires the agency and the form of the migrant's body to mark the physical reality of the migratory movement, the question of migratory experience requires a deeper analysis of the migrant's "consciousness" which would be the reflective space that grants the physical movement of migration an existential meaning. In other words, even at the level of a spatial understanding of migration, it is not enough to simply represent the "object" of this movement — that is the displacement from one place or site to another. The objective description of migration only becomes concretely meaningful when the migratory subject begins to *exist*.

The condition for such an existential meaning of the experience of migration can only be constituted when the migrant not only physically migrates under specific circumstances but also produces a kind of self-relation or even a subjective "knowledge" of this physical fact marked on and borne by the body of the migrant. So within the project of a more or less empirical definition of migration, we are already confronted with a series of conceptual tasks: First, we need to analyse the *historical* circumstances under which the physical movement of the migration takes place. Secondly, we must grasp the structural amplitude or range that supports the physical movement in relation to the circumstances in which they take place. That is to say we need to investigate whether the historical circumstances in which a particular set of migratory movement takes place are *repeated* over a longer period of time. Because if they are then that would mean the immediate migratory circumstance is actually both supported and impelled by a more durable structural logic. The most obvious example of this would be the development of the global circuits of capitalism in at least the last hundred years that have led to both emergent patterns of the migration of labour and accelerated intensity of the very *idea* of migration as inseparable from a globalised capitalist world.

The first two tasks lead to the third and more intractable one of finding out the modes of being of the migrant's existence both in its bodily life and in its reflective consciousness. While the migrant is subject to the particular experience of a physical displacement which is itself determined by certain set of structural conditions, in what forms of thought does the migrant capture her own particular experience and the historical inheritance of structures over which she has very little control? When we speak here of "forms of thought", we must give this phrase as much elasticity as possible: Forms of thought can mean as much intellectual or conceptual knowledge as clusters of subjective feelings or affects implicitly or explicitly referring to modes of *desire*. Does the migrant consent to the larger logic of history that produces her migratory experience? Or even more directly and obscurely, what does the migrant *want*?

Having laid out the minimal ground for the common image of the migrant as the natural subject of migration though at every moment problematizing this naturalness, we would also like to suggest an emphatically different meaning of this subject. Suppose one were to imagine that having gone through the historical and physical experience of migration the so called migratory subject that is the migrant *refuses* this experience...what form of subjectivity would correspond to this refusal? We might quickly put forward the hypothesis that this refusal marks the threshold of a political possibility.

This possibility can only arise from a passionate and difficult traversal of the historical and structural conditions of migrant's existence but it arises also as a certain intellectual refusal of the very conceptual terms of migration commonly used to describe the experience of migration. In other words, between the structural side of history that is representable through a set of stable logical positions and the political side that testifies to a certain individual or collective breaking out from this structure, there lies the elusive but real instance of history. Within the historical instance forms of existence suspend their regular trajectories and itineraries to enforce a new challenge of thought in relation to the given ground of experience as well as its "subject" hitherto considered self-evident and natural.

In what is to follow we will try to illustrate both these sides that confront us when the experience and question of migration arises. We will do this in a somewhat uneven and episodic way. By the time we are ready to conclude this study, we will not at all prescribe a political "solution" to the problem of migration but we hope to be a little closer to the "real of history" that makes it possible to both de-familiarise ourselves to the so called natural conditions of migration and also allows us to think of the minimal existential counter-conditions for a politics released from the *dogma or fetish of migration* imposed by capitalism today.

An Epidemic Mirror to Migrant Existence: Proletarianization without a Proletariat

The recent "epidemic situation" triggered by the spread of the coronavirus (Covid-19) infection has, among other things, exposed both the reality and the dogma of migration on a global scale[1]. In India we have seen this scenario unfold with horrifying vividity. In the last many months, the global exposure of migration as an intrinsic part of economic life obviously possesses a kind of epidemiological parallel with the virus' spread (though the actual migration since the announcement of the pandemic and the lockdown has been a *reverse migration*). This can almost be formulated as a parallel between our economic and biological lives even though the practical dilemma of the present is understood to be one involving a trade-off between "lives" and "livelihoods".

---

[1] Badiou, Alain, "On the Epidemic Situation", 23 March 2020, versobooks.com, https://www.versobooks.com/blogs/4608-on-the-epidemic-situation

Alain Badiou, in his brief intervention early on during the onset of the pandemic, pointed out that while the actual biological threshold of the deadly infection can be located within a specific geographical and cultural contexts — the animal markets of Wuhan in China being a possible context — the real epidemic situation arises when the biological threat circulates and spreads with accelerated intensity globally through pre-existent economic circuits. By this logic the spread of the virus already possesses a pre-given itinerary in the migratory roots which enable capitalism to function as a global market society.

Of course this parallel or articulation between the epidemic and migratory intensity of our present day world does not result in a simple coexistence or even complicity between these two forces. As we all know in our experience of living through the spring of 2020 in its passage to a stunned summer, the combination of biological infection and the economic conditions of migration has not resulted in either simple coexistence or intimate complicities. In fact the combination has produced violent short circuits and exposed stark contradictions in specific societies with global consequences. We will not repeat the great many lacerated descriptions of these phenomena that one has read or seen across the different media. But one peculiar commonality with a paradoxical effect of these accounts is that while they depict the undeniable material reality of migration as an empirical social phenomenon, they also impose the *dogma* of migrant existence as the historical and structural bedrock of contemporary society.

This paradox is also evident in the practical and ethical initiatives taken by several conscientious individuals and groups when they responded with great alacrity to the migrant crisis unfolding after the announcement of the nationwide (and worldwide but we are limiting our gaze to India at this point) lockdown in March 2020. The admirable interventions made at the different nodes of the crisis were nothing less than acts of pulling people back from the brink of individual and collective disasters. These nodes concentrated within themselves the *truth* of migrant existence that the precarity of earning one's livelihood on an unstable daily basis could anytime be exposed to its hidden side where the migrant was unable to reproduce even her minimal biological life. "Street scenes" after the lockdown became terrible manifestations of this truth. So much of the ethical initiative was prompted by accounts, images and testimonies coming from these paradoxical scenes where during a nationwide lockdown to protect our biological lives, a population on the brink of losing the economic support to their physical existence, were thronging the street in desperation. Apart from the governmental question as to whether this paradoxical short circuit could have been anticipated and avoided, it also highlighted the *class-contradiction* that structured the nodal truth of the situation.

This contradiction can be seen from within the example cited above that does not involve the open antagonism of the rich settled classes and the poor precarious ones. Rather we see those from the settled part of the society with a certain ethical sensitivity to human suffering come out to help in indispensable ways a whole part of the people who were suddenly confronted with the cruellest side of the truth of their existence. But even as this ethical and practical joining of hands took place, a discourse was articulated that consolidated the very contradictory nodal structure leading up to this violent paradox. The discourse roughly said that migrants were "essential" to the settled existence of the more "fortunate" parts of society who were, more or less able to carry on undisturbed despite the lockdown. So the subjective impulse towards salutary ethical actions actually came from *justifying* the inegalitarian class structure of society. After all the moment it is said that an element or part of the system is essential to the survival or welfare of the other parts, a logic of objective necessity that justifies the system as it is, has already been launched. The peculiar if non-antagonistic contradiction of this justificatory discourse is that it leads to the feeling of unhappiness or non-reconciliation among those very people who make this enunciation. Such subjective vacillations between justification and non-reconciliation becomes that much more intense when the conscientious members of the settled classes *see* the precarious migrant population walking, falling, dying on the streets.

This subjective pathos of the ethical social agents is a kind of symptom expressing the class-contradiction of society while also denying it. After all it takes but a basic analytical move to grasp the *real* of today's moment, today's history as it were, that the migrant population is lethally stranded on the streets because in the hidden depths of the structure it is denuded of its productive capacity in the current circumstances. That is why when one keeps lamenting the physical miseries of the "migrant", one is failing to notice that the economic system which depends on the actual "services" of migrant labour does not structurally accord this type of labour a truly productive status or capacity. That is why we, even at our most compassionate dispositions, do not notice that the present crisis of the so called migrant population is not essentially one of spatial or territorial dislocation. It is one of *proletarianization* — and proletarianization *wherever they are*. If "proletarianization" means the denudation not just of our economic means of livelihoods but of our very capacity of productive work then the migrant was always on the brink of proletarianization. Marx was himself ambiguous about the valuation of what he called "services" in comparison with the values of productive labour[2]. What the present epidemic situation has exposed is that the part of the migrant population which is predominantly engaged not in "labour" but in "service" lives at incommensurable distance from the other part which could be as much "migrant" but structurally belongs to the classes which enjoy both an organised productive status as well as sedentary territorial one.

This is the core of the epidemic mirror that shows migrant existence in its contradictory truth. The ones who express solidarity for the proletarianized migrant in the name of the slogan "we are migrants too!" actually express their complete incommensurability with the proletariat reality of those they subjectively would like to join with. This is not an ethical incommensurability: it is a *political* one. But what is even more disabling today is that the entire valorisation of the vocabulary of migration to describe our epidemic situation forecloses the invention of a language which speaks in the name of a *subject of politics*. The immediate reason for this lack is that the process of contemporary proletarianization has not visibly resulted in any new political subject we could call the "proletariat".

However at the end of this section we must launch a double inquiry about vocabulary itself. In the epidemic conjuncture or situation, we are evidently inundated by the effects of the discourse of migration and correspondingly poor of a political idiom of the proletariat. Now it is interesting to note that the very basis for speaking of migratory movement originally comes not from human history but from animal behaviour. For example, birds are known to migrate over long distances following seasonal patterns[3]. These

---

[2] Marx in his 1857-58 notebook *Grundrisse* discusses the peculiar deadlock between the piano player and piano maker to the extent that while to manufacture a piano would be meaningless without the existence of the piano player in the system of capitalist exchange of values determined by labour time only the piano maker's labour can be translated into primary "value" and the "service" provided by the piano player always remains subordinated to this primary value form. We'll come back to the virtuosic model of services in global capitalism later in the essay.

[3] This point has been brought out in Badiou's little elegant text *Migrants and Militants*. We will refer to this text, more than once. Badiou, Alain, *Migrants and Militants*, trans. Joseph Litvak (Cambridge, Polity, 2020)

Also see for a latest law passed in Lebanon to protect seasonal migrating birds of prey against the hitherto regular hunting practice of shooting them down and brutally violating the *rhythms* of migration.
https://www.nytimes.com/2020/01/06/science/lebanon-birds-hunting-conservation.html

patterns have a rhythmic manifestation rather than a historical one. It is only with human beings that in their social behaviour they follow conjunctural and inconsistent trajectories of movements and dislocations. And so it is only with human beings that we associate the double features of inevitable historical condition — the condition of capitalism inevitably requiring global migration — and pathetic inconsistency of subjective destiny — the individual migrant though dislocated to an alien place of work always pulled back to her archaic roots.

Just like we can bracket the language of migration to expose its inner equivocations we could probably do the same with the inherited political vocabulary of the proletariat. Though it will not be possible to develop this second inquiry in any detail here, the very question of the proletariat can be posed along the division and hierarchy between the productive labour and service as it comes down to us from Marx's vocabulary. It is not uncommon to hear of a bifurcation of the political subject between the classical proletariat and the contemporary precariat to express the migrant exception as an irreducible condition of neoliberal global capitalism[4]. But we have already seen that the "migrant exception" can actually function as a smokescreen to hide the more precise nature of class-contradiction within migration itself. To that extent no mere extension of the proletariat to the precariat can satisfy our political "desire". And yet that desire cannot simply collapse back into the embrace of the proletariat. This is the extraordinary challenge that the epidemic situation throws up for the thought of any politics today. To respond to this challenge let us consult some associated vocabularies.

Capitalist Vocabularies: Migration and Enterprise

While this imagery has been around for a long time in the history of modern economics, it is only after the early 1990s with the liberalisation of the Indian economy that we heard policymakers and ministers openly speak of promoting "animal spirits" among entrepreneurs in the country[5]. What does "animal spirit" connote in the context of modern enterprise. For one thing it

[4] The invention of this new name resonant with but departing from the classical political name proletariat, can be seen in Guy standing's works.

[5] For example Manmohan Singh during his tenure as the Prime Minister in a speech made in 2012 asked for the revival of animal spirit in the country's economy see. https://economictimes.indiatimes.com/news/economy/finance/prime-minister-manmohan-singh-calls-for-revival-of-animal-spirit-in-economy/articleshow/14435229.cms

seems to incite a kind of predatory *risk taking* that enables innovative investments with a promise of unexpected returns, which in turn becomes an inducement for more enterprise and more activation of these very spirits. In another way, animal spirits points us in the direction of extraordinary physical stamina which makes it possible for living entities to endure great adversity and yet in their face, reach unknown territorial frontiers. Finally the vocabulary of "animal spirits" connotes a sphere of intrinsic disposition or instinct that expresses itself in seasonal or ecological rhythms to produce new habitats and forms of life.

The sum and substance of these possible associations of "animal spirits" in the sphere of economic activity or enterprise is that while the latter is apparently a historical structure and discourse of both government policy and economic theory simultaneously appears to us as the pure product of *nature* hitherto suppressed by the prehistory of capitalism. The very fundamental assumptions of neoclassical economic theory consisting of the free market for all commodity exchange including the commodity called labour and the freedom of individual will to enterprise and innovation ideologically invoke a general climate of rationality and free will that vindicate the so called natural aptitude of human beings to produce a world of work and leisure, labour and profit.

Marx's critical interventions in the history of economic knowledge as ideology — that is Marx's critique of political economy— inaugurally exposed the constitutive contradiction between the freedom of the wage worker to sell her labour power "anywhere" and the freedom of capitalising "anything" in the modern historical epoch. The wage worker's freedom was only realisable in concrete conditions of social and geographical restrictions while the freedom of capital to travel across spaces was paradigmatically encoded in the most malleable and unrestricted "migrant" of all commodities that is *money*. In Marx's section on commodity fetishism in Capital the paradigmatic example of money can be seen as a condensed mixture of total deterritorialized movement or migrancy and a fixed mystical power[6]. The contradiction comes out quite sharply in almost hostile antagonistic terms when we historically witness the reality of the wage worker purged perpetually on the edge of poverty and immiseration while the image of the entrepreneur, even when traversed by the qualities of struggle and resistance does not cease to evoke the horizon of wealth and success.

---

[6] Marx, Karl. *Capital A critique of political economy Volume 1*, trans. Ben Fowkes (London, Penguin, 1990) pp. 163-177

This subjective contrast, in the narratives of nineteenth century political economy always accompanied by the critical shadow of Marx, was structurally anchored in the following dialectical project: in Marx's Grundrisse, his notebooks preceding the writing of Capital, it is proposed that Capital on the one hand aims for the minimisation of labour-time and the optimisation of disposable time to measure the progress of society and the social individual. At the same time, Capital finds labour time to be the source and measure of all wealth. This internal contradiction within the capitalist project can also be expressed as the fundamental division between the constitution of social knowledge of what Marx calls “general intellect” in society which encompasses the productive and intellectual potentially of *everyone*, and the fixation of labour as a kind of automatic extension of nature into the specific activity of producing economic value which is without any intellectuality or capacity for knowledge[7]. Within the classical justification of the capitalist appropriation of what could be called the generic "life process" of humanity it is claimed that the entrepreneurial side of this process contain the capacity for knowledge and innovation while labour is more “metabolical” in character with the qualification that it is an extension of the natural metabolic process to a kind of social metabolism. So even while both labour and enterprise are part of social individuality it is only the latter that almost entirely monopolises the intellectual component of this individuality and the former merely marks the precarious though necessary transition from nature to society.

The concrete historical realisation of this ideological operation insinuated by Capital in nineteenth century to the first half of the twentieth (the age of late capitalism) takes place through the forms of labour that are precariously balanced on the dividing line between imminent penury under minimal condition of its social reproduction and the dogmatic form of the free market. In the nineteenth century in Europe the movement of labouring individuals is caught between social vagabondage (symmetrical to exposure of an animal to a predatory environment) and the local compulsions of participating in the minimally viable market for labour[8]. So while one does see a certain provincial dislocation among labour within the European territories under the pressure of both escaping unbearable poverty in a given locality and the need to find work at the least distance from that original

[7] Marx, Karl. *Grundrisse: Foundations of the Critique of Political Economy*, trans. Martin Nicolous. (New York, Penguin, 1993) p. 700

[8] ibid. also see. Castel, Robert, *From Manual Workers to Wage Laborers: Transformation of the Social Question*. trans. Robert Boyd (London, Routledge, 2017)

reference point to the later displacement, this restricted circumstantial movement can in no way be attributed to any intrinsic migratory or entrepreneurial “spirit” or “instinct”.

In interesting contrast the political economy instituted in this period credits enterprise in all its intellectual inventiveness and risk taking chutzpah, with a migratory *nature*. The highest abstraction into which this nature is metamorphosed is of course capital itself since the primary quality of the latter is its endless exchangeability and mutability. In the later part of the twentieth century when we think of global capitalism in the neoliberal age we actually see the concrete realisation of this capitalist abstraction in the form of production that entails both long supply chain across the territories of the world and frequent turnover of a migrant labouring population working in this supply chain but without any social or intellectual localisation. In this globalised version of capitalism the entire circuit from production to consumption to recirculation, is unthinkable without a properly expropriated migrant population now entirely denationalised and deprovincialized. The other term of the earlier dialectic both historical and ideological which is enterprise now *subsumes* the labouring necessity that was thought to join natural with social metabolism in the nineteenth century political economy. So the subjective figure of the entrepreneur is not anymore only the intellectual adventurer and consequently profitmaker in capitalism (moving into an imagination of the risk taking character who disrupts and creatively destroys all prehistories of latest capitalist movement[9]) contrasted to the natural source of *measurable* wealth that is labour time; the entrepreneur now adopts a strategy of delegating the migratory virtue (or spirit) to the lowest and most minor part of the global assembly line of production. So, peculiarly, the migrant worker employed in the most precarious and non organised economic circumstances— not protected by either contract or unions— is thought to be, at least potentially an *entrepreneur of oneself*[10]. So exactly when the so-called precariat covers the surface of the world a new intellectual subjectivity is imputed to this global (non) class (non) organisation. This extraordinary transformation of both the objective conditions and subjective figure of modern capitalism

[9] For this influential coinage “creative destruction” as the secret of profits earned by capitalist enterprise. see Shumpeter, Joseph. *Capitalism, Socialism and Democracy*. (New York, Harper Perennial Modern, 2008)

[10] For this idea drawn from the Chicago school and Gary Becker’s work in economics and its political function see Foucault, Michel *The Birth of Biopolitics: Lectures at the Collège de France, 1978--1979* (New York, Palgrave Macmillan, 2008) pp 220

begs the question that what kind of intellectuality (or mode of the general intellect) can be attributed to a real people and population who live and work in the most deterritorialized circumstances almost outside the purview of any law or right? The answer that neoliberal capitalism itself provides to this question is that all capitalism today is intellectual capitalism and all its workers, however humble or precarious, are intellectuals. And the ideological syllogism which claims to demonstrate this result is based on the premise that intellectuality is the generic human capacity to *serve.* Not serve anymore in the earlier feudal sense of serving on the lord's land and manor which still entails specific services for a particular master but serve in the sense of a generalised problem "solver" (like a handyman who is called in to deal with a range of problem in a neighborhood with no particular specialisation) or even a virtuoso (in the sense of a performer who is solicited for her ability to perform a range of "items" whether this consists of singing, dancing, comic improvisations etc without the legitimation of being a professional in any art form). So the entrepreneur of oneself is a generic migrant who is open to moving between multiple tasks or problems however improvised or contingent, but at every moment testifying to this very generalised intellectuality of all human beings. By these parameters the meaning of intellectuality is not at all the capacity for specialised knowledge but the openness of one's own *existence* to serve the other's *desire.* The syllogism is completed when this extraction of a new intellectual labour ready to improvise and serve according to the locus of society's "desire" identifies as well as subjectifies itself as an *essential migrant* who has no intrinsic place in any social structure and is meant to move from place to place, or from "service to service" in any structure including the most restrictive ones of society.

Diagnostic vocabularies: the global shudrafication and feminisation of capitalism

Among the several translations of the old Hindu law book *Manusmriti*, Wendy Doniger's version translates a key word featuring in the text's enunciation of the law of the shudra with a specific impact. *Manusmriti* ordains that the shudra must serve the higher *varnas* (brahmins, kshatriyas, vaishyas) and do so "without resentment". Wendy Doniger's translation of the key Sanskrit word *anusuya* as applied to the task of the shudra is "serving these (other) classes without resentment". [11] Other translations have conveyed the same basic meaning but with a more moderate effect –

[11] Donigner, Wendy. *The Laws of Manu.* (London, Penguin, 2000) p 54

for instance, "service without complaining" instead of the far more insistent injunction against the shudra's right to "resentment". No doubt, resentment has a far denser connotation than the more banal image of complaint and the everyday negotiation with that relatively superficial emotion. One could go to the extent of saying that resentment conceals in itself a suppressed reactive act which could as much be a latent revolt against whatever one is resentful of. Or like in the case of Nietzsche's invocation of *ressentiment* there could be deeper sedimentation of not just individual reaction but also a collective intensity building up over generations.[12]

But one can simply infer two analytical possibilities while hearing the enunciation of *Manusmriti* regarding the shudra's duty: the first one is that the shudra, unlike the other varnas, is not meant to perform any *specific* tasks. That is, unlike the brahmin's right to the obligation of performing sacrifices and pursuing knowledge, the kshatriya's ordained capacity for martial glory and the vaishya's civic prescription, the shudra is asked to serve not in this way or that but purely and as a matter of her life's sole rationality. In other words, the shudra is instructed by the text to be perpetually ready to alienate her time for serving the privileged varnas – which could be broadly and interchangeably translated as "class" or "caste" for our present purposes – and the particular content which fills up that time in the shape of her labour or work is a matter of relative indifference. So for one thing the concept of service in this framework appears to be both more capacious and emptier so as to subsume specific types of labour and work. Also the act of addressing the shudra as a subject of customary law does not qualify her as a subject any particular occupational structures or skills. While in the actual operation of a society and economy the shudra could be performing a whole range of tasks demanding several degrees of skills – from very low ones to high-skilled occupations – the essential subjectifying attribute is not either the skill or the faculty of cultivating specific forms of labour but her entire *existence*. So when one infers from the *Manusmriti* that the shudra is meant to alienate her time perpetually and generically irrespective of the specific mode of this alienation then this turns out to be a legal expropriation of the shudra's existential being. In so far as existence is nothing but the temporal unfolding of the subject's relation to herself within the forms of her historical life. In B.R. Ambedkar's *Annihilation of Caste* we learn of the untouchable Balai caste in central India whose members, both men and women are expected to perform a whole range of

[12] For an extraordinary interpretation of ressentiment, slave morality and will to power see. Deleuze, Gilles *Nietzsche and Philosophy.* trans. Hugh Tomlison. (New York, Bloomsbury, 2018)

tasks, each involving a specific discipline and disposition – from singing in marriages, carrying letters of upper caste correspondents to their addressee in distant villages to midwifery. But again the common structural form uniting this multiplicity is the perpetual availability of the time of the untouchable caste to be disposed of in the service of the privileged ones.[13]

The other analytical point of interest we can read into the law of the shudra is that while it is ordained that the latter must serve without resentment (or in a milder form, without complaint) it is hardly apparent that what is the shudra *actually* expected to feel in performing her services. So while it might seem obvious that the *Manusmriti* somehow wants to appropriate the shudra's formal participation if not consent in relation to the *varna* structure of society, it still remains obscure that what *is* the shudra's subjective status compared with the brahmins, kshatriyas and the vaishyas. In each of the upper castes there is not just a structure of occupational obligation but there also exists a kind of subjective incentive – the brahmin's incentive towards purification, the kshatriya's towards glorification, the vaishya's towards civic virtue… – but with the shudra we end up at an impasse, a point of neutralisation when we hear that that latter is meant to serve without resentment but we have no access to the real structure of her subjectivity, the *real of her desire*.

Now Manusmriti which is the most brutal intellectual rationalisation of an inegalitarian caste society can not be expected to grant the shudra-subject any kind of intellectuality or capacity for knowledge. It is this brutal rationality that Gopal Guru so pithily expressed as the division between the *theoretical brahmin* and *empirical shudra*.[14] But for our purposes it is a matter of some interest that the very existential neutralisation of the shudra to a kind of zero-degree serviceability actually becomes the model of the "knowledge worker" in the neo-liberal regime of capitalism in a globalised world. This paradox is not merely a coincidence or a curiosity which an ancient Indian text provides in relation to the devious contemporary logic of expropriation and exploitation; it is at the heart of the inversion of the meaning of intellectuality as it is deployed by the present order of capital. In so far as every one is expected to not merely contribute her labour time in production but also her entire *existence* to the very cause of this

[13] Ambedkar, B.R., "Annihilation of Caste", *BAWS 1* (Edited by Vasant Moon, Bombay: Education Department, Government of Maharashtra, 1979), pp 39

[14] Guru, Gopal. How Egalitarian Are the Social Sciences in India? economic and Political Weekly, Dec. 14-20, 2002, Vol. 37, No. 50 (Dec. 14-20, 2002), pp. 5003-5009

production – which is "enterprise" – everyone is a potential entrepreneur today. And in so far as the classical theory of enterprise in the history of economics grants the entrepreneur the cognitive power, if not genius to force new economic and social forms of life into the world, the contemporary worker seems to be included in this entrepreneurial intelligence. So it is not surprising to hear both forms of praise and criticism: today the worker is praised for actually being able to make her way through employment, career improvement and material success as someone who cuts herself off from erstwhile organisations of workers including labour unions to embrace the precarity of flexible work as a way to finally reach the stage of having become an "entrepreneur of oneself". And the same worker is criticised for not mobilising sufficient entrepreneurial *will* to employ her own self when she complains of the state of the economy and the scourge of unemployment. Within these paradoxical conditions the entrepreneurial intellectual ideology reaches a particular point of extreme convolution when the new "knowledge worker" is imagined and addressed as a pure function of intellectual serviceability. Thus the worker sitting at a desk working on a computer does not serve a specific productive purpose whether that purpose be a certain material product of consumption or the manufacture of capital goods. So this worker also does not experience the specific mode of alienation that Marx diagnosed as the miasma of industrial capitalism enforced by the negative relationship between the producer of values and the body into which these values were crystallised. Unlike the Fordist worker whose alienation is so well imagined in the very degraded glitter of the manufactured body (the shining body of the car, for instance) the knowledge worker at the computer is not alienated. She is *neutralised*. And in so far as the logic of enterprise reaches this extreme convoluted stage the very neutral material that expropriates and appropriates becomes a purely intellectual material rather than a physical or natural one. But this neutral intellectualisation of labour precisely because of the lack of any specific intellectual or productive content, can only be generically flexible or improvised. This virtuosic appearance of labour as a pure formal movement of the "general intellect" as it were across the board from the highest corporate manager to the most menial worker, is underpinned by an ideology of intrinsic or essential migrancy of the intellect.

This is not the free appearance of general intellectuality in the world in the way some Italian autonomist thinkers imagined it to be, bringing together

Marx and Hannah Arendt in a heady cocktail.[15] This so-called intellectual function is a pure function of existential neutralisation that does not highlight the specific alienation of particular types of labour but makes every labouring activity into a delegated network of the intrinsic migrancy which is the primary ideology or fetish secreted by contemporary capitalism. In effect what happens is of course quite stark and ignominious: if in the earlier period of capitalism we started out with the internal contradiction between something like the theoretical migrant (enterprise) and the empirical migrant (labour) in the present regime we witness the extreme gradation and granulation of the theoretical fetish of migration into the least labouring bodies in the global economy. So even when the empirical migrant of history works today at a site far from her home as part of the global supply chain she does not do it in her capacity as either a non-skilled, semi-skilled or skilled worker. She could very well fall into these categories but essentially the migrant worker only and entirely "serves" as a neutral zero-degree agency of that very capacity to serve. It is unforgivably ignominious that this work without qualities (including the quality of alienation) and service without resentment bear the names of intellect and knowledge.

A quick allusion can be made to another old Indian text, indirectly though, in order to render more concrete this neutral, zero-degree and migratory logic of capitalism. In Ambedkar's book *The Shudras,* the author refers to *Narada Smriti* in which one of the analogies for the shudra within the structure of the four varnas is with the "wife"[16]. Ambedkar refers to a long

---

[15] Virno, Paulo, "Virtuosity and Revolution: The political Theory of Exodus", *Radical Thought in Italy: A Potential Politics*, eds. Paolo Virno and Michael Hardt (Minnesota, University of Minnesota Press, 1996) The main difficulty with the autonomist argument represented with superb lucidity in Virno's article is that the historical stage at which the capitalist mode of production invest the very ontological essence of human cooperation and the general intellect for profit becomes the automatic opening up of a horizon of free collective action that is both communistic and Arendtian. However the real challenge is to break this automatism of history such that the question of political organisation and historical change can be thought at a different level from the one at which the automatism and its contradictory character present themselves.

[16] Ambedkar, B.R., The Shudras, *BAWS 7* (Edited by Vasant Moon, Bombay: Education Department, Government of Maharashtra, 1979), p. 306. "It is clear that impure work was done by the slaves and that the impure work included scavenging. The question that arises is: Who were these slaves? Were they Aryans or non-Aryans? That slavery existed among the Aryans admits of no doubt. An Aryan could be a slave of an Aryan. No matter to what Varna an Aryan belonged he could be a

section from the old text alluding to this analogy or this measure of shudra slavery with the effect that the position of the wife in a patriarchal Hindu household becomes an objective mirror for the shudra's subjective figure. Both the wife and the shudra are commanded to serve not in this capacity or that but in the mode of being existentially available perpetually for service. One can extend this analogy to the image of the household in which the wife while being entirely restricted to the four walls of her husband's house has no essential *place* in that set up. Within her confines she must be ready to "migrate" at every instant to whichever other place she is called to serve at. It is this claustrophobic migratory subjectivity that the figure of the wife so graphically illustrates within the familial space of patriarchy. The analogy becomes that much more animated when we grasp that the wife is essentially a service provider to the economy of desires circulating in the households between the different positions and figures to the point that it becomes clear that she is not the husband's wife but the wife of the household itself in which the husband is a particular position/figure. Analogously the shudra is not merely the shudra *of* the master; she is the generic shudra of society itself. So when capitalism is re-imagined as the generalised delegation of theoretical migrancy to its most granulated and empirical migrants then we can also see this movement as the generalised shudrafication and feminisation of capitalism. This characterisation becomes even more vindicated when we consider the subjective world of the wife-shudra as one which remains obscure and insignificant for this convoluted but effective logic of expropriation and exploitation. If from the earlier allusion to the *Manusmriti* we had drawn out an ignominious intellectuality incarnated in the shudra, with the wife we reach the very core of that subjectivity where the feminine essence posited as much for the sexual serviceability as for the economic one blocks us from asking, let alone answering, the fundamental subjective question: What does the wife want? What is her *desire*?

---

slave. A Kshatriya could be a slave. So could a Vaishya. Even a Brahmin was not immune from the law of slavery. It is when Chaturvarna came to be recognized as a law of the land that a change was made in the system of slavery. What this change was can be seen from the following extract from the Narada Smriti: In the inverse order of the (four) castes slavery is not ordained, except where a man violated the duties peculiar to his caste. Slavery (in that respect) is analogous to the condition of a wife".

Conclusion: the real of work and the right to desire

We must be careful not to misunderstand that capitalism excludes desire. It is rather a question of the delegation and imputation of desire in such convoluted yet targeted ways that the very question can be fetishized instead of being allowed to search for its singular form in specific historical circumstances. In other words, the real of desire in articulation with the real of history must be mystified if not entirely blocked by the already available mystical fetishized form of the capitalist commodity. To this extent, everything is mystified and fetishized by capital – from the object of consumption to the subject of production. So it is not only that "things" carry mystical connotations that promise a gratification beyond ordinary sensuous use – the example of brands today is so self-evident that one needn't explain the point – but also the very constitution of human labour is endowed with a magical intelligence and virtuosity. It is as if the very biological fact of human life can directly serve capitalism in so far as this life is already fetishized as pure creativity and capitalizability. That all life is also subject to the contingency of historical existence both at a collective and individual level, is something this ideological circle would seek to control if not forbid.

However when something like the epidemic situation brought on by Covid-19 covering the whole world grips us with such ferocity as it has since at least March 2020 then the real of history does produce a "crisis" that can not be so easily mastered or controlled. Inevitably, certain contingent consequences follow the sheer magnitude of the contingent historical blow such as this one.

It is possible to note that some of these consequences seem to extract from us a reaction that goes in the polar opposite direction from the ideological reflexes of global neo-liberal capitalism. For example, with the explosion of the migrant crisis across the world but with particular reference to Indian conditions, there has been a widespread reaction to the breakdown of global assembly chains, demanding extremely localised and restricted control over economic resources and factors of production. This "anti-globalising" reaction also transforms the subjective attitude to capital in so far as the figure of the "consumer" today is being increasingly asked to adapt her cosmopolitan capacity for desire and gratification to a more autarchic and nationalised one. In India, the economic crisis coupled with the specific confrontation with China on the Himalayan frontiers has resulted in a kind of national-majoritarian insistence that among all our global inducements to desire we must particularly crush the Chinese one. This insistence apparently is hopeful that the actual banning of Chinese companies and softwares will result in an objective replacement of Chinese economic power with a local Indian one. But given that this hope is ill-founded to the extent that Chinese products are part of the same complex global assembly lines (more so because China is the leading global capitalist powers) these systems can not be simply substituted by so-called self-reliant locally delimited production processes. So given its objective impotence the anti-globalising move actually produces the subjective effect of a generalised prohibition of *desire as such*. The effect is mostly a moralising one fuelled by so-called nationalist aspirations but what it essentially does is to forge a purely negative image for the complex, nay, convoluted logic of global capitalism and its delegation of a logic of migratory entrepreneurial desire to the point of its paradoxical limits where the figure of the neutralised zero-degree global shudra/wife/service provider emerges[17]. The utter negative image of this is equally paradoxical because we see the figure of a self-contained and moralised economic agent appear whose neutralisation of desire is indistinguishable from the violent desire to curb all uncontrolled movement and migrancy, all unrestricted scenes of enterprise and innovation. But it can not be missed that this strong provincial reaction in the wake of a global medical crisis to the economic manifestation of this crisis is even in its violent negativity based on the same globalised economic regime. For this type of response the so-called real of history remains limited to a passage between the medical and the economic crisis even though no one will disagree that the greatest torture of living through this passage is borne by the real bodies of migrant workers.

But suppose the real of history is not saturated by either biological or economic life but is instead tied to the historicity of an existence though deeply implicated in biological survival and economic activity, is nevertheless thinkable as a locus of desire released from these very implications…Under

[17] This tendency has also been recently called the uberization of the economy. for a graphic if unnerving prophecy of what the uberized economy will look like post covid 19, see. https://timesofindia.indiatimes.com/blogs/toi-edit-page/why-we-must-uberise-faster-we-can-either-resist-it-and-wonder-where-jobs-vanished-or-tailor-it-to-our-needs/

According to this vision in the future we will tend to have only highly specialised figures of knowledge like scientists and creators (in areas like space research and software developments) and blue collar services like plumbers, electricians, domestic help, chauffeurs the middle level skilled occupation associated with middle class to which the lower rungs of society expire will become more and more redundant. In other words, only knowledge and service will exist, labour will disappear.

such a supposition the stakes are not confined to either promoting circuits of mystified or even fetishized desire through the vehicle of the capitalist commodity nor the reactive moralising suppression of even this degraded form of desire. But an emancipation of desire itself. In the concrete situation of the migrant's expropriation and proletarization this horizon of emancipation is thinkable in two ways: Firstly, a general ethical way can be proposed via which the migrant is re-inserted into the most liberal generous humanist form to which she is joined in a universal way but who is materially suffering relative to other human beings. In these circumstances, the way forward is that the comparatively privileged human subject tries to alleviate her co-human as a matter of universal ethics. Now this proposal leads to the peculiar result that even when the deprived migrant is accorded the most sincere generous assistance by others, it is still done under the principle of *necessity*. Which means the migrant is still thought of at the level of the natural proletarized body on the threshold of animal deprivation which must necessarily be corrected by the necessitarian act of providing food and other basic needs for survival. So the ethical humanist universalism is incapable of granting the migrant in crisis either the principle of freedom or the *right to desire*[18]. In this framework the real of history remains imprisoned within the iron cages of biological life and economic livelihood.

In conclusion, this invocation of a right to desire can only be thought politically. Which is to say that the thought of desire must be articulated at the very instant when the real of history is subjectively experienced and *refused* by those people whose existence is implicated within it. So the "migrants" neither buy into the great capitalist fable of all enterprise being a migratory adventure (given that in this fable all work is already entrepreneurial in essence) nor do they return to a universal womb of humanist co-belonging. But they make an interruptive demand at the very place where they are exposed in their most acute precarity. This demand must simply be the following: "recognise us by the highest measure of

[18] this failure is most penetratingly thought through by alain badiou in his recent text Migrants and Militants where he shows that even the most unconditional ethics of hospitality towards the migrants so eloquently represented in the philosophical position of Jacques Derrida, is unable to truly present the historical construction of migration as a *capitalist* dogma. Which means that any ethics of hospitality is in the danger of mirroring the very ideology of a global hospitalitization of the economy. as we have shown this ideological tendency is itself based on fetishizing the image of a generalised "service provider" who, in being ready to serve is hospitable to all unconditionally, and "without resentment"

universal humanity exactly *where we are* --- at our most precarious and threatened site of historical existence."

At another level, the migrating population demands that its capacity to think is not to be reduced to the value of commodities. The real of its work that is exchanged in the market in the form of commodities is not the calculation or fetishization of its monetised value but something incommensurable with that value – the very thing fetishized by the market as the intellectual capacity of universal enterprise. If there is such a capacity it must be borne anew from the very interruption that a historical crisis produces. But to be born anew means to refuse the terms that this crisis crushes us with. In this sense the subject which experiences the most acute effects of a migrant history in the face of a global medical crisis challenges us to think such a history in excess of and as an exception to the exceptional times that we so readily swear by today.

So the subject of migration is an irreducibly historical instance of the desire to be recognised *as* a subject of desire. That this instance of desire is historical is today indubitably demonstrated by the fact that it is taking place at a time when migration is exposed to nothing less than the law of death even beyond the mortal threat posed by the coronavirus.[19] So on the one hand it seems almost indecent to speak of desire at such a grave hour haunted by mortal danger of more than one kind. But this is also exactly the hour where it becomes imperative to declare the highest principle for the most threatened subject. According to me, this is the principle of "politics" in so far as all political declaration, apart from making specific historical demands attached to particular individuals and groups, is always also a universal declaration of the desire for *politics itself*. So I ask for a political form of thought that would do justice to the migrant existence beyond the purview of either biological life or economic livelihood.

---

[19] The law of death struck its most cruel blows on that very site of desire which the real of history provided the migrants with after a long wait: the *train.* In the special migrant trains that were run to take a sea of humanity back home after the first two months of the lockdown hundreds boarded this means of transportation and among them some never managed to reach their desired destination. As these trains finally arrived at the desired station after many hours of delay it was found that some of these "desiring" migrant subjects had fallen dead *where they were.* Bodies were found in train toilets and images of a migrant mother dead on a station platform with her child sitting next to her went viral on the social media. Clearly, life had given up on these people even while they had not given up on their desire.

Bibliography

Ambedkar, B.R., *Dr. Baba Saheb Ambedkar's Writings and Speeches 1* (Edited by Vasant Moon, Bombay: Education Department, Government of Maharashtra, 1979)

—. *Dr. Baba Saheb Ambedkar's Writings and Speeches 7* (Edited by Vasant Moon, Bombay: Education Department, Government of Maharashtra, 1979)

Badiou, Alain, *Migrants and Militants*, trans. Joseph Litvak (Cambridge, Polity, 2020)

Castel, Robert, *From Manual Workers to Wage Laborers: Transformation of the Social Question*. trans. Robert Boyd (London, Routledge, 2017)

Deleuze, Gilles *Nietzsche and Philosophy*. trans. Hugh Tomlison. (New ork, Bloomsbury, 2018)

Donigner, Wendy. *The Laws of Manu*. (London, Penguin, 2000)

Foucault, Michel *The Birth of Biopolitics: Lectures at the Collège de France, 1978--1979* (New York, Palgrave Macmillan, 2008)

Marx, Karl. *Grundrisse: Foundations of the Critique of Political Economy*, trans. Martin Nicolous. (New York, Penguin, 1993)

—. *Capital A critique of political economy Volume 1*, trans. Ben Fowkes (London, Penguin, 1990)

Shumpeter, Joseph. *Capitalism, Socialism and Democracy*. (New York, Harper Perennial Modern, 2008)

Virno, Paolo and Hardt, Michael ed. *Radical Thought in Italy: A Potential Politics*, (Minnesota, University of Minnesota Press, 1996)

ALIENATION:
NOW DELIVERED RIGHT TO YOUR HOME

JOSEPH AREL

In "The World Delivered to Your Home", the first section of part two of The Obsolescence of Human Beings, Günther Anders writes,

> *But since the king did not like the idea that his son, straying from the main roads, should be wandering all over the land to obtain his own opinions of the world, he presented him with a carriage and horses. "Now you do not need to walk", were his words. What they meant was: "You are no longer allowed to walk." The effective reality: "You can no longer walk."*

The world brought to one's home has the sound of luxury and the society that could make this possible might be considered "advanced" and one with a high standard of living. We should, however, be careful with such new ways of living like these since they may not be as innocent as they seem. To understand this parable better, we should, as Foucault urges, "cut off the king's head" when understanding power in political theory. This means that we should not think of power as emanating from or being vested in some singular figure like a king, president, or CEO. Thinking of power in this way is dangerous because, having found no king out to incapacitate us, we might conclude that there is nobody out to harm us and that we have nothing to worry about. This is the wrong way to think about power and the structure of one's reality. We should look, rather, to the "effective reality" of the changing conditions of our lives regardless of the intentions that there might be in the creation of these conditions. In so doing, we can uncover what new changes might mean for our lives and, like "you can no longer walk", hidden imperatives found in the structures of how we live.

This essay will begin by examining the relationship between alienated labor and the home, with particular reference to working from home (WFH). We will look at some of the complications involved with WFH and how they blur what little line actually exists between alienated labor and one's life away from work. Finally, we turn to loneliness, thinking through how this situation produces loneliness and what our own loneliness can tell us about how we relate to our situation.

1. What is the relationship between alienated labor and the home?

In *What's Wrong with the World*, G.K. Chesterton writes, "to the moderately poor the home is the only place of liberty." Chesterton aims to counter the idea that homelife and domesticity is dull and mundane while the world outside of the home is the real place for excitement and interesting living. He takes this to be a "rich man's opinion." Of the rich person, he writes "His wildest adventure will end in a restaurant, while the yokel's tamest adventure may end in a police court." Thus, the world looks more like a playground when many of the rules do not actually apply to you and you can buy your way out of trouble. If you are not in this position, you are subject to the laws, harassment, and simply the difficulty of existing in many spaces because so much of the commons has been commodified such that without money, it is difficult to be anywhere. Further, in most of the space that one can occupy, there are norms and rules to follow. At work, most of us have sold our labor and this time is not ours, nor are the materials for the production of our labor, the ways that we may wish to act, dress, and even what we might value is dissociated from ourselves during the workday. When we come home, however, this time and space is ours. In one's own home, one can live how one wishes, creatively, even strangely if one wishes: "it is the only place of anarchy," writes Chesterton. If we have exclusive rights to our own home, we can close the door and nobody can enter without an invitation. This makes it possible for us to relax, be ourselves, and recharge in a way that is difficult or impossible if our space is always subject to other's interests or invasions. On this account, the home is where freedom becomes most possible for most of us.

However, if we follow Marx's rejoinder, this view may seem to miss the larger picture of what is happening in the structure of our work-life relations. When discussing the alienated laborer, he writes, "He feels at home when he is not working, and when he is not working he does not feel at home." Marx is claiming that although our time away from work is where feeling at home is possible, the nature of alienated labor has made it difficult to actually feel at home. Upon returning home, the worker has used up essential parts of themself at work and is no longer able to truly access their humanity when off the clock. A typical workday will prioritize the time spent at work above all else. We wake and prepare ourselves for work, and then expend most of our energy during the workday. When we come home, we find ourselves with what's left of our mental, emotional, and physical energy. When these energies are primarily used up while at work, we feel free only in our "animal functions", as Marx writes. These do not represent us in our truest sense of ourselves, and so we are unable to feel at home when we arrive home.

Thus, though this space may be one's own in some legal sense, one's ability to enjoy it and live freely and creatively is shaped by the labor as the orienting force in one's life. Adorno looks at the relationship between work and our "free time" as well. The first thing he notes is that free time is a term "shackled to its opposite", that is, to work or time wherein we acknowledge that we are not free. Adorno writes, "Even where...people are at least subjectively convinced that they are acting of their own free will, this will itself is shaped by the very same forces which they are seeking to escape in their hours without work" (188). Anders titles a similar discussion "Chaplinitis," referring to Chaplin's *Modern Times*. In the film, we see Chaplin's character returning home from the factory "*no longer sufficiently free to free himself from those un-free movements* and anxiously watching his hands dance about like some strange species of animal." Work changes us and we bring this home with us. *Modern Times* shows this point embodied, that though the home may be retained as a potential site for free activity and fulfillment, this is compromised (perhaps entirely) by our working conditions. Tiring and alienating labor calls for something quite different in our "free time." We oppose this time to work and this implies that it should have none of the same qualities as work, like seriousness, thought, or production: "Hence," writes Adorno, "the inanity of many leisure activities" (190). These factors result in the "ruining of our mind" that Marx notes in the Economic and Philosophical Manuscripts. For Adorno, "The reason why people can actually do so little with their free time is that the truncation of their imagination deprives them of the faculty which made the state of freedom pleasurable in the first place" (193). The result, Adorno claims, is that "Free time is nothing more than a shadowy continuation of labor." Here, we find with ourselves and our relation to work some of the hidden imperatives of "free time" or "home life" in a situation of alienated labor: don't be serious, don't think.

Nevertheless, following Engles' analysis in "The Protestant Ethic and the Spirit of Capitalism" and as has been noted often since, we often retain a sense of the need to be productive when not at work, commodifying and analyzing our time in terms of productivity and "returns." This tendency of how our minds have been made to work seems to be another side of what we see in *Modern Times*. So as not to belabor the point, I will share one anecdote in attempt to illustrate how difficult it might be to overcome this. Recently, at an academic conference, one speaker spoke of resisting "late-capitalist productivity" and how one could get out of this mode of constant production. The tongue-in-cheek, though seemingly non-ironic, suggestion was an app where one could track one's time not being spent on production. This, of course, is a trap since it turns "unproductivity" into another mode of production. This "off the clock" time of resistance is in fact to be amassed, analyzed, and commodified, turning "free time" into just another mode of wage-labor type production.

Nevertheless, Adorno finds that the capacity for alienated labor to dominate and dull oneself is not total. Referring to some empirical studies related to investigating the culture industry (though with an incomplete analysis), he finds that people often remain critical and "realistic" with respect to some of the media that they consume. Though they became absorbed in its message at the time, afterwards many "showed themselves to be thoroughly realistic" (1960). The message they were receiving from the culture industry was consumed but did not dominate them altogether. Adorno concludes, "It is obvious that the integration of consciousness and free time has not yet completely succeeded" (196). I would also suggest the same for alienated labor and the home. I wholly agree with the Marxist insight that our time away from work should be understood in relation to work. Nevertheless, we do still retain the possibility and at times the reality of a measure of freedom made possible by having our own space, a place where we can shut the door and separate ourselves from work. This may change, however, in a world where working from home is increasingly the norm.

2. The time and space of work at home

Work from home presents the possibility of a more totalizing form of alienation. We often hear, from ourselves and others, that working from home solves a number of problems. We eliminate the commute as well as taxing and distracting conversations. Staying at home means that we can be more comfortable and see our family more.[1] We also may be "punching a clock" less and are allowed to work flexibly, with the ability to integrate work into our lives as we see fit. Many academics, writers, and others who work from home have known some of the problems with this and the popular press is repeating people's worries that they feel that they are "always on." Never

[1] We should note that women tend to be presented with more significant challenges when working from home.

fully on can also mean never truly off. When the ability to distinguish between time at work and time away from work becomes vague, the integration of work into time off work is made more complete. If our time at work is alienated, and if we begin to feel as though we are always at work, then all of our time is alienated.

Now, let's look at home in terms of space. One way to think about the space of freedom in the home is to think about space that is one's own. The ability to shut our doors and have some physical sense of a separation from work maintains the possibility of non-total alienation from work. Within the confines of what we take to be our "home", we often separate these spaces off into those that are ours and those that are for others or common areas for guests. These spaces might include, for example, the entryway, dining room, or kitchen. In distinction from these, we often maintain some space that is ours, where we can in some sense escape. Current WFH life tends to eliminate any possibility of such a space: zoom meetings are taken in bedrooms, work is done anywhere that one can find some space and quiet. What this means is that the office is everywhere. All spaces are public spaces with the demands that this puts on us. The freedom of the home that Chesterton speaks of becomes less and less a possibility the more what was private becomes public through the surveillance of the camera or microphone, or even simply the requirement that all space available becomes workspace. With both the time and space of work becoming more and more total the alienation that stems from much of our labor also becomes more total. Further, unlike Chaplin in *Modern Times*, we no longer need to bring alienation home with us because we now have it brought right to the home.

3. We should not dissociate from our work

We can first recognize that we are dissociated from our work through alienated labor. Alienated labor is, as Marx says, "external to" the worker. It is not ours and we are already separated from it from the start. We are dissociated from it in the sense our labor time is not ours. There is yet a further form of dissociation found in our ability to relate to or understand the meaning of what we are doing. Anders writes,

> In fact, he is not free, for example, merely because he is excluded from the ownership of 'his' means of production or his products, but because he cannot take in with a single glance the totality of the process of production within which he is integrated; nor does he know the final product or its function...nor does he know the moral or immoral qualities of 'his' product; nor does he know its beneficiaries, its users or its victims. All of these things--

> and with them also his own labor--take place in a certain way behind his back (chap 6, sec. 1)

Most workers find themselves a part of a complex and multi-leveled work environment such that they are far removed from discussions about the ultimate aims and strategies behind their work. One sees only a fragment of the product or process with which one is more truly engaged. Even university professors, for example, are removed from the true meaning of their work. Though we may design our classes, we may not understand why certain classes and not others, why new faculty are being hired in one area and not others. Input may be solicited, but it is often ignored and, if one even goes so far as to attempt to understand the larger picture within which they are involved, one is left only to speculate on the meaning of different decisions made at 'higher' levels. Thus, even in less alienated forms of labor, we tend to be alienated from the larger context wherein we act and are thus dissociated from the true meaning of our actions.

Given that worklife for so many of us is unsatisfying, we rightfully resist identifying with it. Many of us do not want to be identified with our jobs because we rightly do not feel that these jobs are us, or, more in line with how Marx might put it, we are not ourselves while at work. There is also a reaction against a kind of careerist attitude that suggests we should not put everything we have into career success but should find other ways to make life meaningful (no doubt this sentiment makes the most sense when work is alienating). For reasons like these, we often focus exclusively on the non-work parts of ourselves as "ours." "Polite society" has followed suit and it has become a matter of poor etiquette to suggest the importance of one's job in conversation. It is common, upon meeting someone, for one to take cares *not* to ask another what they do for a living. We tell ourselves not to just define others by what they do for work, that there is much more to them than their job, and that, though they may not have an "impressive career", there is much more that may be of value to them as well as ourselves. Thus, for reasons like these, it has become routine to dissociate ourselves and others labor.

There are significant problems with this. First, for those whose work and pay relies on the exploitation of others, and we should not underestimate the size of this group, they are allowed an escape from having to identify as an agent of oppression. Being able to say "it's just my job, but it's not who I am" means that I can say that *I'm* not the cause of oppression. Since one does not associate with one's job, one no longer has the task of thinking seriously about the impact of one's work. When on the clock, I do what I am told, but afterwards, I forget about work. Thus, if one does not think about work when off the clock, in order for one to recognize the nature of their work and how one might be implicated in it, the company will have to make critical reflection on the potentially alienating and oppressive structure of work one of one's paid tasks - something we can safely consider unlikely.

The effect of this is, first, to trivialize what it is that people do with the bulk of their life's energy. This, in turn, makes it easier to hide the relationship that work has to other parts of our lives. In an effort to maintain a part of ourselves that is outside of work, free from the values of the market and the conditions of labor, what may be a reaction against alienated labor ends up maintaining and protecting it. Thus, we find a hidden imperative in the effort to dissociate from our jobs: along with "you aren't your job", we are implicitly told: "don't notice how your life is defined by alienated labor." Instead, of course, we should recognize the role that it plays in our lives, and fight to make work-life, not just endurable, but part of a flourishing life.

4. Loneliness

One of the ways that one can experience this alienation is through loneliness. Most immediately, loneliness is felt as a disconnect from others. We miss people, we feel alone, isolated, and desire a greater degree of intimacy with others. We may feel lonely because we cannot physically be with others, perhaps separated by distance because of a pandemic. These cases are easier to understand but we also know that loneliness should be distinguished from being factically alone.

We are not lonely simply because there is no one around us. Most of us enjoy time alone. Further, being around others does not mean we are not lonely. If one is lost in a crowd, or with others with whom one has little genuine connection, one may feel just as lonely, or more so, than if one is factically alone since those others may serve as a reminder that the problem is deeper than simply the lack of others. As Arendt says, "loneliness shows itself most sharply in company with others" (Arendt 1962, 476). It is not simply the absence of others; rather, loneliness has to do with a felt lack of certain essential connections to others.

Essential connections with others are only forged through some degree of intimacy. The maintenance of a number of superficial relationships will prevent me from feeling like *I* am truly being seen. I must be able to share something of myself as this particular person and not simply one individual among others in order to feel that what is connecting to the other is in fact my self. Further, the other must be open to seeing me. If the other remains indifferent, cold, and closed off, no true intimacy can take place. This is all to say that intimacy requires the active participation of the self and other. To use Hegel's language, we must achieve some degree of mutual recognition.

The loss of an intimate connection with others severs one's connection to oneself. In *Origins of Totalitarianism*, Arendt writes, "What makes loneliness so unbearable is the loss of one's own self which can be realized in solitude but confirmed in its identity only by the trusting and trustworthy company of my equals. In this situation, man loses trust in himself as the partner of his thoughts and that elementary confidence in the world which is necessary to make experiences at all. Self and world, capacity for thought and experience are lost at the same time" (OT 477). Here we can see some of the dialectical interplay between the types of alienation that Marx describes in the Economic and Philosophical Manuscripts. Marx's description of the alienations taking place from the object of labor, the process of work, our "species-being", and from other workers can also be understood to be in dialogue with each other, where each affects the others and vice versa. In this case, alienation from others, or other workers, can cause an alienation from myself. Being deprived of my connection to others robs me of the confirming presence that others provide. This, in turn, weakens the connection I form with myself. At the same time, we can also see that alienation from oneself causes alienation from others. If I am alienated in my home, and this alienation seems to run around the clock, there will be no time where I am my own self. This means that I will lose touch with myself, finding only an alienated self or, as Marx says, I will 'feel free only in my animal functions.' Gadamer, for example, writes that "Only someone who is friends with himself can fit into what is common" (Gadamer 1988, 112). That is, only if I can maintain a self-relation can I be in a position to join with others. If this deteriorated version of myself is the one that I am able to present to others, then I will still fail to achieve any degree of intimacy as my authentic self. Gadamer underscores this point, saying "loneliness is in fact a symptom of self-alienation of the feeling that we do not really belong to ourselves anymore and that we have no place on the face of the earth, a generalized phenomenon in our times. Insofar as the "loneliness' tendency [...] is that a person can no longer extricate oneself from it" (Gadamer 1988, 105). Thus, being disconnected from ourselves will disconnect us with others.

We see this kind of interplay because we are co-constituted by others. We cannot connect with others unless we connect with ourselves, and we cannot connect with ourselves unless we connect with others. There are many arguments for the intersubjective nature of the self in the history of philosophy. In his chapter on self-consciousness, Hegel argues that the self is only made possible through others. In section 26 of *Being and Time*, Heidegger argues that we should understand ourselves most fundamentally as with others and being alone is only a deficient mode of our fundamental relation to others.[2] In accounts like these, we see that it is a fiction to imagine a developed, free individual without reference to others. Others are there with us as we become individuals and are those from whom we identify and distinguish ourselves as we achieve some degree of independence as individuals.

Loneliness seems to testify to our intersubjective nature. If we understand ourselves in our development and primarily as individuals and look at our relationship to others as secondary or perhaps even incidental, loneliness would seem like an option. One should, then, be able to remain stoic and maintain happiness without others since others are not essential to oneself. This viewpoint, in turn, makes loneliness into a kind problem that should be dealt with using one's individual resources alone, since this is taken to be where the problem lies. Following an intersubjective understanding of selfhood, we see that, far from showing a particular weakness of ourselves as individuals, loneliness testifies to our nature as fundamentally a being-with-others. Thus, there is a reason for some degree of optimism for those experiencing the loneliness involved in alienated labor. Many, unfortunately, may not self-consciously experience the alienation present in their lives. Alienation has been fully delivered to one's home and the "Chaplinitis" has overwhelmed the rest of their nature such that they have accepted a fundamentally lonely existence as just what life is like. It follows that experiencing this alienation is good insofar this means we are still in touch with our humanity such that we feel its loss. From out of the alienation of our labor,

[2] This approach is opposed to that of Ben Lazare Mijuskovic in *Feeling Lonesome: The Philosophy and Psychology of Loneliness*, In his book, Mijuskovic asserts loneliness as an essential feature of human life, one that we escape from. We are all primarily lonely, and we flee from this existential dimension of life. This is because Mijuskovic early chapters sketch an account or personhood that contradicts that of thinkers like Hegel, Heidegger, de Beauvoir, or Arendt. Early on (pgs. 2, 5, for example), we get an account of personhood that takes the individual to be primary and to develop without the need of others. I find the arguments presented here unconvincing and so will follow the line of thinking that takes selfhood to have an intersubjective origin.

exaggerated by much of the WFH labor, comes a signal from our own nature: revolt. The loneliness experienced urges resistance against being torn apart from a genuine connection to others and, as a result, to ourselves.

Bibliography

Adorno, Theodor. “Free Time” in *Adorno: The Culture Industry*. Routledge, 1991.

Anders, Gunther. *Die Antiquiertheit des Menschen. Band II: Über die Zerstörung des Lebens im Zeitalter der dritten industriellen Revolution*. C.H. Beck, 1998.

Arendt, Hannah. *The Origins of Totalitarianism*. Mariner Books, 1973.

—. “On the Nature of Totalitarianism: An Essay in Understanding.” Essays in Understanding, 1930-1954: Formation, Exile, and Totalitarianism. Schocken, 2005.

Costache, Adrian. “On solitude and loneliness in hermeneutical philosophy.” *Meta: Research in Hermeneutics, Phenomenology, and Practical Philosophy*. Vol. I, No. 1, June 2013, 130-149.

Chesterton, G.K. *What is Wrong with the World*. Empire Books, 2011.

Engles, Friedrich. *The Protestant Ethic and the Spirit of Capitalism*. Norton Critical Editions, 2009.

Foucault, Michel. “Truth and Power” in Power/Knowledge: Selected Interviews and Other Writings, 1972-1977. Vintage, 1980.

Gadamer, Hans-Georg. "Isolation as a Symptom of Self Alienation." In Praise of Theory. Speeches and Essays, 101-113. New Haven & London: Yale University Press, 1988.

Hegel, G.W.F. *Phenomenology of Spirit*. Translated by Terry Pinkard. Cambridge, 2019.

Heidegger, Martin. *Being and Time*. Translated by Macquarrie and Robinson. Harper, 2008.

Marx, Karl. “Economic and Philosophical Manuscripts” in *Marx: Selected Writings*. Hackett, 1995.

Mijuskovic, Ben Lazare. *Feeling Lonesome: The Philosophy and Psychology of Loneliness*. Praeger, 2015.

FROM SPECIALIZED TO HYPER-SPECIALIZED LABOUR: FUTURE LABOR MARKETS AS HELMED BY ADVANCED COMPUTER INTELLIGENCE

TYLER L. JAYNES

Introduction

Surprisingly, many of the technologies that have been available for years through Google, Microsoft, and other corporations, have only recently been put to corporate-level use as a result of the SARS-CoV-2 (COVID-19) pandemic (Brenan 2020, Desilver 2020, Williams 2020).[1] Although this may be attributed to a lack of corporate "imagination" (Williams 2020), other factors undoubtedly incorporate real concerns—such as cybersecurity, stable access to an Internet connection, and access to corporate-mandated hardware, programs, software, and virtual private networks—into rationales for why these technologies have remained relatively unutilised in recent years. For all of the relative amount of "good" remote work has displayed for the labour market internationally, losses abound in the abrupt "telecommute" transition. These losses do not *just* include the various jobs that many have been furloughed for, but the loss of the home/work barrier (if such a thing ever existed before the pandemic) and meaningful social interactions with the "work family." Even if COVID-19 abides and humanity gains some form of herd immunity against the virus, these *supposedly* temporary transitions *will* become more permanent as organisations see greater worker efficiency outside of the general office settings we have grown accustomed to environing (Forbes 2020).

[1] Specifically attributing to the use of instant messaging or video conferencing software and tools like Microsoft Teams. While these tools have seen use over the years, they have only been sparsely integrated in many corporate environments and were not *as* integral as they have come to be in this current global health crisis.

Underlying these transformations is the endless struggle to balance between repetitive functions that can be entrusted to a human and the ceaseless progression of artificial (or computer) intelligence systems to take these tasks either partially or entirely out of human hands. Of course, there exists a myriad of artificial intelligence programs and software, and each can be applied to a specific task or range of tasks. However, the most common of artificial intelligence systems (Polson and Scott 2018, 13-42; Coeckelbergh 2020, 3-5) are limited in the tasks that they can feasibly automate for humans. Whether for good or ill, however, this will *not* always be the case. Given the changes that *will* come with advanced computer intelligence systems (CIS), and their integration into developing technologies in industries ranging from manufacturing to medicine, a precautionary narrative is *vital* to aiding society towards a developmental path that does not needlessly displace vast portions of the labour force *en masse* upon the implementation of these systems. This chapter is less a discourse on business or professional ethics than it is a broad supposition of what lies ahead for various labour markets, as the future trends of technological advancement are frequently unpredictable or unknown—especially in regard to future career availability and evolution (Lent 2018, 207-208). In terms of cultural workplace norms, the author will make heavy reference to the USA given the unique challenges that nation will face in this coming shift in labour market specialisation.

Before discussing the intricacies of the outlook of the anticipated workforce, however, it would do to remind the reader that CIS are *not* limited to a single program, software system, or piece of hardware. Rather, CIS can exist in a variety of forms and fashions (Jaynes 2020a, 344), so a singular definition to encompass the entirety of computational intelligence is challenging to maintain. For the purposes of this chapter, our focus shall remain upon those CIS that *could* be said to possess intelligence *and* functionality equivalent to that of an average adult human—although other arguments may posit that any CIS attaining a "human-like" status *ought* to be judged from the understood levels of intelligence held by humanity's intellectually-challenged population as representatives of the "lowest" aspect of human intelligence that retains legal protections (Jaynes 2020b; 11, 18). This focus may sharply contrast the CIS some in the field of computer science may be familiar with, which could not feasibly pass itself off as being human under the "right" test conditions.[2]

---

[2] These do *not* include the famous Turing Test, given that the premise for this proposed examination presupposes the concept that one of the entities being examined is not human—which may ultimately yield accuracy akin to a coin toss (Jaynes 2020a, 345).

More than human: The merger betwixt humans and robotics

As many readers are keenly aware, computers have become ever-so prevalent in our daily lives—a stark contrast to the work environment of the 1990s or early 2000s. And based upon general observations of the past two decades alone, computers are bound to encompass more facets of daily life than we could feasibly imagine today. Already, entities from corporations to countries are developing ways in which implantable radio frequency identification (RFID) chips can gain one more relative freedoms by allow the user to interact with their environment in "hands-free" manners (Saadi, Touhami and Yagoub 2017; Savage 2018). Other research has taken a different approach with electronic tattoos (e-tattoos), which serve as a sort of "next-generation" health wearable (Ha et al. 2019, Jeong and Lu 2019, Jeon et al. 2019). The author cannot help but wonder, however, *when* will the figurative "line in the sand" be crossed between greater convenience and means to more accurately monitor our health, and the establishment of a "new" categorisation for human subjects—both taxonomically and legally. When will humanity go "too far" in augmenting our biological forms with technology? This question lies at the heart of the philosophical debate surrounding the morality of human augmentation (HA) and human enhancement (HE), though it should be noted that the author views HE as being bodily modification through chemical means *rather* than bionic or computational means. While this personal note may not have a greater bearing on how academics define HE, it should provide the reader with a more grounded understanding of why "enhancement" may often be substituted for "augmentation" in this dialogue and the semantic rationale for this potentially field-opposing usage.

Those who fear an inequitable treatment of HA and HE technologies advocate for equal access to and fair pricing (or rather, equitability) for the technologies and substances that push our biological forms to their technologic limits (Farah 2010, Galván and Luppicini 2014, Palmerini 2015, Schmidt 2017, Ruggiu 2018). The limitations to artefacts such as e-tattoos and RFID chip implants lie in their availability specifically to those economically stable enough to afford the medical treatment involved with attaining these devices, as is seen in the USA healthcare system. Hence, nations such as Sweden are more capable of enabling their entire population to attain personalised RFID chips, given that their healthcare expenses are factored into their expected incomes and taxes as a result of their policy decisions in the modern era. The problem of equitability is *not* explicitly limited to newer technologies that require invasive procedures (i.e., implants), but ranges to neuro- or psycho-pharmaceutical substances (Farah, 2010, Chatterjee and Farah 2013), to bionic prosthetics (Brown 2013, Bertolini 2015, Sullivan 2018), and even somatic or germline gene editing technologies (Ormond et al. 2017, Enriquez 2019, Primc 2020).

The Issue of "Legal" Work

Especially when we are discussing cases like the utilisation and proliferation of advanced bionic prosthetics, where reliance upon computational intelligence is integral to the device's functioning, other concerns come into play. Specifically, at what line is drawn between a *constitutional* person and a *legally unprotected* entity—as may be the case for some instances of advanced CIS (Jaynes 2020a, Jaynes 2020b). These concerns may seem to come at too early a time for some, but the issues will inherently *need* to be treated as CIS (in particular) gains in sophistication. There is a growing need for certain limitations to be drawn regarding the amount of work that can be processed by a sufficiently sophisticated CIS whose programming is akin to a "black box."[3] For reference, the definition of "work" being used is taken from John Danaher's paper, "Will Life Be Worth Living in a World Without Work? Technological Unemployment and the Meaning of Life;" being "The performance of some act or skill (cognitive, emotional, physical etc.) in return for economic reward, or in the ultimate hope of receiving some such reward" (2017, 43).

Take a scenario wherein a labourer at a construction yard is using a computer-intelligence-dependent assistive bionic prosthetic (CIDABP) to go about their duties. Let us further presume that this CIDABP does not transmit a "pain" signal through the central nervous system, and that strain to it is only feasibly measured in how quickly the patient must return to their preventive maintenance team for adjustments. Respective to how well they can perform their duties, they presumably will be able to lift more than their fellow labourers or be in "less" danger when in areas that could cause harm to the skin or limbs (in the case of a CIDABP that replaces either the entirety or part of one's arm). If the CIS driving the CIDABP does not have a

[3] Generally defined as a device, system or object which can be viewed in terms of its inputs and outputs (or transfer characteristics), without any knowledge of its internal workings.

"limiter" set for the amount of strain the prosthetic can endure,[4] can we *honestly* claim that the labourer's performance is solely due to their ability to perform their tasks efficiently if they are relying upon the CIDABP to take the majority of a given load? And who is then liable for any potential property damage should the CIS malfunction in some fashion? If the CIS is designed in such a manner that it can generate its own code to "adapt" to the environment it is exposed to, at what point can we no longer claim that it is the designer, programmer, manufacturer, maintenance person or team, or patient's responsibility to accept fault for the incident? Thus far, the USA and international law remain bare of sufficient legal jurisprudence regarding this matter—as no such CIS is currently in use in such environments.[5]

Let us take another case, wherein the question at hand is the legality of the work performed by a CI system:

> By suggesting that governments should grant legal protections to NBIs [non-biological intelligence], we are necessarily implying that these interested parties should be altruistic enough *not* to expect an economic return for their investments. How can this be fair? How should these investors be compensated?...If we conclude that NBI systems should compensate the corporation or organisation that developed it, it will need to earn a wage. This conclusion then implies that the system will be *required* to labour and that the nature of this labour will need to be *legal*. As the law is written, workers in the USA are required to prove their citizenship or proof of emigration to become employed legally. If the NBI system was developed in the USA, a case would need to be made that it is a US citizen. If this citizenship is denied on the grounds that an NBI system cannot be "born" like a human can, other methods will need to be devised to ensure that the labour done by the NBI is constitutional. Assuming that the system will only require time enough in the work week to debug its software and update itself, niceties like breaks and limits on work hours will inevitably exceed those required by human workers. What the legal system will also need to decide is whether allowing an NBI system to work more than a human (because it does not have the same biological needs) is legal under market competition

[4] For a set period of time with a given load—although the concept of developing such a system without a limiter may be infeasible if we consider that significantly heavy loads put an undue burden upon the relatively frail human form.

[5] *See generally* Tyler L. Jaynes and Linda MacDonald Glenn, "Direct Nervous System Monitoring and Interaction with Nanorobotics: A Proposed Framework for Novel Convergences," (forthcoming paper); Tyler L. Jaynes, "On Human Genome Manipulation and *Homo technicus*: The Legal Treatment of Non-Natural Human Subjects," (forthcoming paper); Tyler L. Jaynes, "The Legal Ambiguity of Advanced Assistive Bionic Prosthetics: Where to Define the Limits of 'Enhanced Persons' in Medical Treatment," (forthcoming paper).

> considerations. Ultimately, this type of decision will determine the speed at which the job market will decrease on a local and national scale. Should the courts determine that the impact of NBI workers far offset what they are legally capable of ruling upon, other branches of government will be required to then make the determinations judiciaries cannot (Jaynes 2020a, 351, emphasis added).

Although this scenario is likely years away from becoming a reality, we must once again return to the question of the limits of *natural* human intelligence and how they diverge from the CIS equivalent (Lauret 2020). Or rather: if we were to take the computer system away from a given human—be it a desktop or laptop computer, tablet, or smartphone—how much can we expect that human to *know* or be capable of performing (e.g., academically, economically, socially) using non-computerized means? While this may seem like an unfair test to some given how much many of us rely on computerised calculators or "Doctor Google," it is the only *actual* test of the limitations of a natural human—albeit, for this scenario, we would wish to use a subject that grew up before computers were as sophisticated as they are today to know for certain.[6]

Loneliness and Technology

Another issue arises with the sophistication of computerised technologies—namely, in that it increases the relative amount of virtual interaction members of society have with one another. Even once humans begin to augment themselves with RFID-like chips that can synchronise thoughts, or develop wearable devices that project holographic workspaces, the issue remains that the amount of physical interaction we will be encouraged or required to engage in will become increasingly limited. The best example of this phenomenon would be to point to social media platforms, such as Facebook or Twitter. Although these platforms exist to help humanity keep in touch with our friends, family, and colleagues, they have become superficial reflections of our inner psyches—if one chooses to utilise these platforms at all.

Just think for a moment how *genuine* you personally are when you post or "tweet" on these sites. We rationalise that no sane individual puts their

[6] This is stated with the understanding that those members of society who advanced through school in or before the 1960s did not have complete access to the Internet of Things and thus were expected to memorise more "knowledge" than a student proceeding through school around the turn of the millennium. *See generally* "On Human Genome Manipulation and *Homo technicus*."

unfiltered thoughts online, and so we justify ourselves to put a "filter" on ourselves to match the audience we wish to reach out towards. Although this may be one form of communication, there is growing academic concern that excessive time on these platforms is contributing to a lessening of intimacy in interpersonal relationships and difficulty overcoming deficiencies in self-esteem (Hollenbaugh, Ferris, and Casey 2020; Lopez and Cuarteros 2020).

Given that "telecommuting" will become an increasing norm as companies realise the benefits gained from remote work (Forbes 2020),[7] there becomes a real concern that interpersonal communication between members of the same team will gain in superficiality. This trend may not *immediately* seem like a detriment, given how there are often "certain" people in the office one may rather not run into daily. Yet there are those "telecommuters" who have been turning to office noise generators during the current health crisis (King 2020) to fill the quiet space that inevitably permeates a remote work environment. Although these noise generators give the user some authority of the sounds they hear, they are still substituting for something particular—being, of course, the presence of other human beings that are not one's family. These "familiar strangers," as they may be considered, offer an outlet that one's more intimate contacts simply cannot fill—whether that be an outwardly friendly or hostile reaction that only these "familiar strangers" can provide, or some other nuanced interaction that would only occur in an office environment.

The future of market labour

With the emergence of sophisticated CIS will come a revolution to the type of labour required of the average individual. This trend is one that society has seen (arguably) since the dawn of the Industrial Revolution (Danaher 2017, 43-44), where seemingly unskilled labour evolves in such a way that it requires a trade or scholastic training to perform. Unlike how events transpired during the Industrial Revolution, today's rate of technological progression simply *cannot* compare. Although there is a wide range of estimations for when CIS will attain human-like intellectual status (Ford 2018, 528-529), it will likely come sooner than humanity would like if its

[7] Such as the potential cost-savings for providing employees the hardware they may need to perform their job remotely when compared to monthly office space rent, or support for local public transit participation.

development is approached in the "right" manner.[8] As such, a brief look at the various forms computational intelligence *may* adopt will further clarify the gap that will exist between the requirements for "skilled" labour in the current economy and the economy to come.

Dividing Humanity (At Least) Four Ways

Evidently, humanity will reach the point where legal definitions expand to protect various groups that are enhanced or unenhanced as a matter of course—more for the moral considerations of preserving some aspects of where we "originated" from and what we can "become" than to serve as physical barriers (at the onset). Although complications of discrimination will inevitably arise as these categories are legally defined, the fact remains that there is *no* overarching measure of legal protections that can exist for a species that has bionically or chemically augmented themselves beyond the species' base abilities. Simply put, the same legal protections *cannot* be given to both a naturally unaugmented human that has no interaction with computers and a human who only has one aspect of themselves that remains organic.[9]

To begin with, the two categories of human require different things from legal and social systems—for one, protection of their right to remain (as some may state) a "Luddite" beyond those rights granted for religious expression,[10] and the other their right to be only one figurative step away from becoming an entity that only "exists" in Binary code. Another point adds that the interactions these members of humanity have will inevitably become increasingly complex as interpersonal relationships develop and flourish. After all, we do not know (at present) whether one loses the emotive capacity so integral to the human experience as one "swaps" organic material for bionic. As such, we can only assume the limits of human experience from the present moment and remain within the realms

[8] Ideas for what the "right" way to approach computational intelligence development are widely variant, and the author does not subscribe to a single idea given the unpredictability of scientific advancement. However, the author agrees with Lauret (2020) that this approach to a fully "capable" CIS must incorporate some consideration for the realm of intelligence that exists in the human population—psychological or neurological ailments notwithstanding.

[9] Explicated in "On Human Genome Manipulation and *Homo technicus*."

[10] Here referring to communities such as the Amish in the USA, or similarly conservative religious groups internationally.

of living that we are currently familiar with (Jaynes 2020a, 345-346; Jaynes 2020b, 12).

Given these assumptions, one such method of separation may come from a four-stage model: biologically-natural, genetically-manipulated, computer-aided, and cybernetically-enhanced.[11] Distinguishing between individuals who have had their cells treated with genetic manipulation techniques and those who do not is essential insofar as we cannot accurately predict how manipulations to somatic or germline cells affect the individual or their progeny while also guaranteeing humans the right to an unaltered genome (Ormond et al. 2017). As alluded to before, this right to an unaltered genome *should* remain regardless of the technological changes before us for more than just religious practices, given that it is ultimately the culmination of our biologic heritage.[12] Although advocacy for a more "purified" genome may sound enticing, is there *really* anything to tell us what we have lost in attaining this "purified" version of ourselves? Are we not merely practicing the ultimate form of eugenics if we force this practice upon the entire population and discriminate against unaltered individuals, as was dramatized in the 1997 film *Gattaca*? Given the moral and ethical boundaries that would be crossed in that scenario, it is *not* something that should be practiced in our future society in this author's view.

Going beyond the first two categories, modern humans who rely upon their smartphone or Fitbit to aid their daily lives and tasks deserve their own unique category because the level of intelligence they can attain far exceeds the level of intelligence possessed by a natural human. The complication with defining this group of humans, however, is where the line is drawn between a computer-aided human and one who is cybernetically-enhanced (Jaynes 2020b). For instance, do subcutaneous implants like the RFID chip constitute a *cybernetic* enhancement or a *computer* enhancement? This delineation, and others like it, are not ones that have been made legally clear at this date given humanity's lack of available bionic enhancements—and thus become problematic for future labour markets if corporations do not

---

[11] Further defended in "The Legal Ambiguity of Advanced Assistive Bionic Prosthetics," which examines the legal protections with patients in possession of CIDABPs. As this proposed model applies to this work, however, further subclassifications and definitions will need to be considered to grant us a full model to reference (from a legal and judicial perspective, at least). *See further* "On Human Genome Manipulation and *Homo technicus*."

[12] The argument made by this author is in opposition to those made by Primc (2020), though concessions are duly made for the strength of her argument.

keep up with legal determinations on such distinctions. There also exists the question of where neuropharmacology or psychotropics fit into the picture, given that they range from organic substances to synthetically-developed compounds. Although they are *technically* as much of a technologic artefact as electronic computers, there has not been a need to separate them based on origin to this extent.

And finally, the distinction between what constitutes as a computer-original intelligence and an organically-original CIS has to be discerned given that our technological advancements may lead us to produce CIS that can gain a biologic form and vice versa (Jaynes 2020a, 344). Of course, the first step to this is determining the legal protections enjoyed by non-organic computationally-intelligent entities and how they differ from *natural* human or augmented human entities.

"Skill" Level Amidst CI-Augmented Humans

The most significant barrier today's labour force faces is that of education—at least, in terms of how it is defined and classified concerning *actual* job skills. What the labour market has seen, especially in the past few decades, is an influx of higher-educated hopefuls who have pursued some form of degree or trade certificate that *supposedly* translates into tangible skills required for specific positions in the labour market. While this influx cannot be said to be *harmful* in the sense that the general public is gaining necessary knowledge to improve their overall quality of life, it *is* harmful in that a USA Associate's degree or International Standard Classification of Education level 4 or 5 attainers are becoming the industry's "new" secondary education standard rather than maintaining their standing as tertiary educational levels before graduate studies. This shift also applies to jobs that traditionally only required a USA Bachelor or Master-level education to "qualify" as being well-enough educated to fill. Although this has done positive things for the labour market as a whole, many stories of humanities- or arts-focused doctorate holders only finding employment in professions considered to be unskilled (such as fast food or retail) have been on the rise alongside other field-specific doctorates (Ruben 2019, Schein 2019).

The issue intrinsically is *not* that job requirements have gained in sophistication overall,[13] but that the level of competition for the few jobs

[13] Although there *is* something to be said for "entry-level" job postings beguiling new workers with experience expectations that are *not* "entry-level," insofar as such

that require higher levels of education is simply too great considering how they are few and far between to find compared to other positions. This issue only gains complexity when the growth of possible jobs requiring doctorates realistically only extend to those in the science, technology, engineering, or mathematics (STEM) fields, and the failure for the industry to accept and integrate the social sciences, humanities and the arts for people and the economy (SHAPE)[14] fields. Whether this decline in attention to SHAPE fields is based on the perception of how STEM fields comparatively have displayed a physical change in the world we environ[15] or some perceived lack of need for "soft" sciences in a technology-heavy world, its effects are detrimental for those members of the human population who struggle with mathematics or applied scientific concepts. Other movements such as the STEAM (adding "arts" to the STEM category) have been floated to emphasize the importance of the arts to mathematics and physical sciences (Jolly 2014), yet the divide between mathematics-focused fields and those in the realm of the social sciences and humanities continues to grow.

Given how CIS will continue to automate processes previously thought to be solely the responsibility of humans, there is a real threat that less skilled jobs will be lost—from fast food and retail to delivery services and custodial work. Couple this with a move toward CIS potentially handling the labour of several regular white-collar employees at a general firm (Jaynes 2020a, 351-353), and there becomes an increasing dearth of options even for those

positions *ought* to exist to introduce inexperienced labourers to either the labour market as an entity or a particular industry. Expecting more than a year of prior experience in such positions is unrealistic if we consider that many recent university graduates cannot hold full-time salaried work while pursuing their education full-time, on account of in-person class schedules and their respective availabilities in a given institution's register. While a company would obviously prefer to have a more experienced worker in a posting of this sort, young professionals are effectively barred from gaining *any* relevant experience when such practices are encouraged or excessively prevalent in a given community or industry.

[14] Attributed from an editorial from *The Guardian*, posted June 26, 2020, which references the development of a counterpart to the STEM acronym by the British Academy's London School of Economics and Arts Council England. *See* https://amp.theguardian.com/commentisfree/2020/jun/26/the-guardian-view-on-the-humanities-the-importance-of-being-rounded.

[15] As discussed in another opinion piece from *The Atlantic*, published October 1, 2018. *See* https://www.theatlantic.com/letters/archive/2018/10/letters-the-humanities-are-in-crisis/571081/?gclid=Cj0KCQjwl4v4BRDaARIsAFjATPmVW3tOj-0a8vawqvYqs20x qHuaX8xfGvZN8maOKJCxzumt8-RzX2oaAi28EALwwcB.

who are sufficiently "trained" through education. With these potentialities, the call should *not* be for a readjustment of our education systems (Lent 2018; 212, 216),[16] but to find a way for society to sustain its population with citizens working fewer hours as we have been forced to in prior shifts in technologic ages (Marx 1909, 268-330). Such potentiality is shared by scholars of political philosophy; such as Professor Michael Minch, who shared with the author the following observations:

> Obviously, AI will continue the technological trend of eliminating human jobs, and with a vengeance. We need to quickly get beyond the idea of work as the status of nonpoverty, and rethink work in radical ways: perhaps a full-time job needs to be realized at 25 hours a week; perhaps all human beings above a certain age should receive a universal basic income that sustains a decent life, regardless of their working life, and work becomes a bonus circumstance, etc.[17]

Arguably, this is akin to the arguments presented by Marx (1909, 255-330) and would generally be decried in the USA, [18] given its ties to *The Communist Manifesto* and his attacks on the nature of capitalism. Rather than focus on an old, politically-instigated mindset towards one potential system of governance however, society should instead consider how *communal* or *social* various governments have become as technology has advanced in response to the evolving needs of their populations (Tucker 1978, 291-293); seeing as how the nature of supply and demand will inevitably morph into something never before handled by capitalist frameworks. As the mantra goes, *social* safety nets are ultimately *socialist* in their very nature—regardless how much Americans try to argue it being part of a libertarian framework. To decry their societal benefit due to practically ancient resentments towards a specific socio-political climate is the height of ignorance and effectively denies society an avenue to adapt to trials it has never surmounted before.

Conclusion

Ultimately, an intensive focus on education will only benefit society to a certain degree. Too much emphasis on this policy will result in a hefty portion of viable labourers without an avenue to earn a living wage, which

[16] Although such a readjustment may be beneficial to society in other manners.

[17] Michael Minch, Ph.D., Correspondent, email message to author, August 3, 2020.

[18] Although it may arguably not be against libertarian frameworks (referring to the political philosophy, *not* the politically-oriented party of the same name) that structures its society.

in turn strains the existing social networks that may not completely recover after the current international pandemic. As a counterpoint to this, an investment towards HA or HE technologies and medicines may also yield an ineffective solution when considering the long-term impacts their use will have on a society that refuses to grant protections to advanced CIS. Before serious considerations can be made in handling the inevitable changes that will arise with the integration of CIS into various technologies—including nanotechnology, which itself has the potential to transform various industries in its own right completely—a focus *needs* to be centred on the legal treatment of computational intelligence systems and the human-computer mergers that are currently emerging in medicine. By developing litigation and jurisprudence to sufficiently treat these unique cases, society can then begin the complicated process of mitigating the impact CIS-driven technologies will have on the labour market and the future shape it will take.

Conflict of Interest Statement

The author of this work is serving as the Chair for the IEEE Nanotechnology Council Standards Committee, and actively serves as the Secretary for the IEEE P2863™ – Recommended Practice for Organizational Governance of Artificial Intelligence – Standard Development Group (organized under the IEEE Computer Society Standards Activity Board). All statements made herein are of entirely those of the author, and do not reflect the opinions of the IEEE, IEEE Standards Association, or related Councils or Societies under their jurisdiction; nor those of the P2863™ Standard Development Group as an entity or its affiliated members (notwithstanding of the author). Furthermore, the author's statements are not reflective of the Alden March Bioethics Institute at Albany Medical College as an institution, its staff, or its curriculum, given their standing as a student enrolled in the Master of Science in Bioethics programme and lack of direct employment by the institution or programme (including through federal work-study tuition subsidies).

Bibliography

Bertolini, Andrea. "Robotic Prostheses as Products Enhancing the Rights of People with Disabilities: Reconsidering the Structure of Liability Rules." *International Review of Law, Computers & Technology* 29, nos. 2-3 (2015): 116-136. http://doi.org/10.1080/13600869.2015.1055659.

Brenan, Megan. "U.S. Workers Discovering Affinity for Remote Work." *Gallup*. April 3, 2020. https://news.gallup.com/poll/306695/workers-discovering-affinity-remote-work.aspx.

Brown, Bayard. "A Farewell to Arms (And Legs): The Legal Treatment of Artificial Limbs." *Columbia Journal of Law and Social Problems* 47, no. 1 (2013): 69-102.

Chatterjee, Anjan, and Martha J. Farah, eds. *Neuroethics in Practice: Medicine, Mind, and Society*. New York: Oxford University Press, 2013.

Coeckelbergh, Mark. *AI Ethics*. Cambridge, MA: The MIT Press, 2020.

Danaher, John. "Will Life Be Worth Living in a World Without Work? Technological Unemployment and the Meaning of Life." *Science and Engineering Ethics* 23, no. 1 (2017): 41-64. https://doi.org/10.1007/s11948-016-9770-5.

Desilver, Drew. "Before the Coronavirus, Telework was an Optional Benefit, Mostly for the Affluent Few." *Pew Research Center*. March 20, 2020. https://pewrsr.ch/2Qwk1zt.

Enriquez, Paul. "Editing Humanity: On the Precise Manipulation of DNA in Human Embryos." *North Carolina Law Review* 97, no. 5 (2019): 1147-1240.

Farah, Martha J., ed. *Neuroethics: An Introduction with Readings*. Cambridge, MA: The MIT Press, 2010.

Forbes, Steve. "Could You be Taxed for Working from Home?" *Forbes*. November 17, 2020. https://www.forbes.com/sites/steveforbes/2020/11/17/could-you-be-taxed-for-working-from-home/?sh=5d38223510e2&utm_source=LINKEDIN_COMPANY&utm_medium=social&utm_content=4168639188&utm_campaign=sprinklrForbesMainLI.

Ford, Martin. *Architects of Intelligence: The Truth About AI from the People Building It.* Birmingham, UK: Packt Publishing, 2018.

Galván, José M. and Rocci Luppicini. "Redefining the Boundaries of Humanity and the Human Body: From Homo Sapiens to Homo Technicus." In *Evolving Issues Surrounding Technoethics and Society in the Digital Age*, edited by Rocci Luppicini, 1-8. Hershey, PA: IGI Global, 2014. https://doi.org/10.4018/978-1-4666-6122-6.ch001.

Ha, Taewoo, Jason Tran, Siyi Liu, Hongwoo Jang, Hyoyoung Jeong, Ruchika Mitbander, Heeyong Huh, Yitao Qiu, Jason Duong, Rebecca L. Wang, Pulin Wang, Animesh Tandon, Jayant Sirohi, and Nanshu Lu. "A Chest-Laminated Ultrathin and Stretch-Able E-Tattoo for the Measurement Of Electrocardiogram, Seismo-cardiogram, and Cardiac Time Intervals." *Advanced Science* 6, no. 14 (2019): 1900290. https://doi.org/10.1002/advs.201900290.

Hollenbaugh, Erin E., Amber L. Ferris, and Daniel J. Casey. "How Do Social Media Impact Interpersonal Communication Competence? A Uses and Gratifications Approach." In *The Psychology and Dynamics Behind Social Media Interactions*, edited by Malinda Desjarlais, 137-163. Hershey, PA: IGI Global, 2020.

Lauret, Julian. "GPT-3: The First Artificial General Intelligence?" *Towards Data Science*. July 22, 2020. https://towardsdatascience.com/gpt-3-the-first-artificial-general-intelligence-b8d9b38557a1.

Jaynes, Tyler L. "Legal Personhood for Artificial Intelligence: Citizenship as the Exception to the Rule." *AI & Society* 35, no. 2 (2020): 343-354. https://doi.org/10.1007/s00146-019-00897-9.

Jaynes, Tyler L. "Citizenship as the Exception to the Rule: An Addendum." *AI & Society*: https://doi.org/10.1007/s00146-020-01105-9.

Jeong, Hyoyoung, and Nanshu Lu. "Electronic Tattoos: The Most Multifunctional but Imperceptible Wear-ables." *Proceedings of SPIE 11020, Smart Biomedical and Physiological Sensor Technology XVI* (2019): 110200P. https://doi.org/10.1117/12.2518994.

Jeong, Hyoyoung, Liu Wang, Taewoo Ha, Ruchika Mitbander, Xiangxing Yang, Zhaohe Dai, Shutao Qiao, Linxiao Shen, Nan Sun, and Nanshu Lu. "Modular and Reconfigurable Wireless E-Tattoos for Personalized Sensing." *Advanced Materials Technologies* 4, no. 8 (2019): 1900117. https://doi.org/10.1002/admt.201900117.

Jolly, Anne. "STEM vs. STEAM: Do the Arts Belong?" *Education Week*. November 18, 2014. https://www.edweek.org/tm/articles/2014/11/18/ctq-jolly-stem-vs-steam.html.

King, Noel (host). "Miss the Noise of an Office Environment? A Device to the Rescue." *NPR*. April 22, 2020. https://www.npr.org/2020/04/22/840717836/miss-the-noise-of-an-office-environment-a-device-to-the-rescue.

Lent, Robert W. "Future of Work in the Digital World: Preparing for Instability and Opportunity." *The Career Development Quarterly* 66, no. 3 (2018): 205-219. https://doi.org/10.1002/cdq.12143.

Lopez, Ayla G., and Kennet G. Cuarteros. "Exploring the Effects of Social Media on Interpersonal Communication Among Family Members." *Canadian Journal of Family and Youth* 12, no. 1 (2020): 66-80. https://doi.org/10.29173/cjfy29491.

Marx, Karl. *Capital: A Critique of Political Economy, Volume I: The Process of Capitalist Production*. Trans. from the 3rd German edition by Samuel Moore and Edward Aveling, ed. Frederick Engels. Revised and amplified according to the 4th German ed. by Ernest Untermann (Chicago: Charles H. Kerr and Co., 1909). 7/21/2020. https://oll.libertyfund.org/titles/965#lf0445-01_head_063.

Ormond, Kelly E., Douglas P. Mortlock, Derek T. Scholes, Yvonne Bombard, Lawrence C. Brody, W. Andrew Faucett, Nanibaa' A. Garrison, Laura Hercher, Rosario Isasi, Anna Middleton, Kiran Musunuru, Daniel Shriner, Alice Virani, and Caroline E. Young. "Human Germline Genome Editing." *The American Journal of Human Genetics* 101, no. 2 (2017): 167-176. https://doi.org/10.1016/j.ajhg.2017.06.012.

Palmerini, Erica. "A Legal Perspective on Body Implants for Therapy and Enhancement." *International Review of Law, Computers & Technology* 29, nos. 2-3 (2015): 226-244. http://doi.org/10.1080/13600869.2015.1055664.

Polson, Nick, and James Scott. *AIQ: How People and Machines are Smarter Together*. New York: St. Martin's Press, 2018.

Primc, Nadia. "Do We Have a Right to an Unmanipulated Genome? The Human Genome as the Common Heritage of Mankind." *Bioethics* 34, no. 1 (2020): 41-48. https://doi.org/10.1111/bioe.12608.

Ruben, Adam. "When Ph.D. Stands for Problematic Hiring Detriment." *ScienceMag.org*. January 23, 2019. https://doi.org/10.1126/science.caredit.aaw7746.

Ruggiu, Daniele. "Implementing a Responsible, Research and Innovation Framework for Human Enhancement According to Human Rights: The Right to Bodily Integrity and the Rise of 'Enhanced Societies.'" *Law, Innovation and Technology* 10, no. 1 (2018): 82-121. https://doi.org/10.1080/17579961.2018.1452177.

Saadi, H., R. Touhami, and M.C.E. Yagoub. "Automatic Identification and Data Capture Techniques by Radio Frequency Identification RFID Tags Applied to Reader Authentication." In *Communication, Management and Information Technology*, edited by Marcelo Sampaio de Alencar, 227-234. London: Taylor & Francis Group, 2017.

Savage, Maddy. "Thousands of Swedes are Inserting Microchips Under Their Skin." *NPR*. October 22, 2018. https://www.npr.org/2018/10/22/658808705/thousands-of-swedes-are-inserting-microchips-under-their-skin.

Schein, Daniel Roy Torunczyk. "Universities Must Recognize Their Role in the Crisis, but in the Short Term, Governments Must Help PHDs to Integrate into The Job Market." *Policy Options*. July 30, 2019. https://policyoptions.irpp.org/magazines/july-2019/the-phd-employment-crisis-is-systemic/.

Schmidt, Albrecht. "Augmenting Human Intellect and Amplifying Perception and Cognition." *Pervasive Computing* 16, no. 1 (2017): 6-10.

Sullivan, Carol A. "Going Out on a Limb: Advocating for Enhanced Legal Protections for Advanced Prosthetic Limbs." *Suffolk University Law Review* 51, no. 4 (2018): 669-694.

Tucker, Robert C. (ed.). *The Marx-Engels Reader, Second Edition.* New York: W.W. Norton & Company, 1972.

Williams, Joan C. "The Pandemic Has Exposed the Fallacy of the 'Ideal Worker.'" *Harvard Business Review*. May 11, 2020. https://hbr.org/2020/05/the-pandemic-has-exposed-the-fallacy-of-the-ideal-worker.

THE PHENOMENOLOGY OF PARASOCIAL RELATIONS AND LONELINESS – BUBER AND STEIN

THOMAS J. SPIEGEL

1. Introduction

The phenomenon of parasocial relationships (or parasocial interaction) has been first described by sociologists in the second half of the 20th century (Horton & Wohl 1956).[1] Parasocial relationships feature at least one person featured in a (mass) medium like television and at least one other person consuming and interacting with this mediated presence. This relationship is necessarily lopsided and asymmetric: both sides of this relationship have limited and essentially different means of engagement, making a form of imagination one of the defining features of parasocial interactions (Valkenburg & Peter 2006). While parasocial relationships technically precede the advent of modern mass media (a believer's relation to a deity is parasocial by design), they attain a new quality with the emergence of contemporary online social media, most notably through platforms like Instagram or Twitter and streaming providers like Twitch. The main difference between these forms of parasocial engagement and traditional ones is the specific quality of reciprocity and interaction which suddenly became possible. Despite the term being established in sociology, psychology and media studies, the phenomenon has received virtually no attention in philosophy generally or social ontology specifically. What truly *are* parasocial relationships? How do they differ from regular interactions on a deeper level? What is the social ontology of parasocial relationships?

---

[1] "One of the most striking characteristics of the new mass media–radio, television, and the movies–is that they give the illusion of face-to-face relationship with the performer [...] We propose to call this seeming face-to-face relationship between spectator and performer a para-social relationship." (Horton & Wohl 1956, 215)

The main movement of thought this article develops goes like this. Loneliness is a secondary, yet fundamental existential condition of being human which consists in the absence of the second person. Trivially, loneliness is problematic in many different ways. Parasocial relations promise to curb loneliness through connecting people digitally in an effort to (re-)introduce the second person. But drawing on the work of Martin Buber and Edith Stein, it becomes clear that parasocial relationships of the kind enabled by contemporary social media technologies do not qualify as relationships of the kind which would be able to dissipate loneliness. This is because parasocial relationships do not feature the second person at all, as shall be explained. The specific mode of interactive engagement, while pretending to traverse the 'gulf' between the first and the second person, serves to mask this fundamental disconnect – a disconnect which is not present in genuine I-Thou relationships. The article closes by pointing towards the connection between loneliness and totalitarianism famously posited by Hannah Arendt to the effect that parasocial relationships, rather than combatting loneliness, might be conducive to the rise of totalitarianism.

Before we begin, there are a few terminological preliminaries to get out of the way. Firstly, parasocial relationships have to be distinguished from (what I call here) *genuine* social relationships. Genuine social relationships are those that make up to core of our social life: friendships, romantic relationships, having acquaintances, having colleagues, classmates, family, and so forth. Genuine social relationships are typically personal, i.e. not typically mediated through some kind of mass medium, and are essentially not lop-sided but rather feature symmetric recognition relations (in contrast to parasocial relationships). Genuine social relationships are those kinds of relationships that seem to be in important ways essential to being human.

Secondly, the genus of parasocial relationships itself can be divided further into two species: traditional parasocial relationships and modern parasocial relationships.[2] I call traditional parasocial relationships those which were

[2] It is interesting to see that this difference is not really present in the research. However, looking at research in the early 2000s, it can become obvious that people were not able to foresee the ways in which parasocial relations would change in nature in the upcoming years. For example, Ballantine & Martin (2005) aim to analyze online parasocial relationships in a research framework from stemming from the 80s and 90s which predominantly focussed on parasocial relationships via TV. Rojek (2016, 33) introduces a distinction between Category A and Category B parasocial relationships, the former referring to parasocial interactions with

available and prevalent when the phenomenon of parasocial relationships was first described, i.e. the parasocial relations to TV figures, celebrities, and even deities. In contrast to this, I stipulate that *modern* parasocial relationships are those which are qualitatively different in important aspects which will be further described in the upcoming sections; qualitative differences which are closely connected to the kind of lopsided interactivity and reciprocity enabled by internet powered mass media, specifically influencer culture of Instagram or TikTok and interactive video and streaming services like YouTube and Twitch.[3]

Thirdly, I follow the terminological distinction found in Klimmt et al. (2006) according to which parasocial relationships generally consist of a *persona* and an *audience*. While many parasocial relationships may have the broadcasting person in question not performing a persona, and while the audience is often not simply confined to listening anymore, this distinction is apt at bringing out the essentially asymmetrical character of parasocial relations.

A last (non-terminological) caveat is that analyzing the kind of parasocial relationships afforded to us by mainly the internet is not aimed at simply stating technology is 'bad' or 'evil'; I do not aim to propose prescriptions that we ought to return to a 'simpler' or 'better' time. Regardless of one's own convictions, the main reason for the rejection for such a putative return to 'innocence' is that it is impossible to turn back time and undo the effects of technological 'innovations' once they have taken a foothold. Some may come to the conclusion that parasocial relationships (especially the ones I call "modern") ought to be eschewed; but such judgments, if they are to be made properly, should be grounded in a social-ontological analysis of parasocial relationships first.

---

celebrities, the latter to less focussed, unidentified mass, e.g. the kind of sympathy we feel with survivors of the nuclear disaster in Fukushima.

[3] Some may wonder why I do not explicitly name online gaming (like World of Warcraft), message boards or social platforms (like Facebook, LinkedIn). The reason is that while these forms of interaction do in fact feature and allow for parasocial relationships, they are still widely (perhaps even predominantly) as an extension of genuine social relationships.

2. Loneliness: The Second Person Disappearing

It has been widely observed that the last century has seen a dramatic diminishing of the time people in industrialized countries spend *together*.[4] Sociologists estimate that the time we spend in the presence of others (talking, in silence, laughing, crying) has been cut in half compared to the 19th century. This effect is at least partially enabled by the rise of nearly instantaneous communication technologies (telegrams, phones, the internet first on desktop PCs and now portable internet-accessing devices). Simultaneously, the multifaceted need for connection is what drives the development of more technologies of the same kind which in turn enable us to spend less and less time in the actual presence of others. While tele-communication through space and time qua writing (most notably: writing letters) has been part of non-oral cultures for millennia now, it would be conceited to claim that parasocial relationships would therefore be 'nothing new'. There certainly is something new about the kind of parasocial relationships which are only now enabled through new technologies. One of the main aspects of what is new about parasocial relationships of this kind is their connection to an epidemic of loneliness swathes of people in industrialized countries experience. The history of the 20th century can, among other things, also be written as the history of loneliness.

What is loneliness? We all know what loneliness is and what it feels like even if putting it into words can elude us.[5] Loneliness as a phenomenon outruns our attempts at putting it into words. Loneliness feels unpleasant. While being alone can be joyous, it is analytically true that feeling lonely is

---

[4] This is closely documented for North America: The average US-American citizen spends 2,8 hours a day watching television versus 38 minutes per day socializing in person (cf. https://www.bls.gov/news.release/pdf/atus.pdf). Interestingly this seems to be reflected in our linguistic usage: In 1674, the word "loneliness" was "in a list of infrequently used words, and defined it as a term to describe places and people 'far from neighbours'. A century later, the word hadn't changed much." (Hill 2020).

[5] One of the better 'flowery' descriptions of loneliness as a feeling is found in the writing of psychiatrist John McGrath: "Loneliness not only refers to the absence of the desired other's presence but this very absence is perceived as a presence, albeit a presence that is felt in the manner of an absence, that is, as a privation or deprivation of the other. Hence, it is not only the other's absence and the felt presence of its absence that constitute loneliness, it is also that this absence creates a lack or loss within the lonely self such that one feels porous and drained. Consequently, when the other is absent, the lonely person feels that something is wanting within one's self. One feels emptied (the lack of intimacy) and hollowed (the lack of meaning)." (McGrath 1995, 44).

terrible. Loneliness is a negative state–deprivation of something, more specifically: someone. This someone is usually not a specific person as one usually does not require a *specific* person to not experience loneliness. This someone is rather the generalized second person.

While anyone knows by acquaintance what loneliness feels like, it would be incorrect to identify loneliness as a mere feeling. Loneliness is neither *only* a feeling or emotion as some authors, predominantly psychologists, imply (Roberts & Krueger [forthcoming], Murphy & Kupshik1992, Cacioppo & Patrick 2009, Ettema 2010). Loneliness is more than an emotion. Loneliness can be accompanied by emotions, but loneliness itself is an existential category. Rather, loneliness is a subject-transcendent existential phenomenon. As Heidegger notes, being-with-others (*Mitsein*) is ontologically fundamental: we always already find ourselves with others; all Robinson Crusoe-style thought experiments to the contrary are hypothetical exercises. If being-with-others is a primary existential state, then being-without-others is a secondary, if irreducible, existential state. It is therefore not mere coincidence that "one of the fundamental experiences of every human life" (Arendt 1973, 475, cf. also Shuster 2012, 474). Since being-with-others is an existential condition, its privative form–loneliness–is, too, 'baked' into what it means to be human.

Hence, I shall understand loneliness here at its core as the lack or disappearance of the second person, the generalized person that is not oneself. Loneliness as an emotion is, under this aspect, not a binary, all-or-nothing state; one can feel vastly different degrees of loneliness and isolation, regardless of whether the second person is present. And it is certainly not the case that any and all people in industrialized Western countries feel lonely, i.e. wholly deprived of other people. Some are lucky to never experience true loneliness. Yet, there is a definite trend of loneliness connected to our changing forms of life.

The question then remains: what is the relationship between parasocial relationships and loneliness? Modern parasocial relationships are designed to help curb loneliness. Their promise is human connection. Nowhere is this idea expressed more clearly than in Facebook's ubiquitous CSR statements, in Mark Zuckerberg's own words:

> "I started Facebook to connect my college. I always thought one day someone would connect the whole world, but I never thought it would be us. I would have settled for connecting my whole dorm. We were just college kids. But we cared so much about this idea -- that all people want to connect.

> […]
>
> It's not enough to simply connect the world, we must also work to bring the world closer together." (Zuckerberg 2017)

Facebook, the juggernaut of social media, is all about "connecting" people. And it has indeed been a research topic in psychology and communication studies whether social media technologies are effective in 'fighting' loneliness. The results are mixed (Miller 2020). It might be an empirical matter whether certain people *feel* more or less lonely with social media (e.g. Rubin et al.1985). Yet, it is not an empirical matter, all things considered, what the relation between modern parasocial relations, facilitated by such technologies, and loneliness truly is. This non-empirical link is the general frame for what follows. This is because loneliness is as shall become clear, an existential phenomenon, *not* simply one that may or may not have developed in the history of mankind. Therefore, modern parasocial can curb loneliness as a phenomenon if and only if they make the second person (re-)appear.

3. Parasocial Relationships: The Second Person Reappearing?

Technological optimists will rejoice at this point. Some will state that while the second person gradually disappears, this disappearance is accompanied by a coeval rise and development of parasocial relationships. Parasocial relationships are relationships which a "viewer or user holds to a media person, which includes specific cognitive and affective components" (Schmid & Klimmt 2011).

Fittingly, political scientist Chris Rojek states that parasocial relationships facilitate and operate on what he calls *presumed intimacy* which enables "distanced ontological identification with strangers" (Rojek 2016, 39). Presumed intimacy can be viewed as a form of soft power which does not openly coerce, yet asserts forms of dominance through a disclosure of empathy. Presumed intimacy can be established between truly anonymous strangers (the survivors of catastrophic incidents broadcasted through the news) and relationships with celebrities (Rojek 2016, 11). Parasocial relationships create a quasi-familiarity through presumed intimacy, the strange person is "no longer precisely vague or general", becoming what Rojek calls "pixillated people" (Rojek 2016, 32). Interestingly, genuine social relationships create emotional involvement through a development of intimacy by getting to know and understand the person's life and character.

In parasocial relationships with merely presumed intimacy, emotional "involvement is urged to precede" our familiarity with the persona (Rojek 2016, 32). Such preliminaries are helpful. Yet, we can further characterize parasocial relationships through the following aspects: asymmetry, pretense, and commodification.

Firstly, parasocial relationships are asymmetric insofar as typically only audience forms a cognitive or emotional bond with the persona. And in situations where there is some form of interaction between audience and persona, the bulk of cognitive and emotional engagement is typically on the side of the audience. This will, of course, be relative to the medium involved and other factors. Traditional parasocial relationships mediated by way of television are usually entirely one-sided whereas, say, a musical performer responding publicly to a fan's question on Twitter is slightly less one-sided. Contemporary forms of streaming services like Twitch allow for a minimal simulated form of reciprocity where, depending on the celebrities 'clout' and audience, the relationship to their viewer-base may be more or less intensive. For example, a professional Twitch streamer with an audience in the ten thousands can engage in virtually no individualized contact with his viewers whereas a smaller streamer with an audience of a few dozen or a few hundred is in a position to engender such interactions. It is, finally, constitutive of parasocial relationships that this distance is never fully closed. While it is usually the purpose of genuine social relationships to lessen and perhaps make disappear the perceived distance between the friends, colleagues, acquaintances in question, parasocial relationships can, by definition, only be maintained as long this distance is maintained. A parasocial relationship whose constitutive distance gradually disappears simply becomes a genuine social relationship.

This is intertwined with a *second* characteristic of parasocial relationships: pretense. Pretense applies especially to the more modern forms of parasocial relationships. As an example of traditional parasocial relationships, A-List Hollywood actors (e.g. Scarlett Johansson or Leonardo DiCaprio) do not need to pretend to be within grasp of their fanbase (regardless of whether some fans may feel some celebrity's social proximity). This is not to say that such celebrities do not feel pressure to seem approachable or likable, but rather that the audience by far and large does not expect any form of specific interaction (beyond, say, signing paraphernalia at a movie premiere) by those venerated almost like demigods. In contrast, contemporary influencer and streaming culture (as representations of modern parasocial relationships) almost necessitates the need to style oneself as someone who could, in principle, be socially *reached*, i.e. as someone to whom the social 'gulf' could realistically be bridged. Part of this game of pretense is to pretend that there is no asymmetry or that *their* user engagement is less asymmetrical than that of their competition or that the asymmetry could in principle vanish or be alleviated. Parasocial relationships, especially modern ones, create an illusion of companionship, intimacy, identification, community, and sometimes even friendship. For example, it is standard procedure of the vast majority of Twitch streamers to refer to themselves as "we" in a manner that is supposed to include the chat: "we did it!", "we won", "we will end the stream here". The word "chat" in these contexts is used as a name for the amorphous, everchanging, growing, shrinking mass entity of consumers which can engage with the streamer during the stream via chat interaction and donation messages. Simply put, "chat" is used as a proper name in such contexts in statements such as "chat thinks that p". And more often than not, this way of talking about "us" and "ourselves" is adopted by large parts of any given "chat". Contrast this with the way in which traditional celebrity athletes tend to refer to their fans and viewership. For example, athletes in a team sport like football will rarely use statements like "we won" or "we played badly in the first half" to refer to their team *plus* the fanbase, but rather to themselves, their team and its support infrastructure. (Conversely, it is not rare that fan-talk includes using "we" and "us" as a means to refer to the team plus themselves as fans.) The "we" of modern parasocial relationships is an artificial "we", a pretend-we.

The main incentive for pretense in modern parasocial relationships lies with the *third* aspect: commodification. Parasocial interactions of the relevant interest here are almost always transactional, hardly ever somehow without the motive of some form of monetary gain.[6] Examples of commodifying parasocial relationships even date back to times when radio was the most relevant mass medium: singer and radio star Kate Smith raised §39 million USD in donations for the Second World War in a one-day marathon of broadcasting (Rojek 2016, 13). While this extreme early example is obviously impressive, commodification has become much more pervasive, trite, and normalized in modern forms of parasocial interactions. So-called

---

[6] There are some counter examples, at least anecdotal ones, for some personae looking for human connection rather than financial gain:

> "The reason I started streaming was that I was kind of looking for human connections," said Richárd Szélesy, a streamer who has spent the last few years mostly broadcasting hardcore games to zero viewers.[…] "[I streamed to] escape loneliness and depression," he said. While he has mostly been streaming without an audience, every so often an errant person will drop by and stick around." Hernandez (2018)

'influencers' and other smaller and larger media personalities often receive direct payment for individualized engagement with some fans, subscription services, or access to 'candid' pictures of the 'influencer' in question (Sokolova & Kefi 2020). (This is indeed the main purpose of platforms like *Onlyfans*). Another example is the interesting, so-far largely unique phenomenon called *Cameo*, a website on which celebrities (of truly different popularity statuses–most you will never have heard of) offer 'shout-outs' (short personalized video messages) to fans for prices starting at around $10 up to several thousand US dollars. Streaming platforms like Twitch have become highly influential, highly profitable social media platforms. On platforms like Twitch, so-called streamers broadcast themselves to an audience, usually playing video games, although recent years have seen the rise of other forms of entertainment on that platform (for example, real-life streams or workout streams). The audience can interact with the streaming persona using a screen-name via a chat, however, without their own visual or auditory representation, thus creating a more or less asymmetrical communicative situation. Streamers have a financial incentive: viewers can "subscribe" to a channel for §5 (USD) and they can donate money directly to the streamer, making both the platform and the partnered streamer money. The most successful streamers are millionaires, mid-sized streamers can still make a very good living. The so-called "cheer"-mechanic alone generates a collective net-gain of $10 million for streamers alone (Spangler 2017), the main driving force motivator to "cheer" being social integration (Wohn & Freeman 2020) and a sense of community (Hilvert-Bruce et al 2018). Such forms of social media "codify and managerialize" central aspects of human connection by "commercializing and standardizing" interactions and related emotions (Rojek 2016, 136). Similar instantiations of commodifying relationships and attention can be found in virtually all forms of modern parasocial relationships.

The upshot is that parasocial relationships consist in interactions between a first and a second person, like genuine social relationships–at least in the standard picture. The difference to genuine social relationships is that parasocial relationships are constrained by their constitutive asymmetry, pretense, and commodification in the form of monetary gain. While genuine social relationships are sometimes permeated by aspects of pretense and commodification, these aspects are usually seen as a detractor of what one would want their genuine social relationships to be. For example, some marriages are built on pretense and commodification (e.g. marrying for money or to attain citizenship), yet this is reasonably seen as a corruption of an idealized idea of marriage. Thus the second person does appear in modern parasocial relationships, but as defective or incomplete. The second person is never *really* there. In what follows, it shall become apparent why that is the case.

4. Stein and Buber on the Indispensability of the Second Person

It would be an absolutely naive understatement to say that the role and value of the second person has been studied before. Philosophy, sociology, sociobiology, psychology, psychoanalysis, cultural studies, communication science and many other disciplines research the nature of the second person and sociality more broadly speaking. One could then accordingly view the phenomenon of parasocial relationships through any and all of these different lenses. For the specific social-ontological aspects of recent kinds of parasocial relationships, we can look to two thinkers in the phenomenological tradition whose analysis of the role of the second person gets to the roots to the question in what sense the relation between the first and the second person is fundamental. Presumably, it may turn out to be these roots which also underlie the (mostly negative) social and psychological ramifications that accompany loneliness understood as the disappearance of the second person.

The fact that the second person is never really there in parasocial relationships has, of course, not eluded these disciplines. Traditionally, psychology and sociology focus on certain superficial traits of parasocial relationships, both positive and negative. For example, parasocial relationships are sometimes attributed the property of being conducive to one's character development, identity formation, and self-reflection (Madison & Porter 2015). Or conversely, parasocial relationships are sometimes said to be partially responsible for an increase in aggression or the development of body image disorders (Maltby et al. 2005). From a philosophical (more specifically: a phenomenological) perspective, the conceptual ramifications of parasocial relationships can be investigated on a 'deeper' level.

The work of Martin Buber and Edith Stein can serve to highlight certain unexplored blind spots in the available thought on the nature, impact and ramifications of parasocial relationships. They each can provide us with a different reason for the following key-thought: parasocial relationships are not relationships in which a first person *truly* encounters the second person. In Stein's thought, this idea is implicit in her account of the transcendental role the second person's body plays for the constitution and experience of the first person. Even more problematically: If we take Buber's account of

I-Thou relationships seriously then, it turns out, parasocial relationships are not even relationships between an I and a Thou, but rather between an I and an It (in his terminology). I will not argue for the truth of either of Stein's and Buber's accounts. It is, instead, a conditional claim: if Buber and Stein are correct about their respective accounts of the second person, then we bring into view seemingly novel ways in which parasocial relationships essentially differ from genuine social relationships. Both of them show us different ways in which the second person is indispensable, yet is left absent in parasocial relationships.

In her doctoral thesis *On the Problem of Empathy*, Edith Stein seeks to fill a theoretical lacuna in the work of her teacher and arguably greatest influence, Edmund Husserl. One of the then greatest research desiderata for a complete phenomenological account of experience was the experience of the other person, more specifically the mind of the other, second person to which the experiencing subject does not have the same privileged access it has to its own experience. Stein first establishes the role of the experiencing subject's own spatially situated body (*Leib*) as essential to experience as such. Some thinkers in the Germanophone phenomenological tradition famously distinguish between a *Körper* and *Leib*, two different concepts which have no simple linguistic differentiation in English:

> The living body [*Leib*] in contrast with the physical body [*Körper*] is characterized by having fields of sensation, being located at the zero point of orientation of the spatial world, moving voluntarily and being constructed of moving organs, being the field of expression of the experiences of its 'I' and the instrument of the ''I's' will. (Stein 1989, §5, 63)

The living body, according to Stein, is most notably characterized by being the spatial center of one's experience, being able to be moved voluntarily (contrasted with involuntary reflexes of the merely physical body), by being *literally* living, and being the center of the experiencing subject's will. Stein then delves deeper into what the generalized second person's body's role plays for the experience of the first person. In what follows, I provide a brief, abridged recounting of Stein's conception of empathy with regards to the lived body of the second person in a manner that is tailored to the aims of this paper:

Firstly, sensual empathy (*Empfindungseinfühlung*) is made possible in virtue of the subject being able to change to position of its body as well as the subject analogously altering its lived body's properties in imagination (Stein 1989, §5, b, 65f.). This imaginative capacity is what enables the subject to imagine what it would be like to be (in the position of) the other person.

Secondly, empathetically projecting oneself into the second person's lived body ("einfühlend in ihn versetze...", Stein 1989f, §5, d, 68), the second person's lived body becomes a new "zero point of orientation" (ibid.) in addition to the subject's original point of orientation which is its own lived body. While one's own original point of orientation is *primordial* to oneself, the second person's lived body provides a *non-primordial* point of orientation. The second person is a point in space just like oneself. In having acquired another non-primordial spatialized point of orientation, the subject is now in a position to understand its own point of orientation not as *the absolute* point of orientation *as such*, but rather as one among many. Moreover, the subject also comes to understand that its own lived body (*Leib*) is merely a physical body (*Körper*) for the second person, just like the second person's body is a lived body for them, but merely a physical body for the subject.

Thirdly, Stein uses the results thus far to motivate her conception of the concept of world:

> The world I glimpse empathically is an existing world, posited as having being like the world primordially perceived. The perceived world and the world given empathically are the same world differently seen.
>
> [...]
>
> Were I imprisoned within the boundaries of my individuality, I could not go beyond 'the world as it appears to me.' At least it would be conceivable that the possibility of its independent existence, that could still be given as a possibility, would always be undemonstrable. But this possibility is demonstrated as soon as I cross these boundaries by the help of empathy and obtain the same world's second and third appearance which are independent of my perception. Thus empathy as the basis of intersubjective experience becomes the condition of possible knowledge of the existing outer world [...]. (Stein 1989, §5, g, 71f.)

Thus, according to Stein, the world is that which the subject experiences both qua its lived body and through that which is given to it through acts of empathy or empathizing. Furthermore, empathy is what allows one to transcend one's "boundaries of individuality" in a way that enables access to an intersubjectively shared world which is the transcendental enabling condition ("condition of possibility") for knowledge of the world as such.

This is in the briefest of terms Stein's account of the relevance of the lived body of the second person for experience as such. It is important to note that this is a decidedly *transcendental* account. That is, this is not a story about how–phylogenetically or ontogenetically–we come to be with others. It is rather theoretical dissection of transcendental layers which enable the full content of experience as such in the first place, i.e. that which must be the case for there to be at all an experiencing subject with access to the world.

How then does this relate to the phenomenon in question, i.e. parasocial relationships? Parasocial relationships are characterized by the fact that they are essentially disembodied, making the relationship always a spatially distant one, even if this distality is attempted to be overridden by different means of tele-communication and reciprocity. The streaming personality I follow on Twitch may employ certain maneuvers to simulate a decrease of distance in manifold ways (by chatting, reading my messages etc.). Yet, it is constitutive of the streaming experience as such that the streamer to whom I have this parasocial relationship is not present, only an image of his lived body on a screen. Thus, the lived body of the streamer cannot serve as a second point of direction in space; namely, because the streamer (as an image on the screen) does not share a space with me. Accordingly, there is no lived body with which I could come to understand that my lived body is simultaneously a physical body for the other. This goes, by the way, *vice versa*: The streamer herself does not have her viewers present as (lived or physical) bodies such that her relationship to her viewers does not support Stein's analysis either. Consequently, the parasocial relationship cannot play the transcendental function of constituting an intersubjectively shared world in which the first and second person come to find themselves, again due to the absence of the body of the second person–either persona or audience. In this sense, a reading of Stein demonstrates that parasocial relationships do not implicate a second person the full sense.

Of course, Stein's story, again, is neither supposed to tell an either phylogenetical or ontogenetical story. Yet, her account implies that the *fundamental* relationship to a second person with all these important transcendental features is a genuinely social relationship. If Stein's account is true, this assessment then supports the following counterfactual: If there was a world in which individuals could only entertain parasocial relationships, then the subjects in that world would not be able to have experience of a non-subjective world at all. But this seems like an obvious contradiction. Of course, this then implies that parasocial relationships are parasitic on social relationships: there are *a priori* (not merely empirical sociological) reasons why there need to be social relationships for there in order to be parasocial relationships. And while such a counterfactual world may perhaps not be realistically possible, it demonstrates that parasocial relationships are profoundly deficient insofar as they cannot, in principle, serve the fundamental role of co-constituting the experiencing subject as such. The simple, yet crucial main point we can extract from Stein's transcendental analysis of the second person is that the very fact that parasocial relationships do not involve a lived body makes them defective and ontologically parasitic upon genuine social relationships in an essential manner.

There may be some misleading exceptions. For example, a fan can briefly shake hands, take a picture, and exchange three or four words with their object of admiration at a 'meet-and-greet' event or a film premiere. This objection leads us to Buber's view of the role of the second person. For, while there is certainly a living body present in such moments, it might be the case that this is not properly called a *relationship* to another person (a Thou) at all–at least if Buber has something to say on that matter.

Martin Buber's philosophical thought is notoriously difficult to situate. A deeply religious thinker, Buber is often not canonically counted as a phenomenologist; his *I and Thou* can be read at least in a phenomenological spirit that is compatible with thinkers like Stein and other's.[7] Buber uses the word pairs I-Thou and I-It to stress that these modes are a priori, that is *always already*, established. For Buber, it does not make sense to speak of an I that is not in engagement with an I or a Thou.

The I-It mode is perhaps more readily understood. In I-It relationships I treat things as things, usually as a means to an end. The It can be animate or inanimate. For example, I use a hammer to put nails into a board. I can engage with the cow as a source of meat and milk. I talk to the clerk at the post office in order to get my mail sent. More generally, Buber states that the It-World is the world of experiencing: I experiences an It, the It is disclosed to the I in experience. It is not only the mode of teleological engagements with the world (Heidegger's *um zu*, Heidegger 2006), but rather a mode of engagement with the world as it is in dependency to me. This also includes other people: in the mode of I-It, another person is merely

[7] Kojima (1987) and Zank (2020) both call his thought "phenomenological" without supplying further reasons. He is also often mentioned alongside Levinas, e.g. Atterton et al. (2004). There are a few seemingly methodological remarks in the otherwise wholly unacademic *I and Thou*, for example: "For I speak only of the actual human being, of you and me, of our life and our world, not of any I-in-itself and not of any Being-in-itself" (Buber 1970, 65). This remark seems wholly in line with the phenomenological tenet to let oneself be guided in one's inquiry by the phenomena themselves.

a He or She (not a Thou).

That being said, I-It engagements can even be reciprocal too: I sometimes treat living beings as an It who also, in turn, treat me as an It. For example, try as I might, my colleague's Chihuahua simply views me as a living food dispenser, perhaps as I may only see it as a source of entertainment and play.[8] Likewise, a prostitute and her suitor treat each other as an It: the suitor (a He) is a source of income for the prostitute, the prostitute (a She) is a way to satisfy the suitor's desire temporarily. Contrast this with the relationship between an I and a Thou. Buber uses the term "relationship" (*Beziehung*) terminologically. Where the I-It mode is one of experiencing, *relationships* can only be between an I and a Thou. This also means that a Thou is *not* experienced on Buber's account. The mode of engagement in an I-Thou relationship is not of the kind that gives us an experience as such, but rather something different. The Thou is not a *thing* or *object* to which an I would relate.

The I-You mode can be between an I and nature, an I and another human person, or between an I and mental beings (*geistige Wesen*) (Buber 1970, 56f.). For example, the I-Thou can be between me and any sentient being, a tree, a dog, or a human person. I-Thou engagements have three defining characteristics. Firstly, they are *unmediated*:

> "The relation to the You is unmediated. Nothing conceptual intervenes between I and You, no prior knowledge and no imagination; and memory itself is changed as it plunges from particularity into wholeness." (Buber 1970, 62f.)

The I and Thou are in *direct* contact. Note that this is not meant in a spatial sense: the Thou does not need to be in close proximity.[9] This is relevant due to the second characteristic.

The second characteristic is *reciprocity*. It is not entirely certain how Buber conceives of the reciprocity of I-Thou relations. This is because in one place he stresses that they are reciprocal (*gegenseitig*, Buber 1970, 58), while shortly after stressing that the

---

[8] In contrast, my aunt's Border Collie does respond to me as a Thou, just as I treat him as a Thou, in a manner that is difficult to explicate in language.

[9] "Before the immediacy of the relationship everything mediate becomes negligible. It is also trifling whether my You is the It of other I's ("object of general experience") or can only become that as a result of my essential deed" (Buber 1970, 63).

> "relation can obtain even if the human being to whom I say You does not hear it in his experience. For You is more than It knows. You does more, and more happens to it, than It knows." (Buber 1970, 60)

He thereby makes it appear as if the question whether an I-Thou relation obtains is entirely up to the I itself. And indeed, this needs to be the case for two reasons. First, otherwise no I-Thou relation between the I and non-sentient nature would be possible. Second, otherwise an I-Thou relation between the I and an unresponsive God would not be possible; and that is simply not feasible for Buber. In fact, for Buber, the primordial, most fundamental I-Thou relation possible is between the I and God. Yet, this relation cannot be the same as between an I and another human person.

The third characteristic of I-Thou relationships is *purposelessness*.

> "No purpose intervenes between I and You, no greed and no anticipation; and longing itself is changed as it plunges from the dream into appearance. Every means is an obstacle. Only where all means have disintegrated encounters occur." (Buber 1970, 62)

I-Thou relationships do not allow for instrumental concerns. A Thou cannot be treated as a means to an end. The Thou cannot be used for anything or be hold as anything or can be approached with ulterior motives, otherwise it is merely an It. This is for conceptual reasons if we follow Buber: the Thou in the I-Thou relation is not a "something" that one could use as a means to an end. The necessary condition for us to enter an I-Thou relationship is to not treat the Thou as something at all.

Buber stresses that both modes of engagement are irreducible although he is certainly not using this term. Yet, Buber clearly prioritizes the I-Thou mode as more important. It is more important because *all actual life* occurs in the mode of I-Thou (Buber 1970, 62). He calls it the "sublime melancholy of our lot that every [*Thou*] in our world must become an It" (Buber 1970, 68). It is not possible to always treat sentient beings as a Thou. It seems to be a hard, metaphysical necessity that we treat others as an It. For example, in my everyday life, I treat the cashier at the supermarket as an It. Reciprocally, she does the same with me. She is the means to an end for me, and I am simply an affordance that comes with her job. But it might just be the case on a lazy Saturday morning that I am the only customer at the super market and I start, for some reason, a conversation with the cashier that goes beyond the necessary pleasantries (politeness is most certainly part and parcel of the It-world). And if the conditions are right ("if will and grace are joined", Buber 1970, 58), then we may enter an I-Thou relationship. In an

I-Thou relationship, the I and Thou enter a new mode, without experiencing ("erfahren") each other.

What does this now have to do with parasocial relationships? Buber's notion of the I-Thou discloses that parasocial relationships–especially modern parasocial relations–might not deserve the title *relationship* at all. In other words, it is very questionable whether parasocial relationships can even count as I-Thou relationships; they are seemingly better understood as I-It relationships.

Counterintuitively, the asymmetry between audience and persona is not the decisive factor though. After all, Buber admits that the second person does not have to directly reciprocate. Although, realistically speaking, the viewers probably usually engage with the streamer in a manner that is in an I-It mode, the viewer might even find himself in the mood conducive to an I-Thou relationship. Hence, the crucial moment is not the asymmetry between streamer and viewer. This has to be the case since Buber conceives of the relationship between I and God as the prime form of an I-Thou relationship.

Instead, the relevant characteristic is the third aspect of I-Thou relations previously specified: purposelessness. The lack of instrumentalization is a necessary condition for there to be an I-Thou relation. Audience and persona are more like consumer and producer. The engagement between consumer and producer, however, is an I-It par excellence. The viewer is a commodity to be milked. The producer depends on the audience watching. Commodification–money for entertainment and simulated closeness–remains the main theme of their relation. It is perhaps the most pernicious aspect that the viewer is conned into treating the streamer as a Thou as one without ulterior motive.

Therefore, if we follow Buber, a parasocial relationship merely simulates and pretends to be a genuine social relationship. Parasocial relationships cannot be genuine I-Thou relationships because they are virtually never purposeless.

5. Glossy Loneliness and Totalitarianism

We can take stock and provide an overview of the relationship between parasocial relationships (specifically modern ones) and loneliness. Loneliness is the absence of the second person. Modern parasocial relationships promise to introduce and make acquainted with the second person. Yet, as a reading of thinkers like Buber and Stein, lays bare, modern parasocial relationships do not *really* feature a second person at all, rather a simulation of the second person. Therefore, modern parasocial relationships do not do away with loneliness; instead, they are apt to perniciously perpetuate it.

There is no point in 'blaming' the actors themselves for, perhaps, not realizing this. The audience who may wish to fill their otherwise silent houses with the voice and face of an interactive human being cannot be blamed for trying to alleviate their loneliness. Nor can the personae trying to make a living and entertain people at the same time be made to feel at fault. As Buber already saw, the It-world offers a kind of soothing calmness. By contrast, engaging in an I-Thou relation is a gamble on Buber's account because. Just like I do not risk anything in playing with a stuffed toy, I do not risk or gamble anything engaging in a parasocial relationship (other than perhaps the content of my wallets).[10]

Technological determinists claim that technological advancement drives human advancement and well-being. Specifically in this context, the central promise of technological advancement was the promised creation of McLuhan's *Global Village* (McLuhan 1962), the vague idea that mankind becomes 'closer' through information and communication technologies. The phenomenological analysis drawing on Buber, Stein, and to a lesser degree, Heidegger demonstrates that technology of the kind that engenders modern parasocial relationships is not apt to fulfil McLuhan's promise: a village, even a metaphorical one, is partially characterized by the immediate proximity to the second person. Yet, as seen, the second person remains absent in modern parasocial relationships. Perniciously, modern parasocial relationships are borne as a technological alleviative solution to loneliness which was in the first place partially caused by the technological advance

---

[10] Interestingly enough, Buber's main example for the ones fleeing the world of relationships (*Begegnung*) was the academic intellectual:

> "To be sure, some men who in the world of things make do with experiencing and using have constructed for themselves an idea annex or superstructure in which they find refuge and reassurance in the face of intimations of nothingness. [...] But the It-humanity that some imagine, postulate, and advertise has nothing in common with the bodily humanity to which a human being can truly say You. The noblest fiction is a fetish, the most sublime fictitious sentiment is a vice." (Buber 1970, 65)

It stands to speculate how harsh a judgment Buber would have passed on modern parasocial relationships.

that accompanied the process of social atomization. Rather than offering a solution, modern parasocial relationships are more like a colourful patch on a gaping wound.

Given the pervasiveness of modern parasocial relationships, it may yield unsettling results to think them together with Hannah Arendt's analysis of totalitarianism. Arendt famously posits the controversial thesis that there is an intrinsic link between totalitarianism and human loneliness:

> "What prepares men for totalitarian domination in the non-totalitarian world is the fact that loneliness, once a borderline experience usually suffered in certain marginal social conditions like old age, has become an everyday experience of the ever-growing masses of our century." (Arendt 1973, 478)

It has become a platitude to claim that we are (again) in an age of totalitarianism with world leaders like Putin Erdogan, or Trump, yet this time around furnished with more so-called "fake news" and conspiracy theories.[11] If this is correct, and if there is anything to Arendt's idea that totalitarianism thrives on loneliness, then modern parasocial relationships deserve a more thorough, and decidedly more critical treatment than virtually all of the current research endeavours. Having tried to establish the intrinsic connection between modern parasocial relationships and loneliness, a subsequent inquiry would now have to deal with the question how this ties into Arendt's thesis of the intrinsic connection between loneliness and totalitarianism.

Bibliography

Arendt, Hannah (1973): *The Origins of Totalitarianism*, San Diego: Hartcourtbrace.

Atterton, Peter; Calarco, Matthew & Friedman, Maurice (2004): *Levinas & Buber: Dialogue and Difference*, Duquesne University Press.

Paul W. Ballantine and Brett A. S. Martin (2005): "Forming Parasocial Relationships in Online Communities", in NA – Advances in Consumer Research Volume 32, eds. Geeta Menon and Akshay R. Rao, Duluth, MN: Association for Consumer Research, 197-201.

Buber, Martin (1970): *I and Thou*, transl. Walter Kaufmann, Charles Scribner's Sons. Ettema,

[11] It would be an impossible endeavour to try and name even just the most salient publications in 2020 alone on the rise of (quasi-)totalitarian leadership in different countries around the world. This topic is simply anywhere and everywhere.

Cacioppo, John & Patrick, William (2009): *Loneliness. Human Nature and the Need for Social Connection*, New York & London: Norton.

Hill, Samantha Rose (2020): "Where Loneliness can lead", *Aeon*, https://aeon.co/essays/for-hannah-arendt-totalitarianism-is-rooted-in-loneliness?fbclid=IwAR3k6iv4Y6DN0_0guDmceYjrJLXenkGgTi6pN3ptH1kfcE7CkhDXO5gqiq0, last viewed 15.10.2020.

Hilvert-Bruce, Z., Neill, J. T., Sjo¨blom, M., & Hamari, J. (2018). Social motivations of livestreaming viewer engagement on Twitch, Computers in Human Behavior 84, 58–67.

Heidegger, Martin (2006): *Sein und Zeit*, first published 1927, Tübingen: Niemeyer.

Hernandez, Patricia (2018): "The Twitch Streamers who spend Years broadcasting to No One", https://www.theverge.com/2018/7/16/17569520/twitch-streamers-zero-viewers-motivation-community, last viewed 16.10.2020.

Horton, Donald and Wohl, Richard (1956): "Mass communication and para-social interaction: Observations and intimacy at a distance", *Psychiatry*, 19, 215–229.

Klimmt, Christoph; Hartmann, Tilo & Schramm, Holger (2006): "Parasocial Interactions and Relationships", in Jennings Bryant & Peter Vorderer (eds.), *Psychology of Entertainment*, Lawrence Erlbaum Associates Publishers, 291-313.

Kojima, Hiroshi (1987): "The Phenomenology of the Thou", *Morality within the Life - and Social World*, Tymieniecka Anna-Teresa (ed.), Analecta Husserliana (The Yearbook of Phenomenological Research), vol 22. Springer, Dordrecht, 337-342.

Madison, Phillip & Porter, Lance (2015): "The People we Meet. Discriminating Functions of Parasocial Interactions", *Imagination, Cognition, and Personality* 35 (1), 47-71.

Maltby, John; Giles, David; Barber, Louise & McCutcheon, Lynn (2005): "Intense-personal celebrity worship and body image: Evidence of a link among female adolescents", *British Journal of Health Psychology* 10 (1), 17-32.

McLuhan, Marshall (1962): *The Gutenberg Galaxy*, University of Toronto Press.

Murphy, Murphy & Kupshik, Gary (1992): *Loneliness, Stress, and Well-Being. A Helper's Guide*, London & New York: Tavistock/Routledge.

McGraw, John (1995): "Loneliness, its Nature and Form", *Man and World* 28, 43-64.

Roberts, Tom & Krueger, Joel (forthcoming): "Loneliness and the emotional experience of absence", *Southern Journal of Philosophy*.

Miller, Eric (2020): "Loneliness in the Era of COVID-19", *Frontiers in Psychology* 11, 1-3.

Rojek, Chris (2016): *Presumed Intimacy. Parasocial Relations in Media, Society and Celebrity Culture*, Cambridge, UK: Polity Press.

Rubin, Alan M., Elizabeth M. Perse, and Robert A. Powell (1985), "Loneliness, Parasocial Interaction, and Local Television News Viewing", *Human Communication Research* 12, 155-80.

Shuster, Martin (2012): "Language and Loneliness: Arendt, Cavell, and Modernity", *International Journal of Philosophical Studies* 20 (4), 473-497.

Sokolova, Karina & Kefi, Hajer (2020): "Instagram and YouTube bloggers promote it, why should I buy? How credibility and parasocial interaction influence purchase intentions", *Journal of Retailing and Consumer Services* 53, 1-9.

Spangler, Todd (2017): "Twitch will let more streamers earn money, after users spend over $12 million on cheering emoji", *Variety*, https://variety.com/2017/digital/news/twitchaffiliate-program-cheering-12-million-dollars-1202392024/, last viewed 12.10.2020.

Stein, Edith (1989): *On the Problem of Empathy*, in Mary Beshard (ed.), The Collected Works of Edith Stein volume 3, transl. Waltraut Stein, Dordrecht: Kluwer.

Valkenburg, Patti & Peter, Jochen (2006): "Fantasy and Imagination", in Jennings Bryant & Peter Vorderer (eds.), *Psychology of Entertainment*, London & New York: Routledge, 177-196.

Zank, Michael and Zachary Braiterman (2020): "Martin Buber", *The Stanford Encyclopedia of Philosophy*, Edward N. Zalta (ed.), URL = https://plato.stanford.edu/archives/fall2020/entries/buber/, last viewed 14.10.2020.

Zuckerberg, Mark (2017): "Bringing the World Closer Together" https://www.facebook.com/notes/mark-zuckerberg/bringing-the-world-closer-together/10154944663901634/, last viewed 14.10.2020.

Wohn, Donghee Yvette & Freeman, Guo (2020): "Live Streaming, Playing, and Money Spending Behaviors in eSports", *Games and Culture* 15 (1), 73-88.

CONTRIBUTORS

Anton Heinrich Rennesland is a PhD researcher and faculty member of the Department of Philosophy, University of Santo Tomas, Manila, the Philippines. He is a managing editor of *Kritike: An Online Journal of Philosophy*, and his research specializations are Friedrich Nietzsche, Peter Sloterdijk, and Comparative/Multicultural Philosophy.

Charles Djordjevic is a senior researcher at the Hong Kierkegaard Library, St. Olaf College, MN, US. Before this, he was a researcher at the TINT Centre for the Philosophy of Science and the University of Zurich. He focuses on philosophical anthropology and its implications for philosophical methodology.

Cristopher Morales has studied Philosophy at the universities of La Laguna, *Technische Universität* Berlin and University of Barcelona (UB), where he finished his doctoral thesis in 2013 on the Situationist International. Since then, he has published numerous articles in various national and international journals. He is currently a member of the research group "Biopolitics and Bioethics" at the University of La Laguna.

Christoph Jedan is Professor of Ethics and Comparative Philosophy of Religion in the Faculty of Theology and Religious Studies, University of Groningen. His research focuses on the intersections of religion and philosophy, especially on the themes of religion and politics, postsecularism, and the history and continuing relevance of consolation for death and loss.

Georgios Karakasis obtained his PhD in Philosophy at the University of the Basque Country. His main research interests include, among others, the later thought of Martin Heidegger, the (neo)fascist thought and philosophy, the re-emergence of (neo)fascist movements as well as the philosophy of Julius Evola.

Hanneke Muthert is Professor of Psychology of Religion with special attention to spiritual care and wellbeing in the Faculty of Theology and Religious Studies, University of Groningen. Her research focuses on concrete shapes and forms of 'speakable spirituality' in health care as well as in profit and not-for-profit organizations.

Heidi Jansen is a PhD candidate at the Faculty of Theology and Religious Studies at the University of Groningen (Netherlands). Her project is entitled *Meaning: Inquiries into the Future of Work*. She specializes in work and meaningfulness. She is also the co-director of a postgraduate training for career advice.

Irene Ortiz is a researcher at *Universidad Francisco de Vitoria*. She has a PhD in Philosophy from *Universidad Autónoma de Madrid*, Spain. She has been a visiting researcher at *Scuola Normale Superiore* in Florence, Italy. Her research is focused on biopolitics, philosophy, and Italian thought.

Joseph Arel is a Hegel scholar and works on Critical Theory and Continental Philosophy, broadly construed. He is also a translator and the founder and General Editor of localphilosophy.org. He lives on a sailboat, somewhere along the east coast of the United States.

Navjot is a Research Scholar and Teaching Assistant in Philosophy in the Department of Humanities and Social Sciences, IIT Delhi, India. Her area of research is Ancient Greek Philosophy, with particular focus on the works of Aristotle and his reception in the Islamic world.

Pritika Nehra teaches at Delhi University, India. She has a Ph.D from I.I.T, Delhi.

Soumyabrata Choudhury is Associate Professor at the School of Arts and Aesthetics, Jawaharlal Nehru University. He has authored *Theatre, Number, Event: Three Studies on the Relationship between Sovereignty, Power and Truth*, *Ambedkar and Other Immortals: An Untouchable Research Programme* and articles on ancient Greek liturgy, the staging of Ibsen, psychoanalysis, Nietzsche, Schiller and Hegel. His latest book is *Now It's Come To Distances: Notes on Coronavirus and Shaheen Bagh, Association and Isolation*.

Thomas J. Spiegel studied philosophy at the Freie Universität Berlin and King's College London. He received his PhD from the University of Leipzig and has been assistant professor and lecturer at the University of Potsdam since 2018. His research focuses on (critiques of) naturalism and scientism, social ontology, Wittgenstein, and Phenomenolgy.

Tyler L. Jaynes is an independent ethicist, whose research interests include bioethics and technology ethics (and all subcategories within those disciplines). He has presented at several international venues during his higher-educational pursuits, and is currently engaged in developing research on the merger between deepfakes, virtual avatars, and deep neural networks.